WHEN MATT MURDOCK WAS A KID, HE LOST HIS SIGHT IN AN ACCIDENT INVOLVING A TRUCK CARRYING RADIOACTIVE CHEMICALS. THOUGH HE COULD NO LONGER SEE, THE CHEMICALS HEIGHTENED MURDOCK'S OTHER SENSES AND IMBUED HIM WITH AN AMAZING 360 RADAR SENSE. NOW MATT USES HIS ABILITIES TO FIGHT FOR HIS CITY. HE IS THE *MAN WITHOUT FEAR.* HE IS...

DAREDEVIL

IN THE MONTHS SINCE HIS RETURN TO NEW YORK, FORMER DEFENSE ATTORNEY MATT MURDOCK HAS NOT ONLY BECOME A PROSECUTOR FOR THE CITY OF NEW YORK, HE'S ALSO SOMEHOW MANAGED TO REGAIN HIS SECRET IDENTITY AND ERASE ANY PRIOR PUBLIC KNOWLEDGE THAT HE IS IN FACT DAREDEVIL.

WITH A NEW LEASE ON LIFE — AND THE HELP OF HIS PROTÉGÉ BLINDSPOT — THE MAN WITHOUT FEAR NOW PROTECTS HIS CITY WITH COMPLETE AUTONOMY. AND WHILE EVERYTHING SEEMS TO BE GOING WELL, THE PAST HAS A WAY OF CATCHING UP...

CHARLES SOULE
WRITER

MATTEO BUFFAGNI (*Nos. 6-7*),
GORAN SUDŽUKA (*Nos. 8-9*) &
VANESA R. DEL REY (*Annual No. 1*)
ARTISTS

MATT MILLA (*Nos. 6-9*) &
MAT LOPES (*Annual No. 1*)
COLOR ARTISTS

"FRAGMENTS"
WRITER **ROGER McKENZIE**
ARTIST **BEN TORRES**
COLOR ARTIST **MIROSLAV MRVA**

VC'S CLAYTON COWLES
LETTERER

BILL SIENKIEWICZ (*Nos. 6-7*),
GIUSEPPE CAMUNCOLI &
DANIELE ORLANDINI (*Nos. 8-9*) AND
VANESA R. DEL REY (*Annual No. 1*)
COVER ART

CHARLES BEACHAM &
CHRIS ROBINSON
ASSISTANT EDITORS

SANA AMANAT &
MARK PANICCIA
EDITORS

COLLECTION EDITOR **JENNIFER GRÜNWALD**
ASSOCIATE EDITOR **SARAH BRUNSTAD**
EDITOR, SPECIAL PROJECTS **MARK D. BEAZLEY**
VP, PRODUCTION & SPECIAL PROJECTS **JEFF YOUNGQUIST**
SVP PRINT, SALES & MARKETING **DAVID GABRIEL**
BOOK DESIGNER **ADAM DEL RE**

EDITOR IN CHIEF **AXEL ALONSO**
CHIEF CREATIVE OFFICER **JOE QUESADA**
PUBLISHER **DAN BUCKLEY**
EXECUTIVE PRODUCER **ALAN FINE**

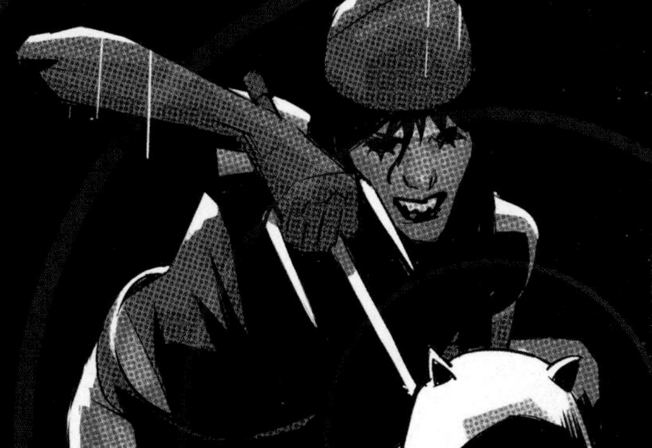

DAREDEVIL: BACK IN BLACK VOL. 2 — SUPERSONIC. Contains material originally published in magazine form as DAREDEVIL #6-9 and ANNUAL #1. First printing 2016. ISBN# 978-0-7851-9645-7. Published by MARVEL WORLDWIDE, INC., a subsidiary of MARVEL ENTERTAINMENT, LLC. OFFICE OF PUBLICATION: 135 West 50th Street, New York, NY 10020.

Printed in Canada. ALAN FINE, President, Marvel Entertainment; DAN BUCKLEY, President, TV, Publishing & Brand Management; JOE QUESADA, Chief Creative Officer; TOM BREVOORT, SVP of Publishing; DAVID BOGART, SVP of Business Affairs & Operations, Publishing & Partnership; C.B. CEBULSKI, VP of Brand Management

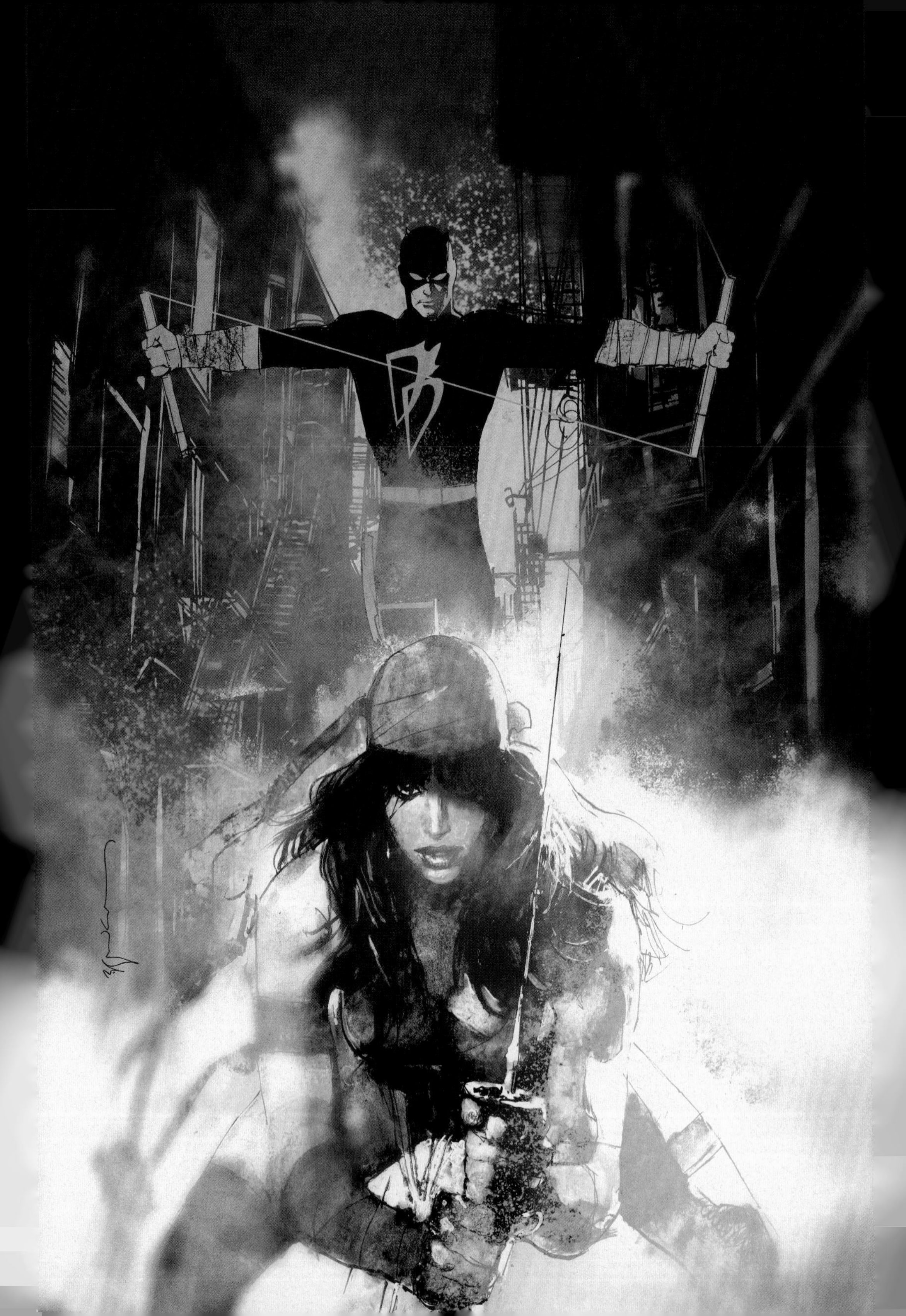

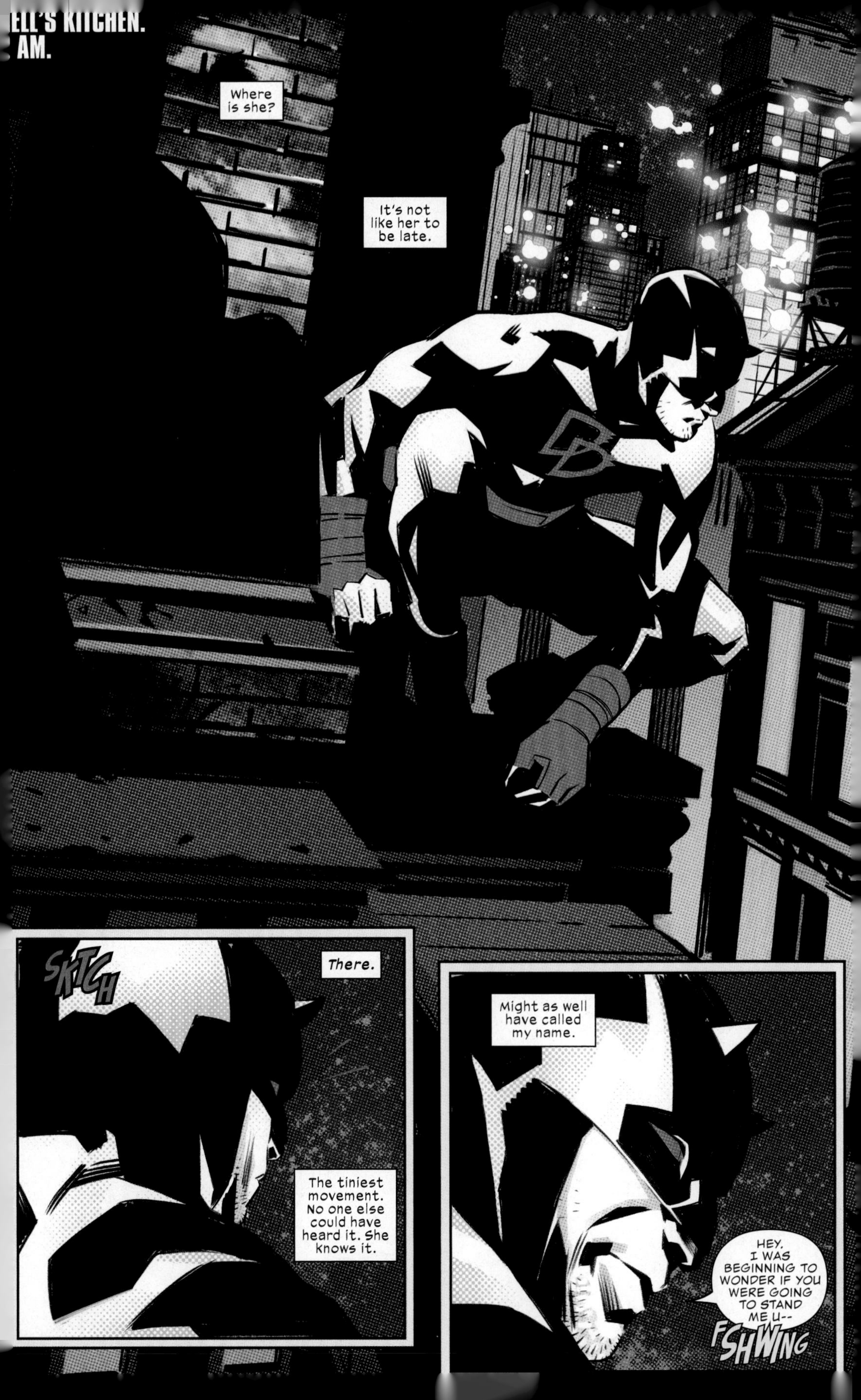
ELL'S KITCHEN.
AM.
Where is she?
It's not like her to be late.
SKTCH
There.
The tiniest movement. No one else could have heard it. She knows it.
Might as well have called my name.
HEY, I WAS BEGINNING TO WONDER IF YOU WERE GOING TO STAND ME U--
FSHWING

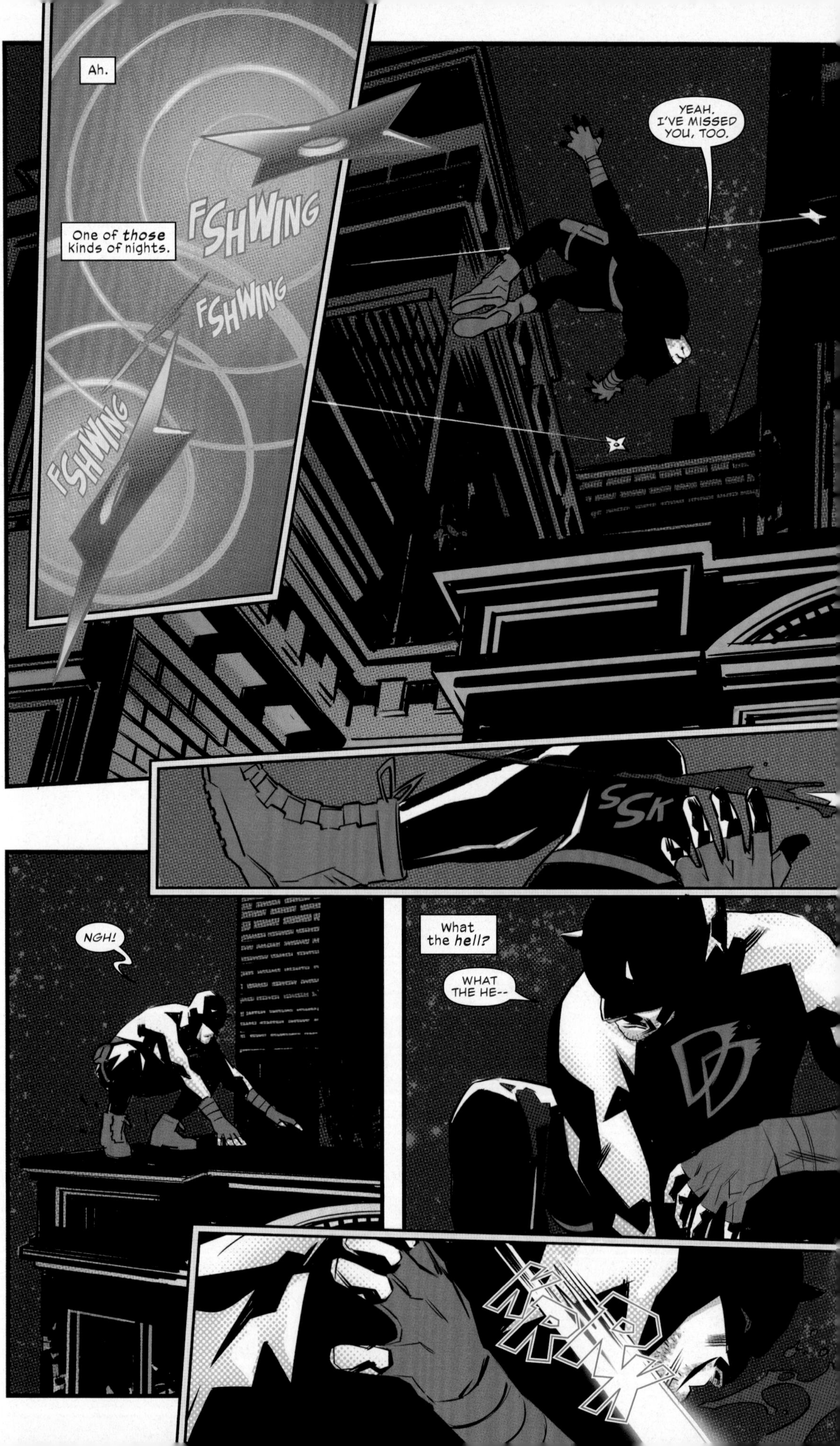
Ah.
One of those kinds of nights.
FSHWING
FSHWING
FSHWING
YEAH. I'VE MISSED YOU, TOO.
SSK
NGH!
What the hell?
WHAT THE HE--

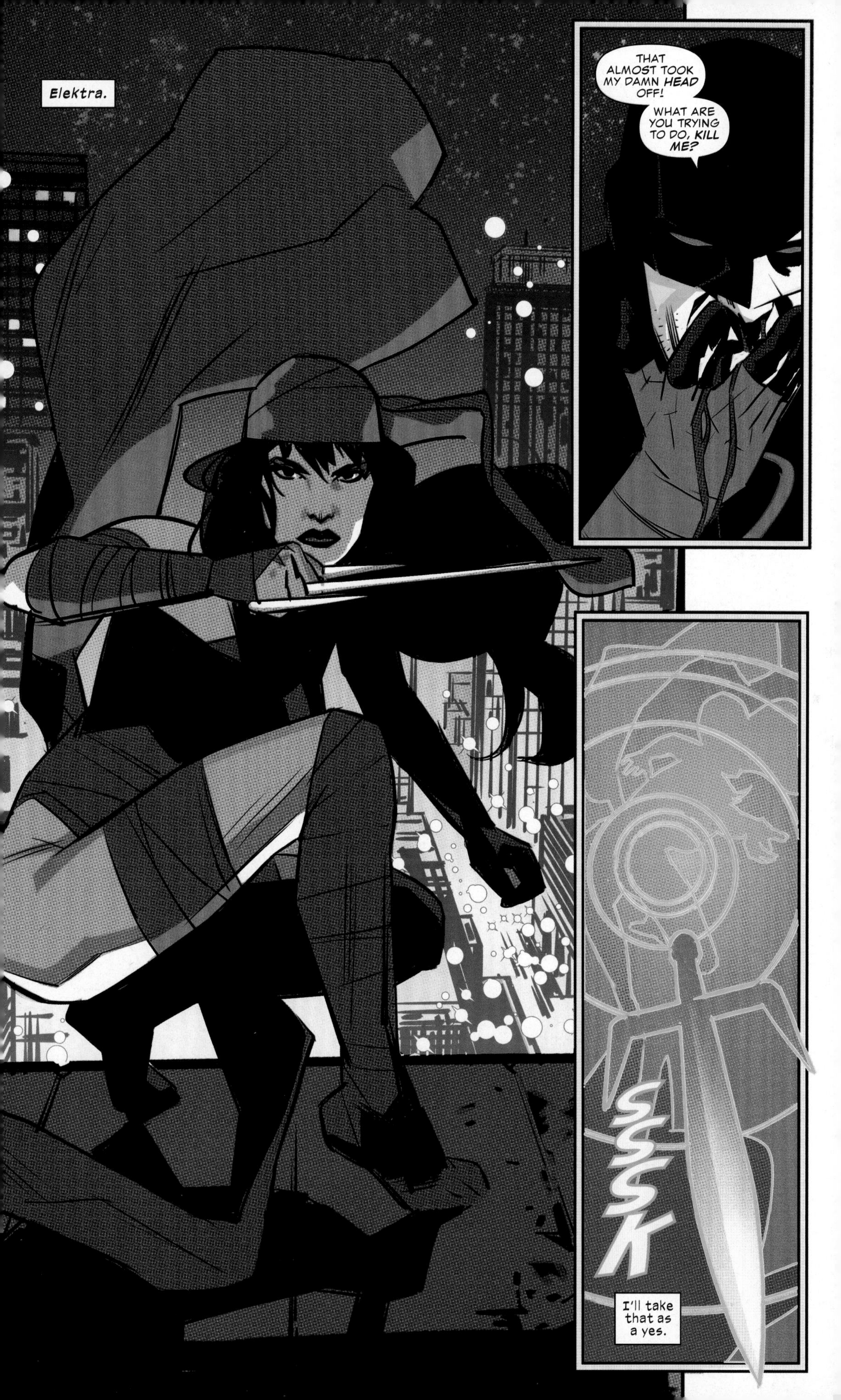
Elektra.
THAT ALMOST TOOK MY DAMN HEAD OFF!
WHAT ARE YOU TRYING TO DO, KILL ME?
SSSK
I'll take that as a yes.

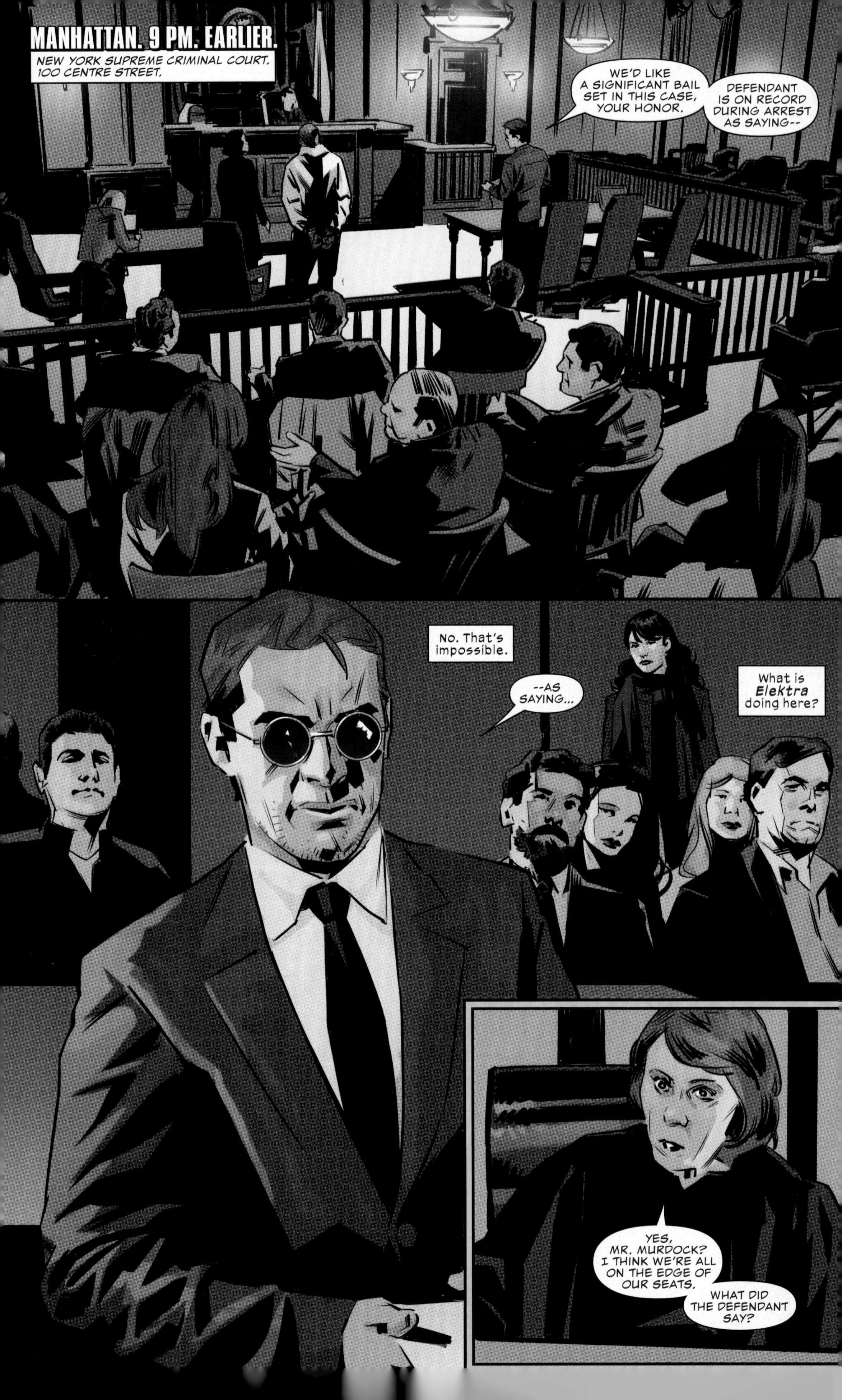
MANHATTAN. 9 PM. EARLIER.
NEW YORK SUPREME CRIMINAL COURT. 100 CENTRE STREET.
WE'D LIKE A SIGNIFICANT BAIL SET IN THIS CASE, YOUR HONOR.
DEFENDANT IS ON RECORD DURING ARREST AS SAYING--
No. That's impossible.
--AS SAYING...
What is *Elektra* doing here?
YES, MR. MURDOCK? I THINK WE'RE ALL ON THE EDGE OF OUR SEATS.
WHAT DID THE DEFENDANT SAY?

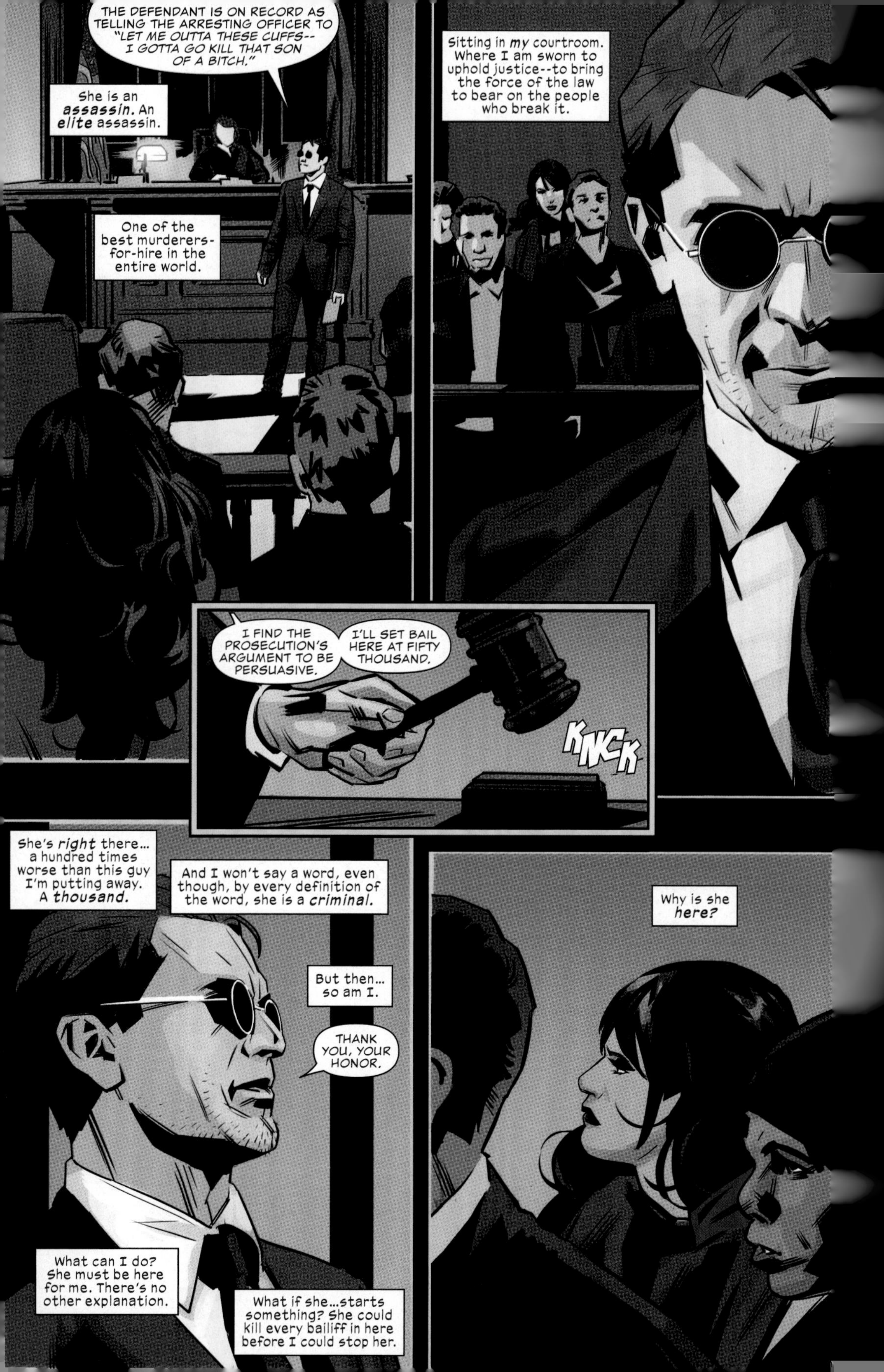
THE DEFENDANT IS ON RECORD AS TELLING THE ARRESTING OFFICER TO "LET ME OUTTA THESE CUFFS-- I GOTTA GO KILL THAT SON OF A BITCH."
She is an assassin. An elite assassin.
One of the best murderers-for-hire in the entire world.
Sitting in my courtroom. Where I am sworn to uphold justice--to bring the force of the law to bear on the people who break it.
I FIND THE PROSECUTION'S ARGUMENT TO BE PERSUASIVE.
I'LL SET BAIL HERE AT FIFTY THOUSAND.
KNCK
She's right there... a hundred times worse than this guy I'm putting away. A thousand.
And I won't say a word, even though, by every definition of the word, she is a criminal.
But then... so am I.
THANK YOU, YOUR HONOR.
What can I do? She must be here for me. There's no other explanation.
What if she...starts something? She could kill every bailiff in here before I could stop her.
Why is she here?

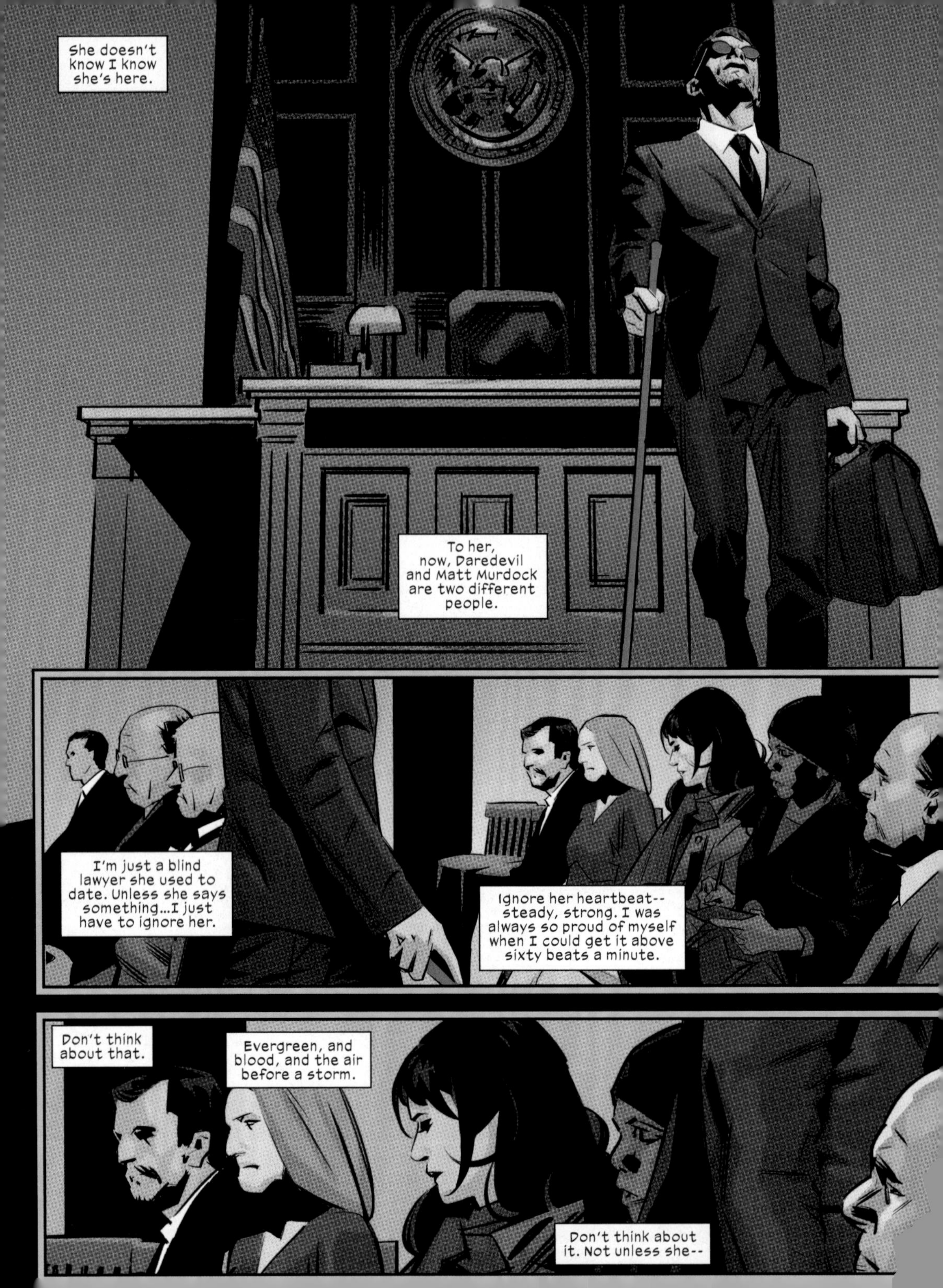

She doesn't know I know she's here.
To her, now, Daredevil and Matt Murdock are two different people.
I'm just a blind lawyer she used to date. Unless she says something...I just have to ignore her.
Ignore her heartbeat--steady, strong. I was always so proud of myself when I could get it above sixty beats a minute.
Don't think about that.
Evergreen, and blood, and the air before a storm.
Don't think about it. Not unless she--

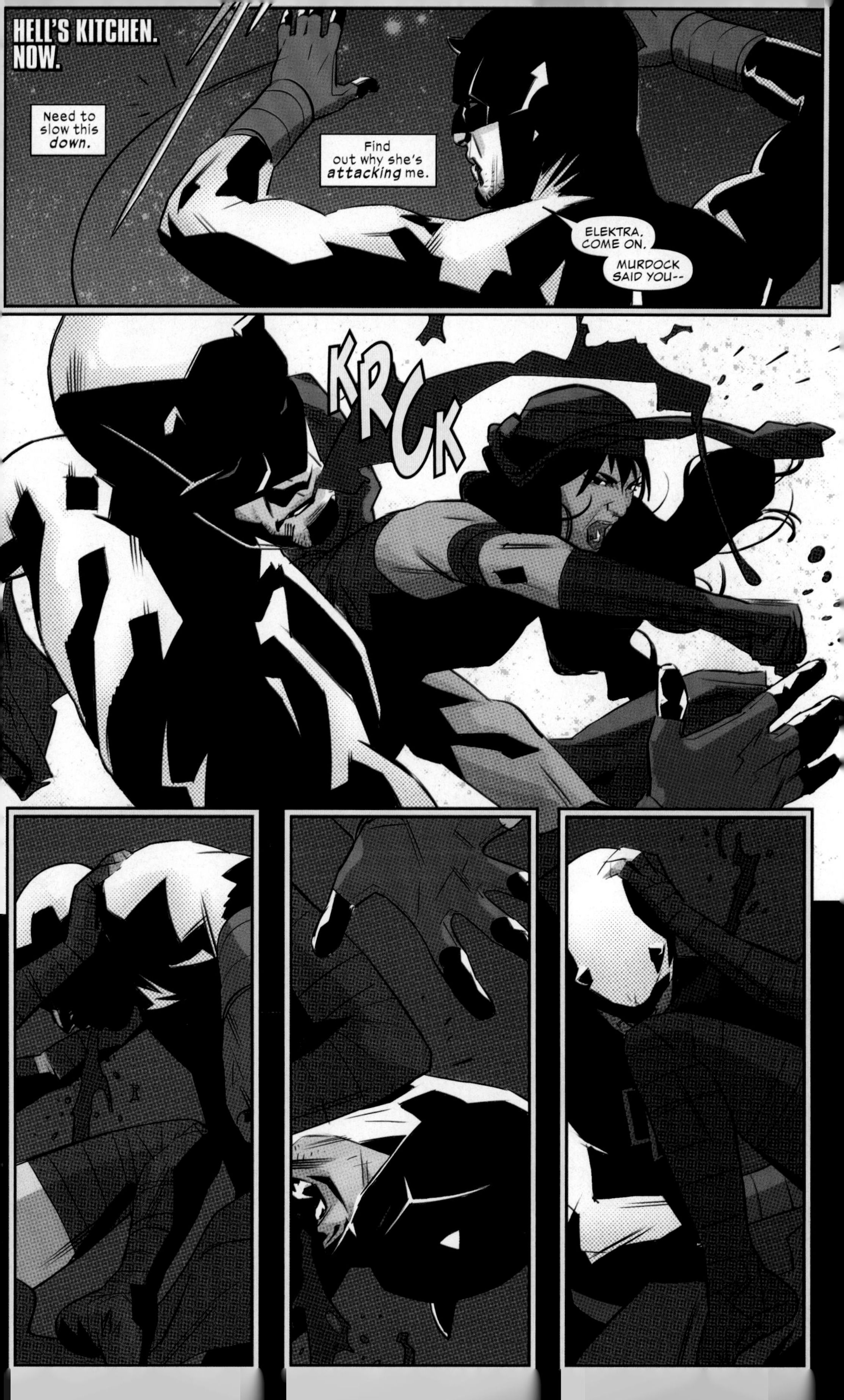
HELL'S KITCHEN. NOW.
Need to slow this down.
Find out why she's attacking me.
ELEKTRA, COME ON.
MURDOCK SAID YOU--
KRCK

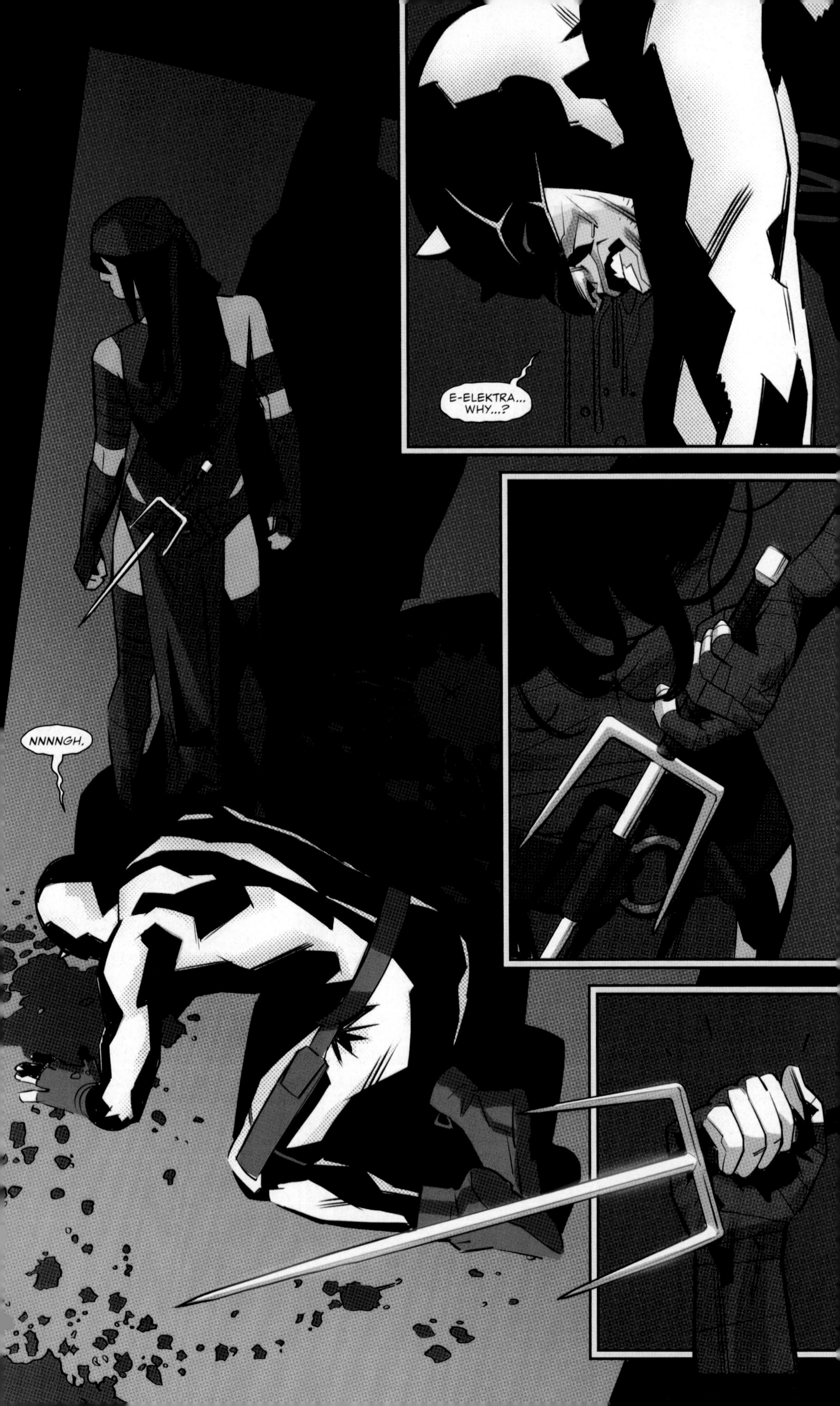
E-ELEKTRA...
WHY...?
NNNNGH.

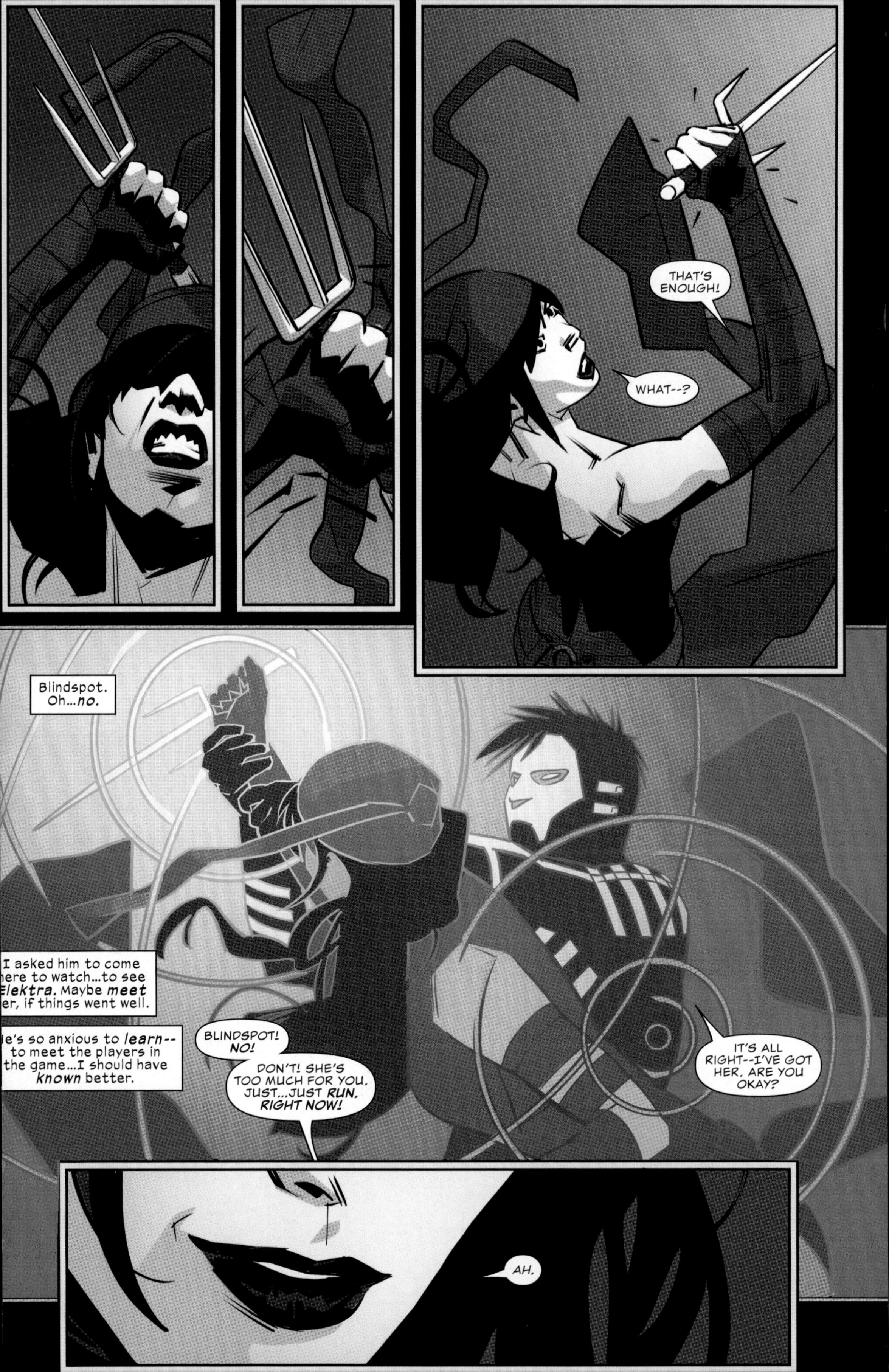
THAT'S ENOUGH!
WHAT--?
Blindspot. Oh...no.
I asked him to come ere to watch...to see lektra. Maybe meet er, if things went well.
e's so anxious to learn-- to meet the players in the game...I should have known better.
BLINDSPOT! NO!
DON'T! SHE'S TOO MUCH FOR YOU. JUST...JUST RUN. RIGHT NOW!
IT'S ALL RIGHT--I'VE GOT HER. ARE YOU OKAY?
AH.

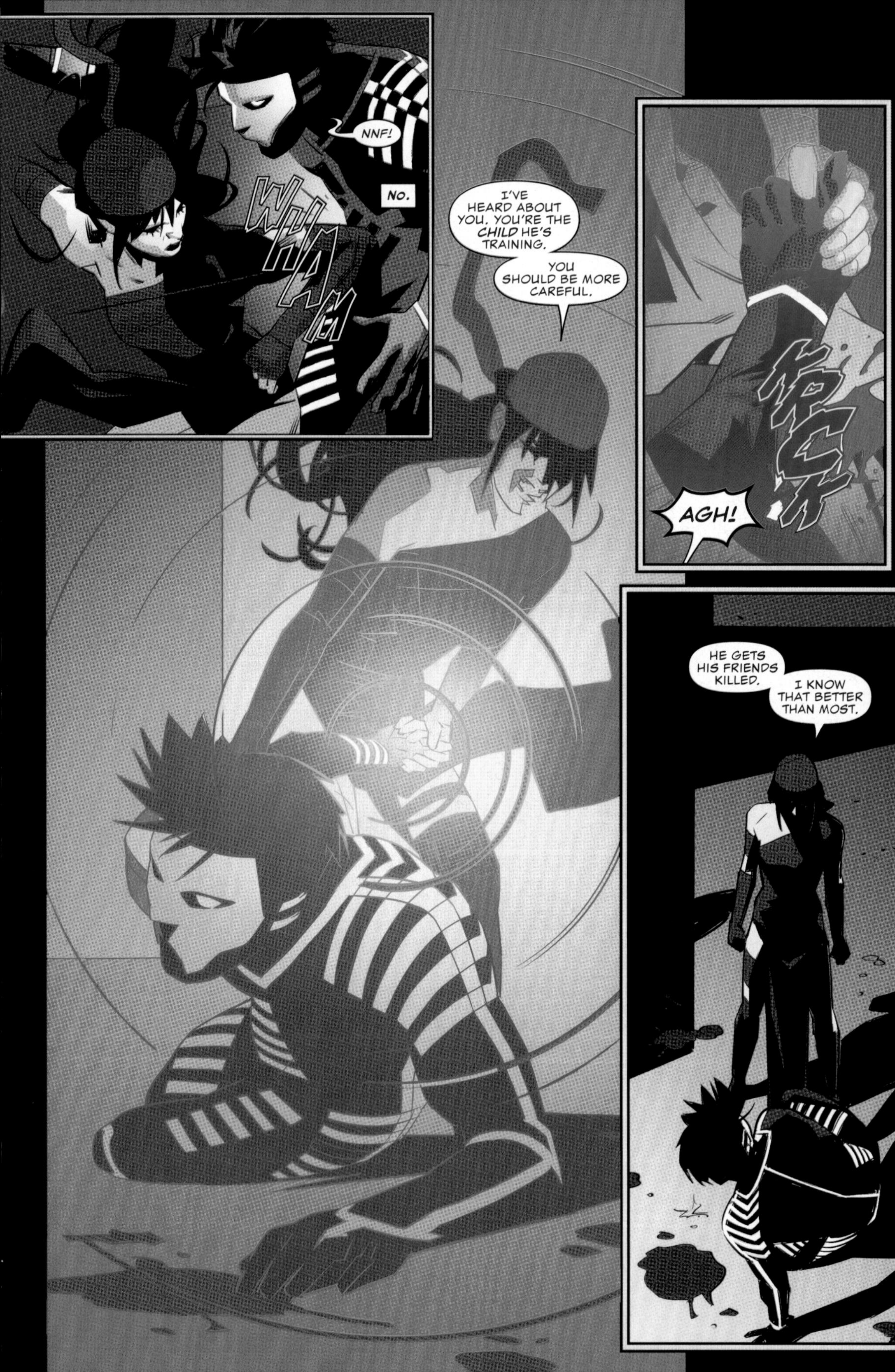

NNF!
WHAM
NO.
I'VE HEARD ABOUT YOU. YOU'RE THE CHILD HE'S TRAINING.
YOU SHOULD BE MORE CAREFUL.
KRCK
AGH!
HE GETS HIS FRIENDS KILLED.
I KNOW THAT BETTER THAN MOST.

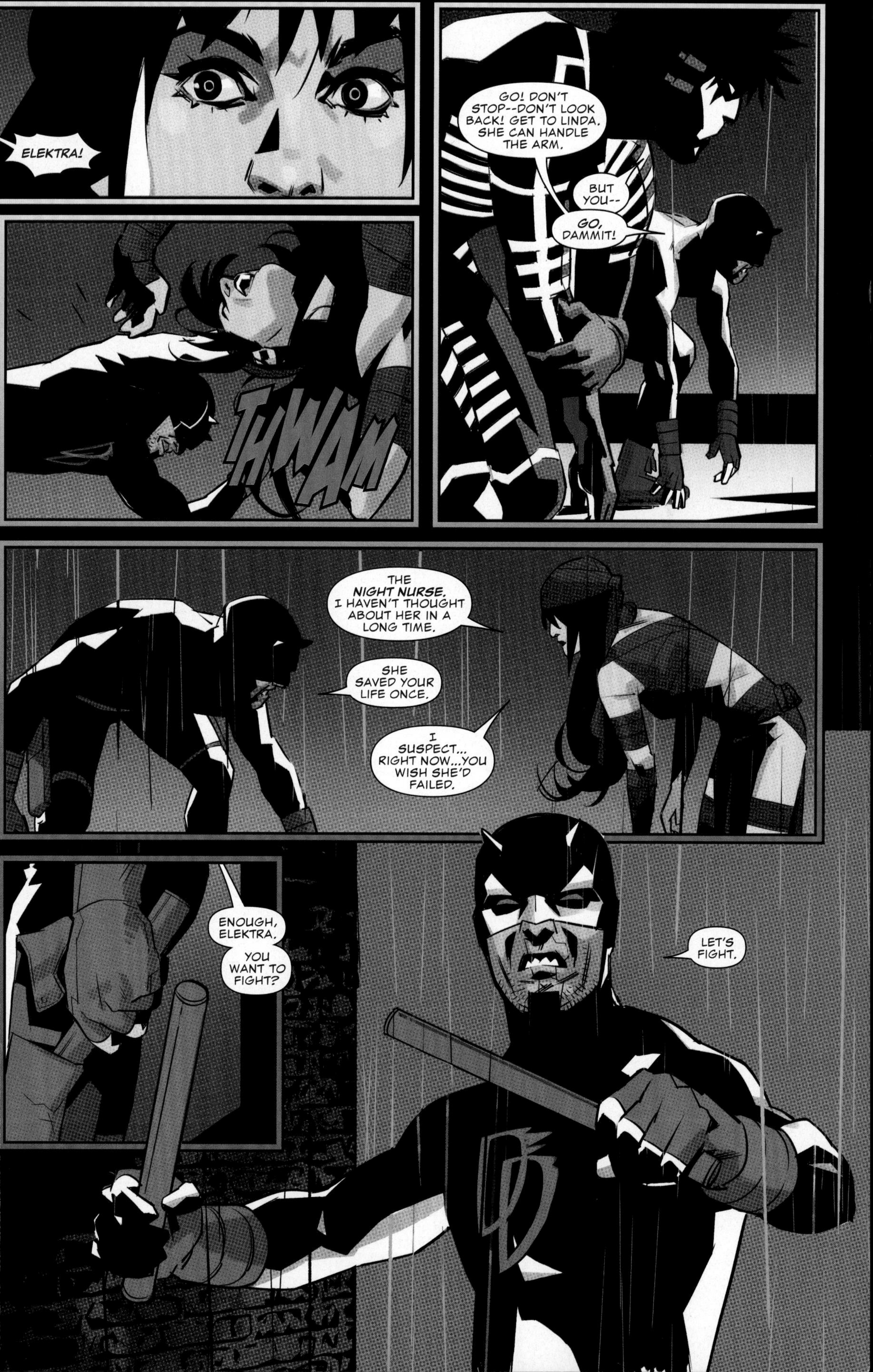
ELEKTRA!
THWAM
GO! DON'T STOP--DON'T LOOK BACK! GET TO LINDA. SHE CAN HANDLE THE ARM.
BUT YOU--
GO, DAMMIT!
THE *NIGHT NURSE.* I HAVEN'T THOUGHT ABOUT HER IN A LONG TIME.
SHE SAVED YOUR LIFE ONCE.
I SUSPECT... RIGHT NOW...YOU WISH SHE'D FAILED.
ENOUGH, ELEKTRA.
YOU WANT TO FIGHT?
LET'S FIGHT.

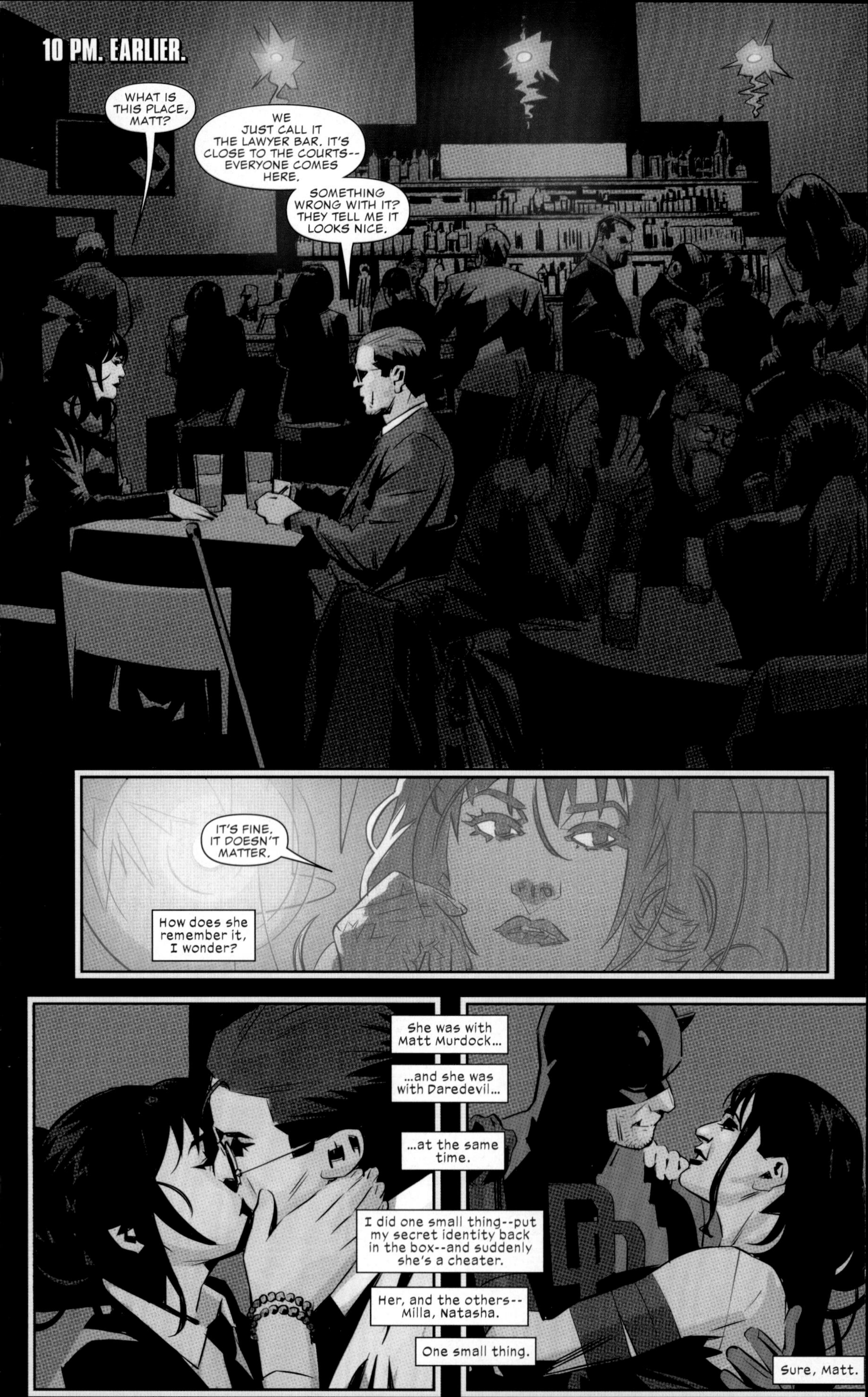
10 PM. EARLIER.
WHAT IS THIS PLACE, MATT?
WE JUST CALL IT THE LAWYER BAR. IT'S CLOSE TO THE COURTS--EVERYONE COMES HERE.
SOMETHING WRONG WITH IT? THEY TELL ME IT LOOKS NICE.
IT'S FINE. IT DOESN'T MATTER.
How does she remember it, I wonder?
She was with Matt Murdock...
...and she was with Daredevil...
...at the same time.
I did one small thing--put my secret identity back in the box--and suddenly she's a cheater.
Her, and the others--Milla, Natasha.
One small thing.
Sure, Matt.

WHY ARE YOU DOING THIS, MATT? PUTTING PETTY CRIMINALS IN JAIL? ARGUING ABOUT *BAIL*, IT SEEMS...BENEATH YOU.

I'VE BEEN ASSIGNED TO SOMETHING CALLED E.C.A.B.--EARLY CASE ASSESSMENT BUREAU. GETTING CASES INTO THE FLOW--MOSTLY STREET-LEVEL STUFF.

I SCREWED UP A BIG CASE NOT LONG AGO. THE D.A. PUT ME IN E.C.A.B. AS...*PUNISHMENT*, I GUESS. MORE LIKE A CHANCE TO PROVE MYSELF. SEE IF I CAN STICK IT OUT, I THINK.

I'M LUCKY TO BE ABLE TO PRACTICE LAW IN NEW YORK AT ALL. I'LL TAKE WHAT I CAN GET.

ANYWAY, EVERY PART OF THE SYSTEM IS IMPORTANT. IT NEEDS SKILL AND ATTENTION AT EVERY LEVEL.

MM.

...

WHY ARE YOU HERE, ELEKTRA? NOT THAT IT'S NOT *WONDERFUL* TO SEE YOU, BUT...

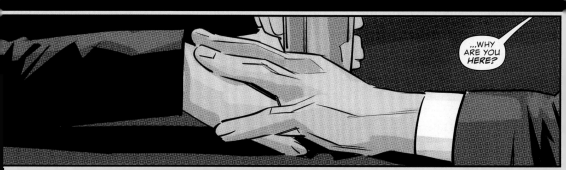

...WHY ARE YOU *HERE*?

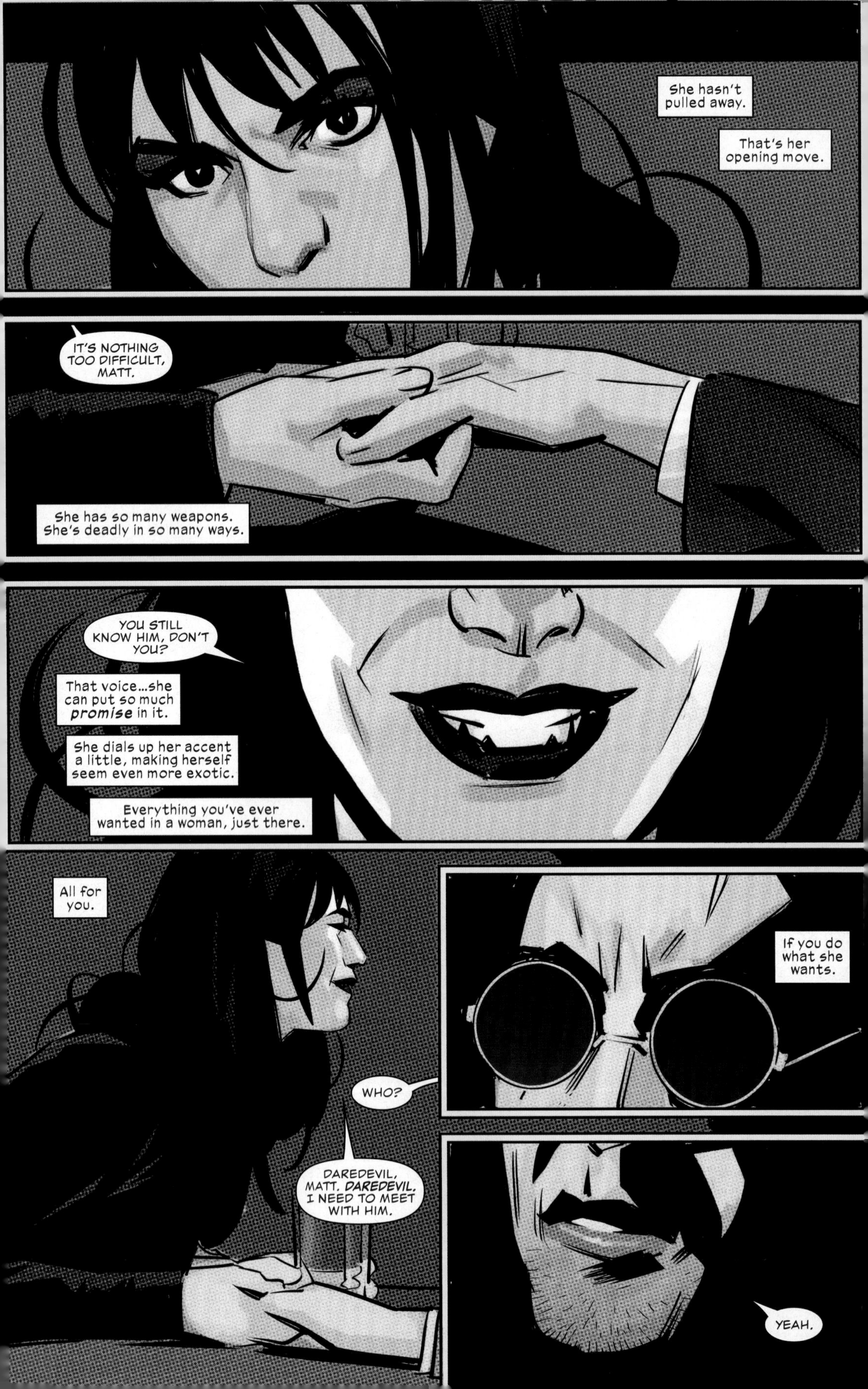
She hasn't pulled away.
That's her opening move.
IT'S NOTHING TOO DIFFICULT, MATT.
She has so many weapons. She's deadly in so many ways.
YOU STILL KNOW HIM, DON'T YOU?
That voice...she can put so much *promise* in it.
She dials up her accent a little, making herself seem even more exotic.
Everything you've ever wanted in a woman, just there.
All for you.
If you do what she wants.
WHO?
DAREDEVIL, MATT. *DAREDEVIL.* I NEED TO MEET WITH HIM.
YEAH.

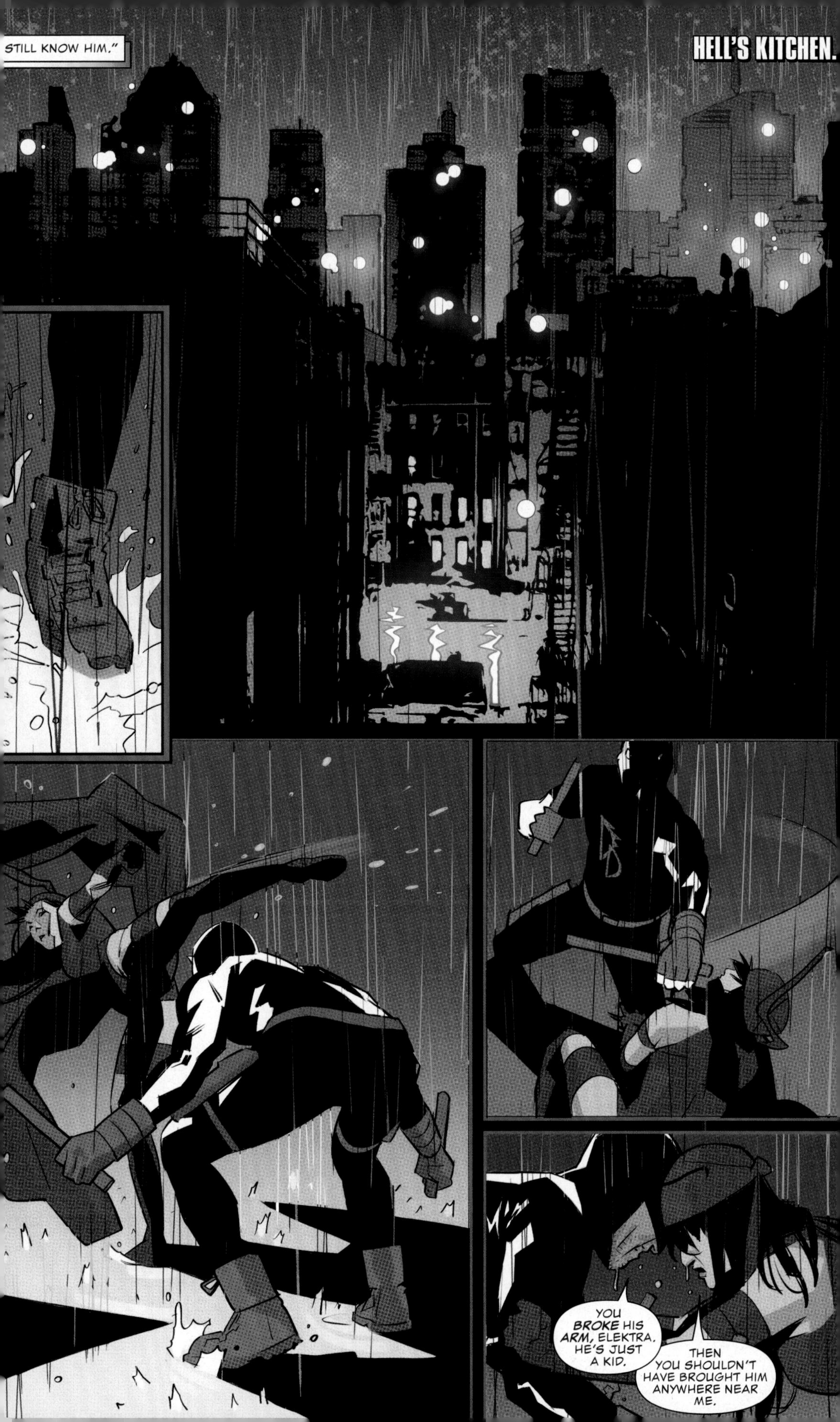
STILL KNOW HIM."
HELL'S KITCHEN.
YOU BROKE HIS ARM, ELEKTRA. HE'S JUST A KID.
THEN YOU SHOULDN'T HAVE BROUGHT HIM ANYWHERE NEAR ME.

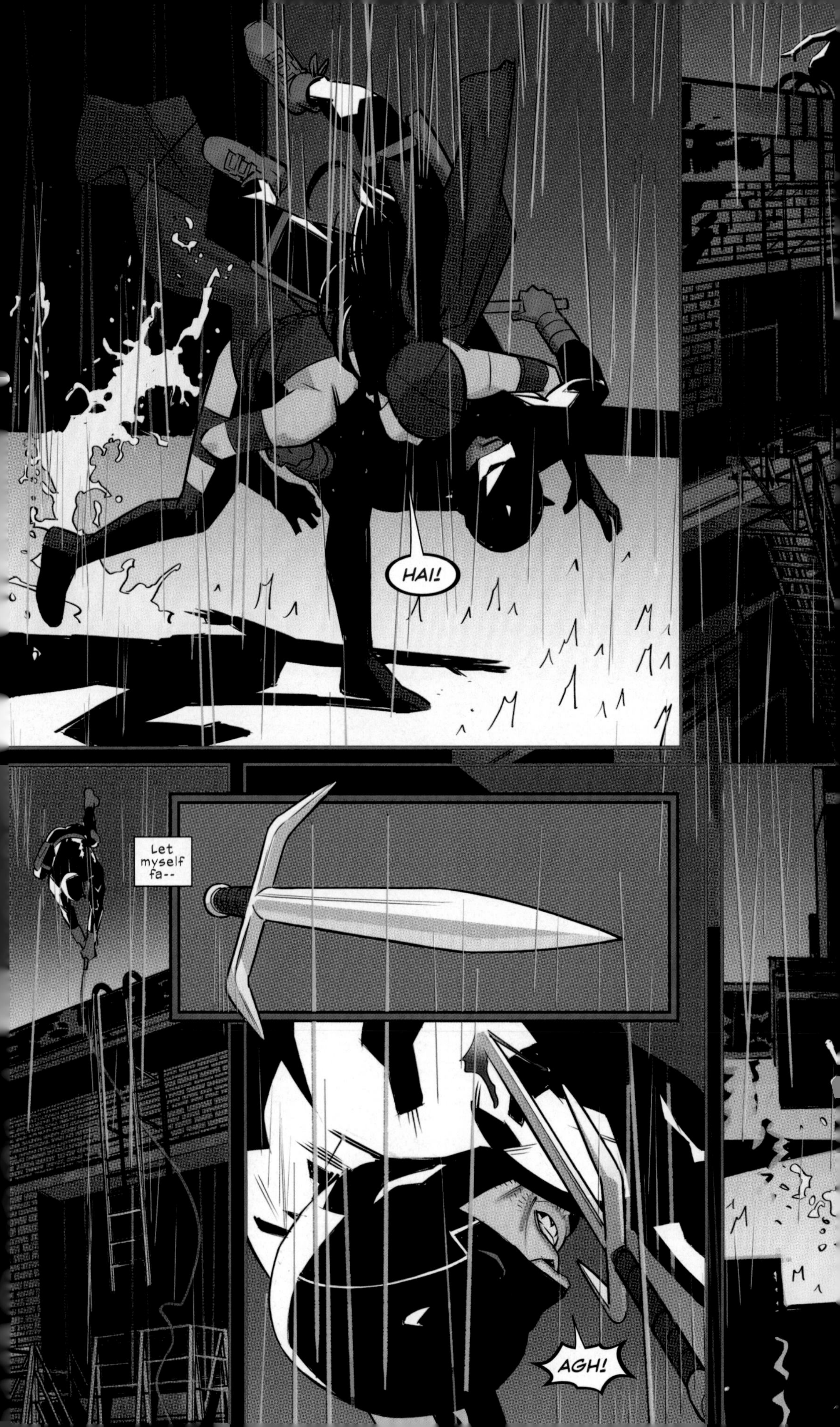
HAI!
Let myself fa--
AGH!

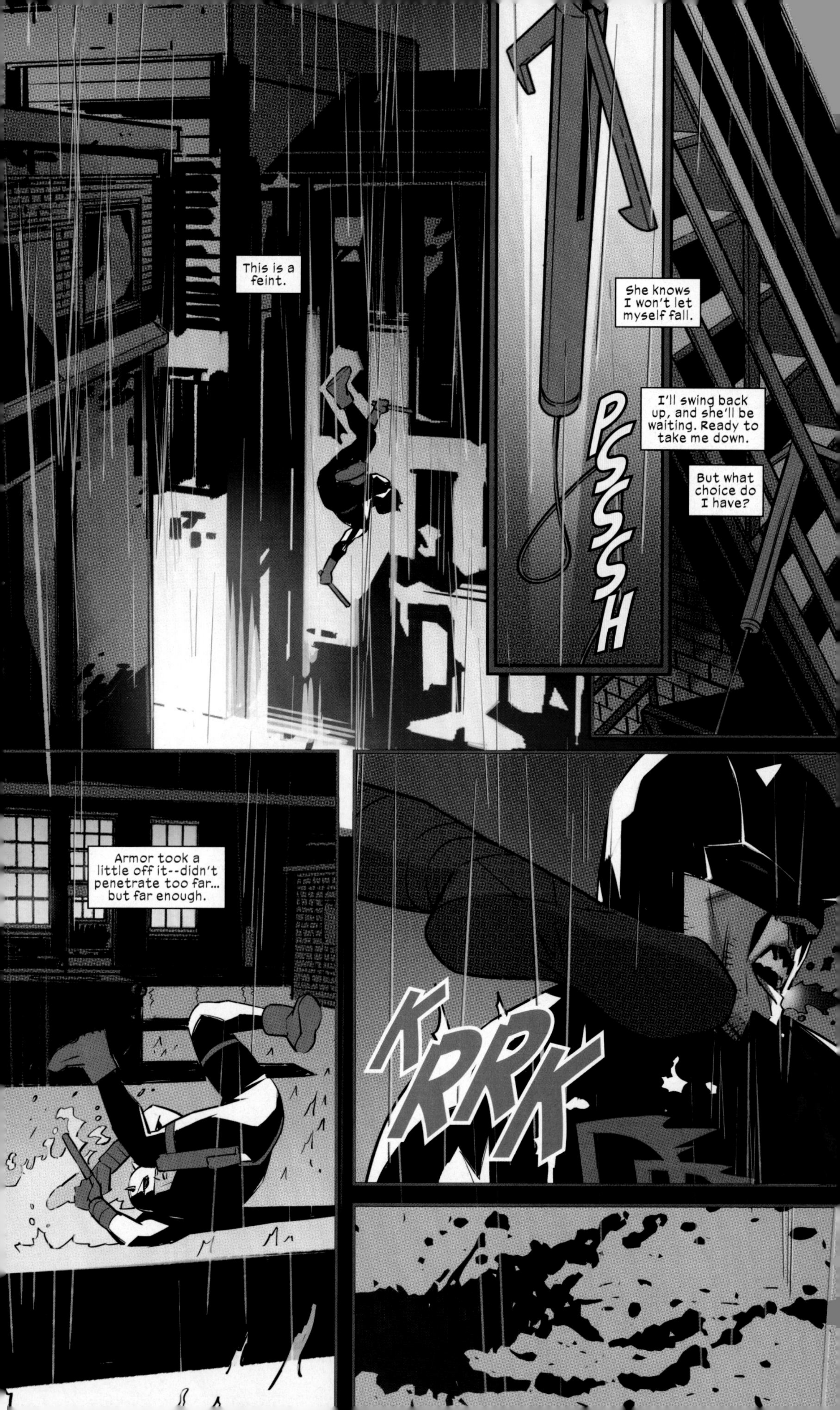
This is a feint.
She knows I won't let myself fall.
PSSSH
I'll swing back up, and she'll be waiting. Ready to take me down.
But what choice do I have?
Armor took a little off it--didn't penetrate too far... but far enough.
KRRK

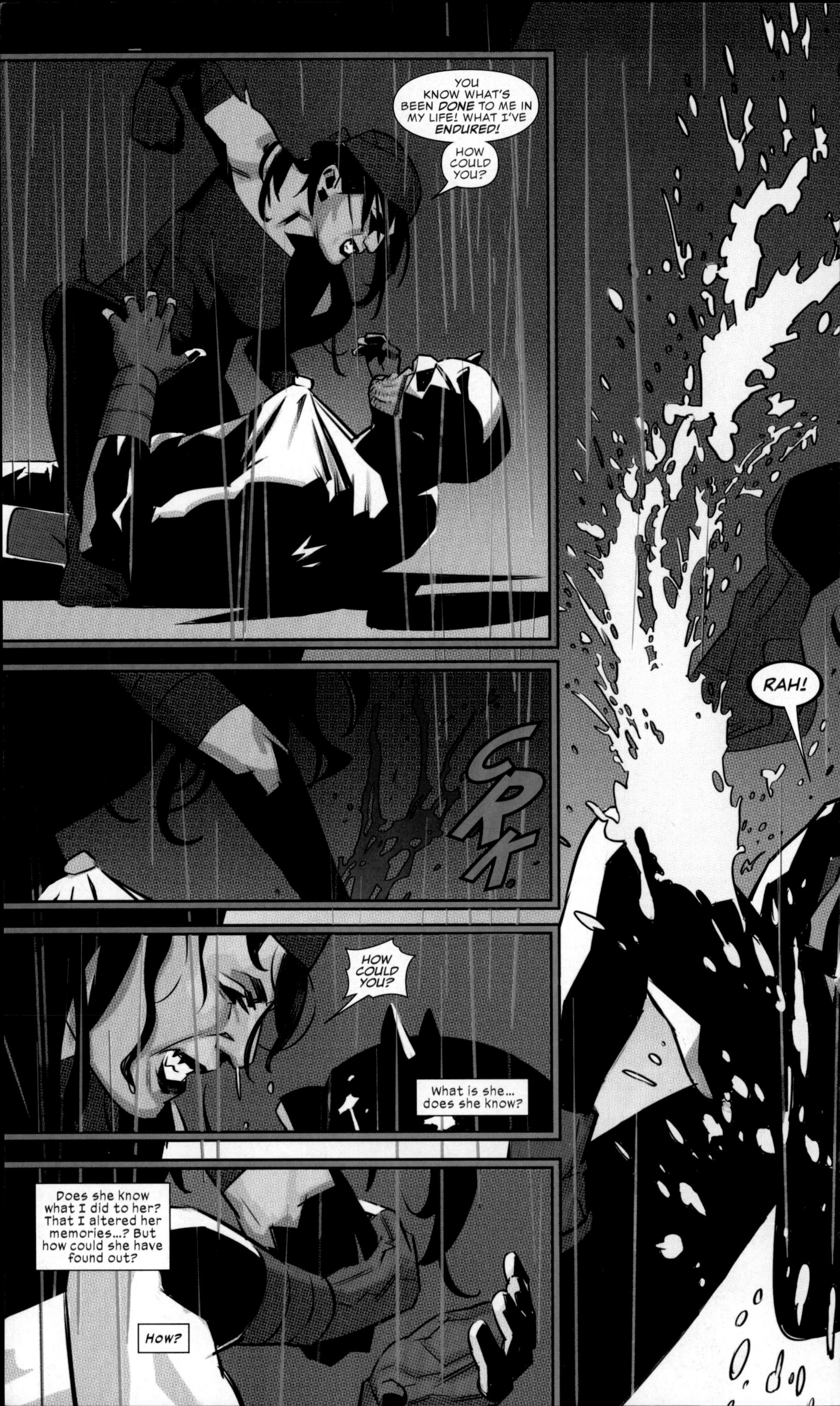
YOU KNOW WHAT'S BEEN DONE TO ME IN MY LIFE! WHAT I'VE ENDURED!
HOW COULD YOU?
RAH!
CRK
HOW COULD YOU?
What is she... does she know?
Does she know what I did to her? That I altered her memories...? But how could she have found out?
How?

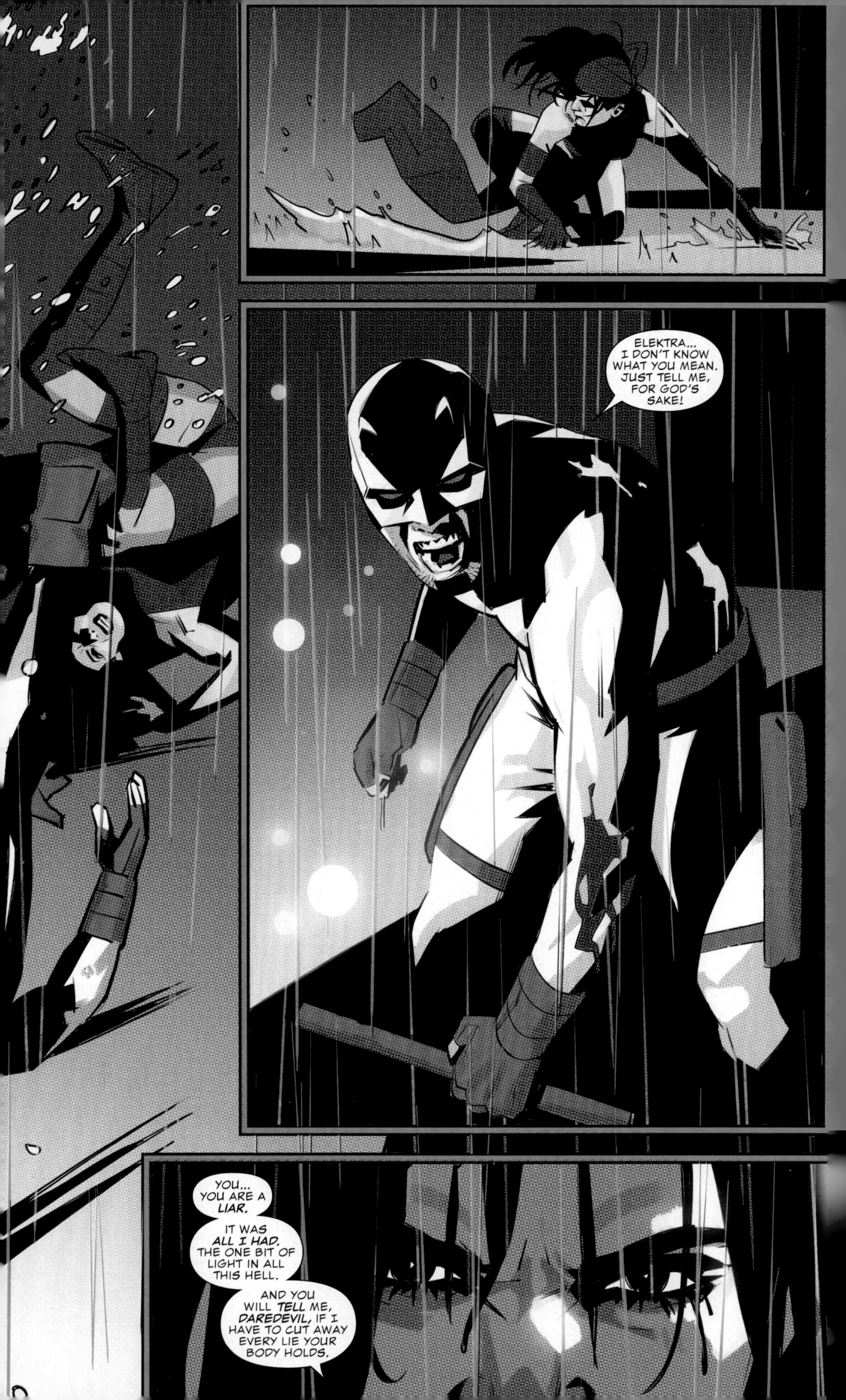
ELEKTRA... I DON'T KNOW WHAT YOU MEAN. JUST TELL ME, FOR GOD'S SAKE!
YOU... YOU ARE A LIAR.
IT WAS ALL I HAD. THE ONE BIT OF LIGHT IN ALL THIS HELL.
AND YOU WILL TELL ME, DAREDEVIL, IF I HAVE TO CUT AWAY EVERY LIE YOUR BODY HOLDS.

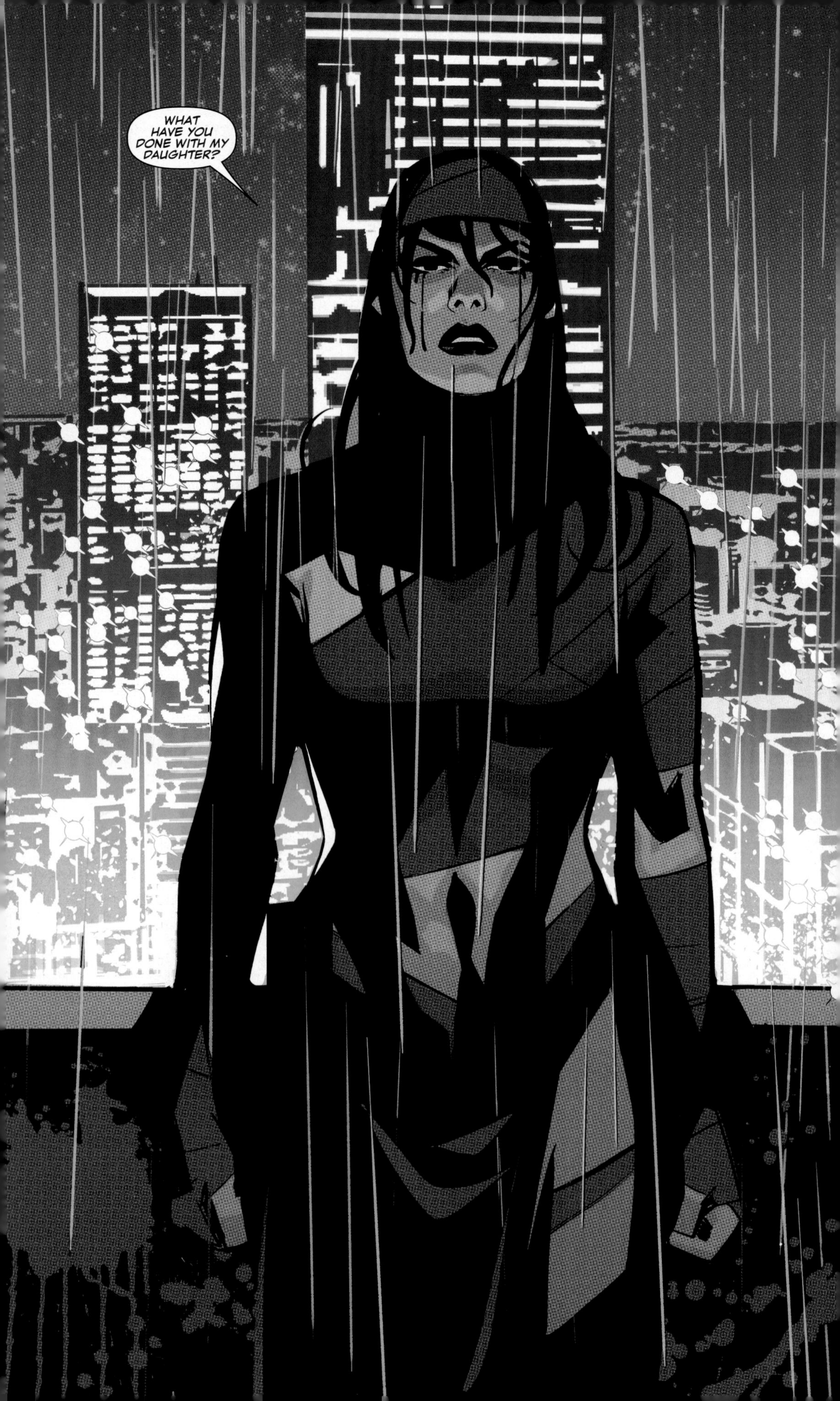
WHAT HAVE YOU DONE WITH MY DAUGHTER?

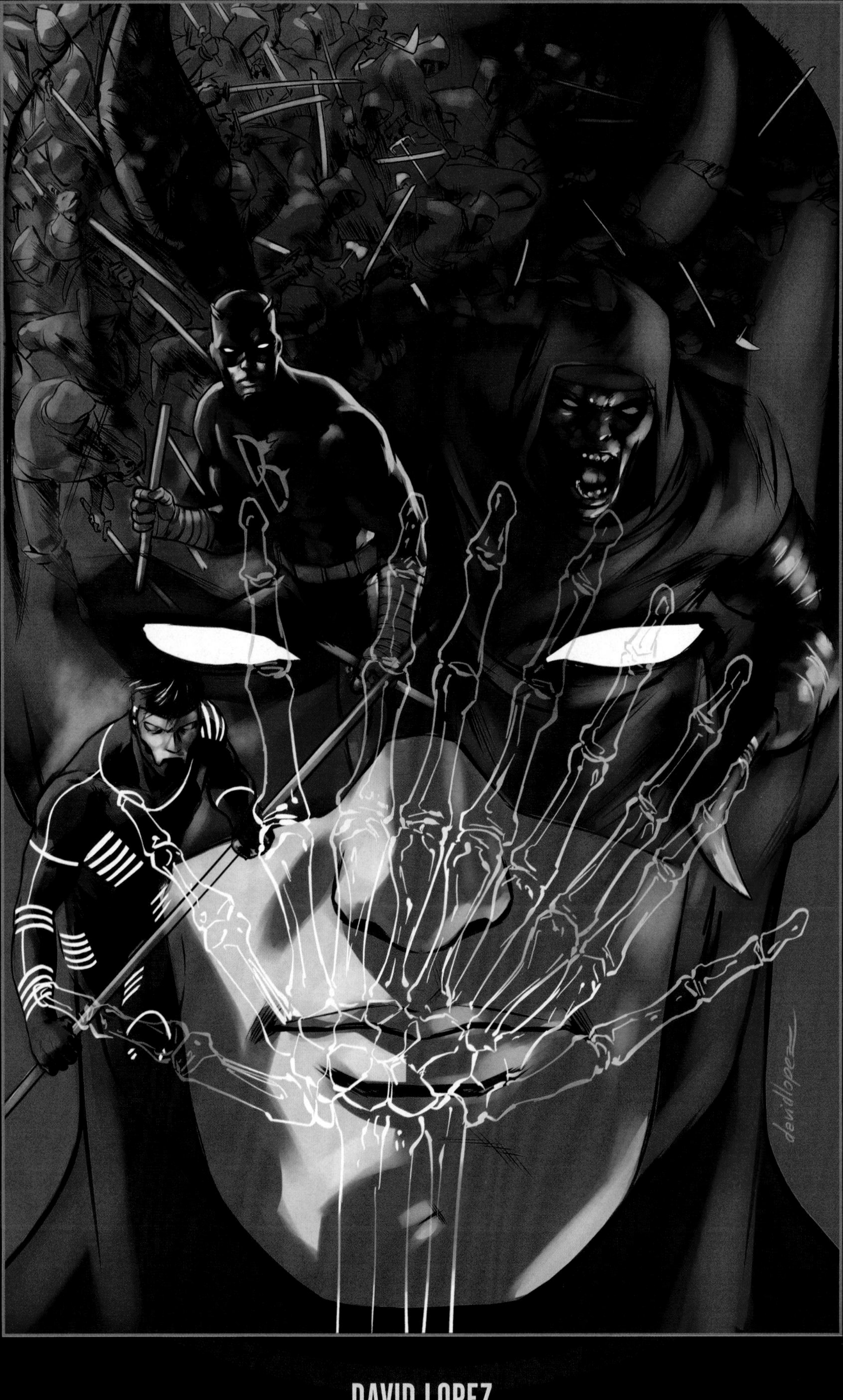

DAVID LOPEZ

No. 6 STORY THUS FAR VARIANT

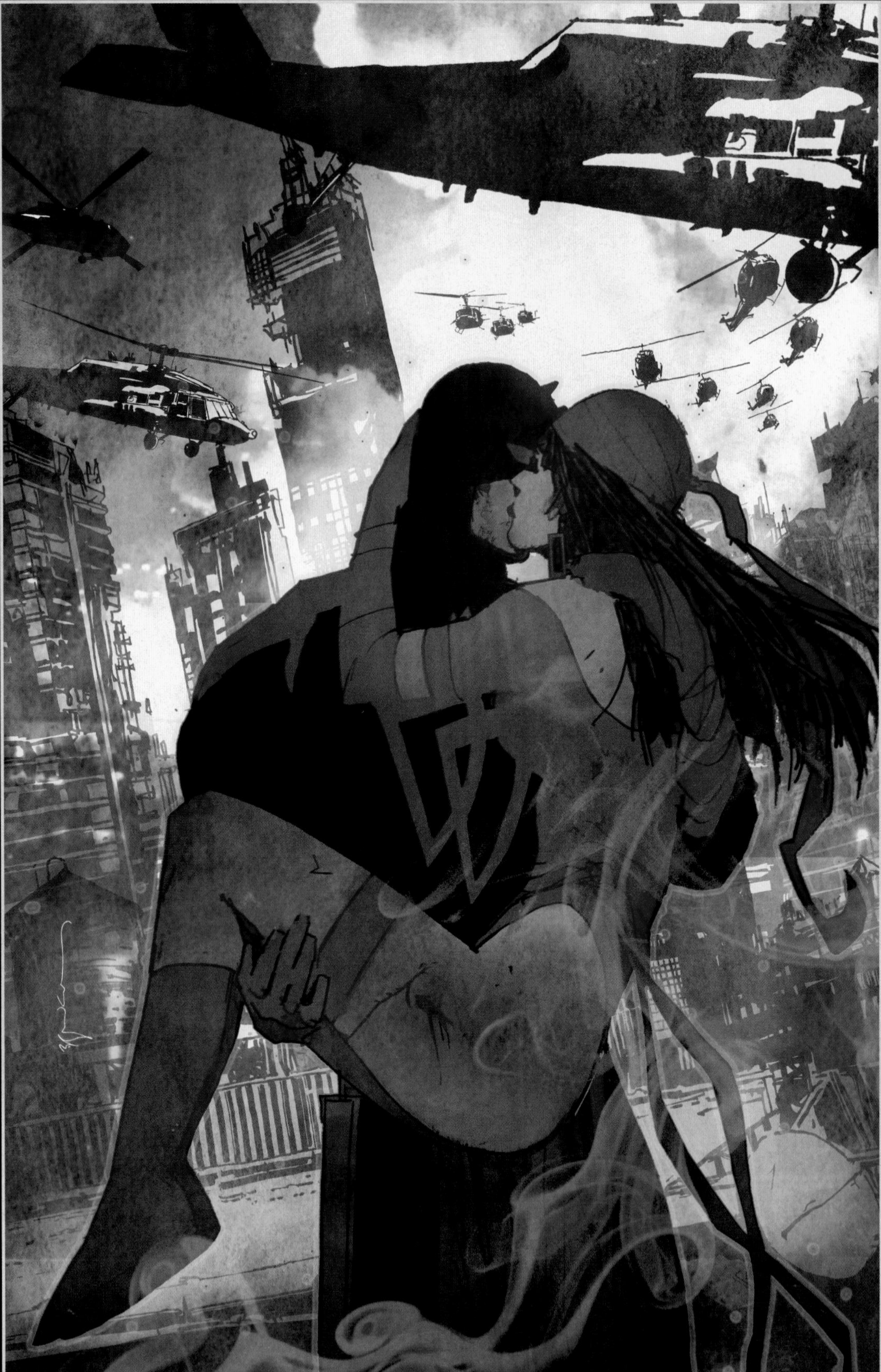

:: 7: ELEKTRIC CONNETION PART 2 ::

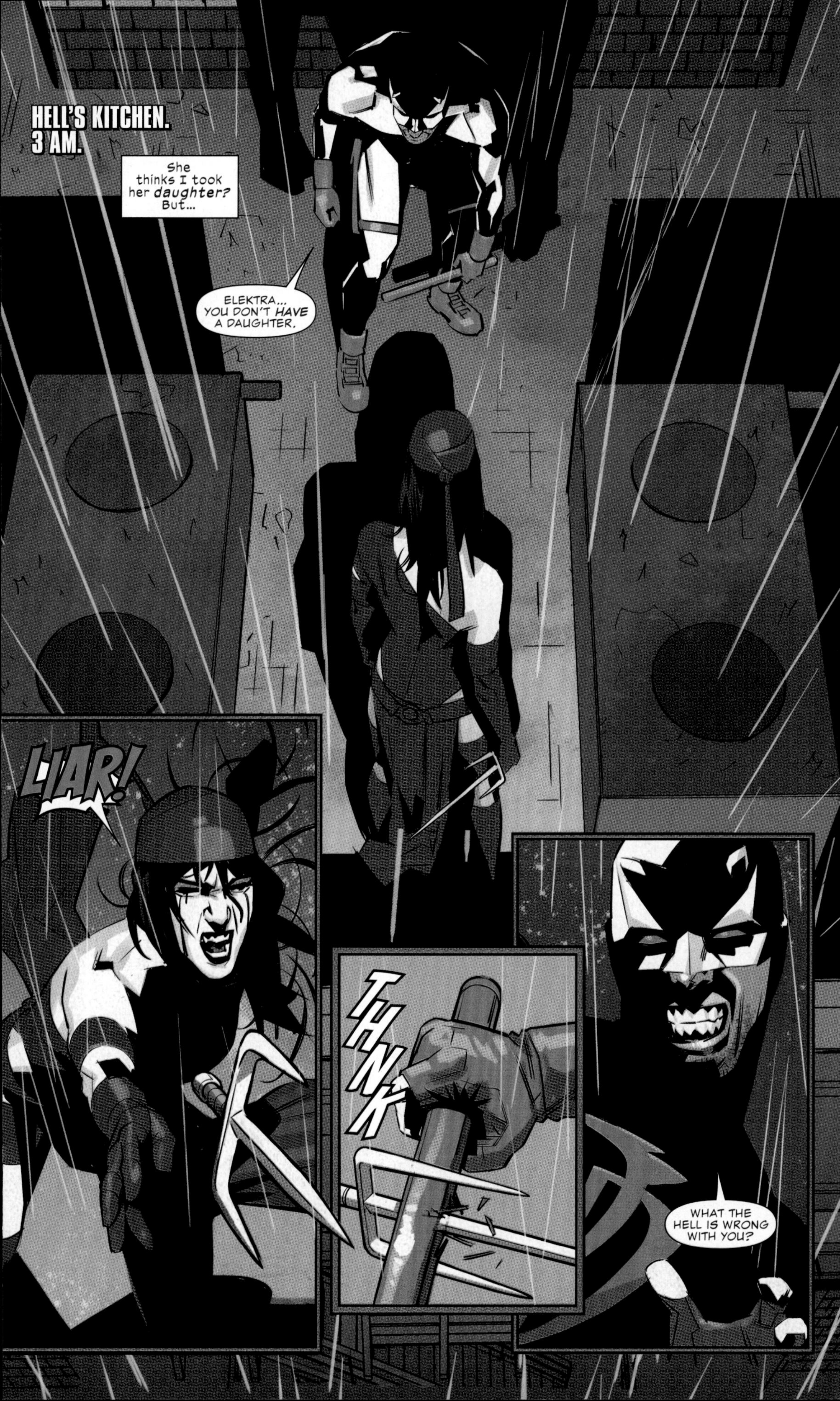
HELL'S KITCHEN.
3 AM.
She thinks I took her *daughter?* But...
ELEKTRA... YOU DON'T *HAVE* A DAUGHTER.
LIAR!
THNK
WHAT THE HELL IS WRONG WITH YOU?

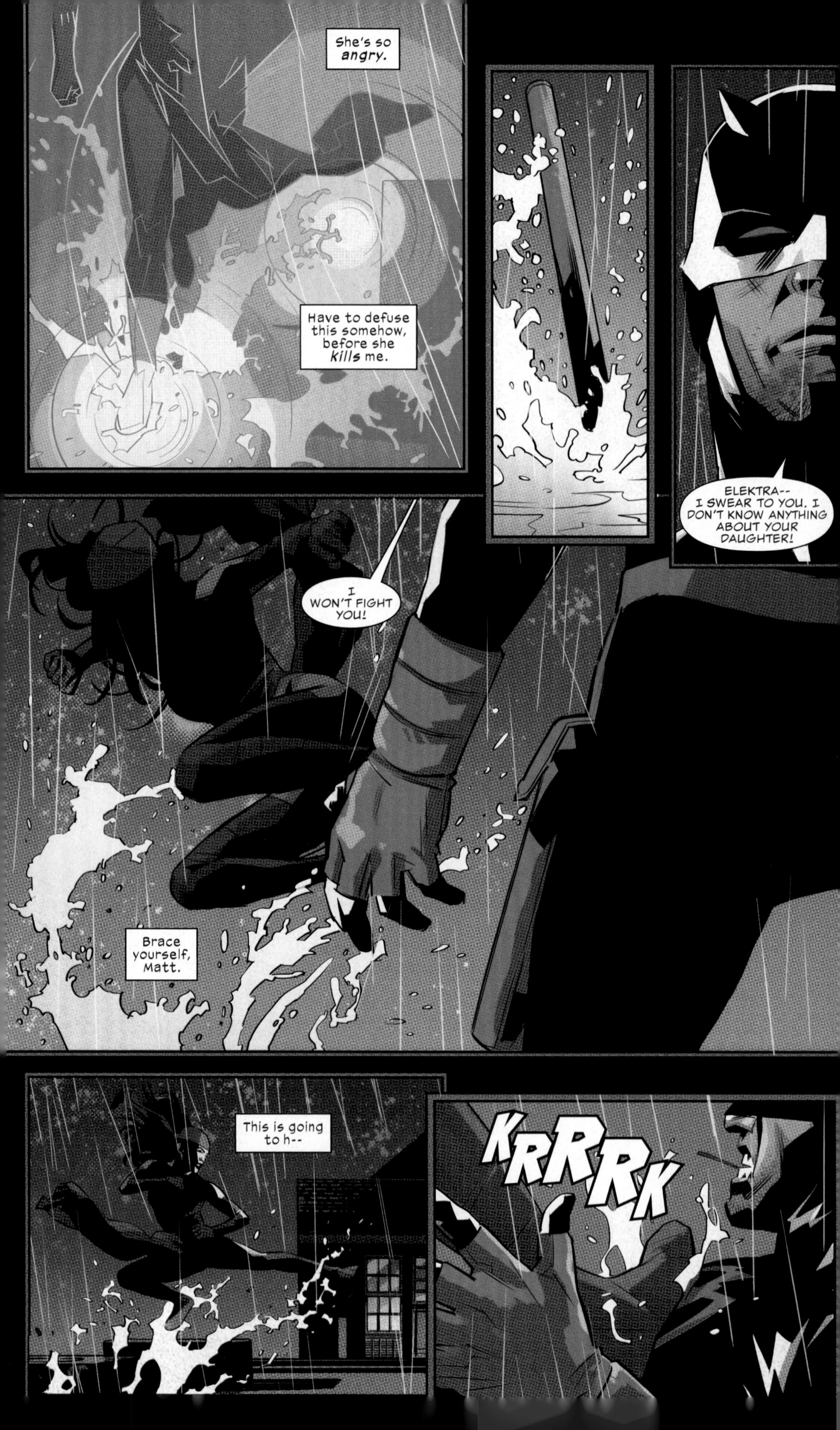
She's so angry.
Have to defuse this somehow, before she kills me.
ELEKTRA-- I SWEAR TO YOU. I DON'T KNOW ANYTHING ABOUT YOUR DAUGHTER!
I WON'T FIGHT YOU!
Brace yourself, Matt.
This is going to h--
KRRRK

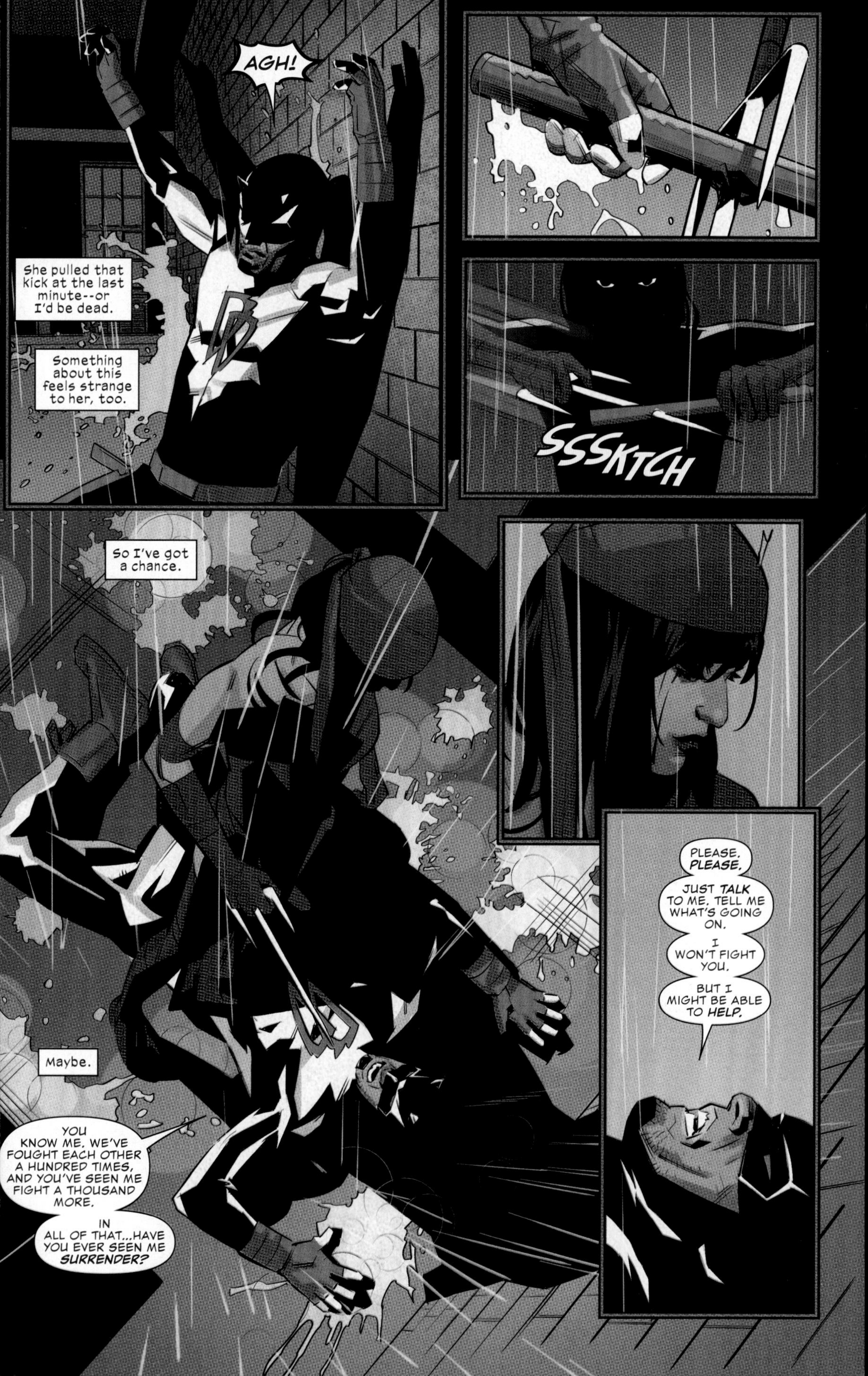
AGH!
She pulled that kick at the last minute--or I'd be dead.
Something about this feels strange to her, too.
SSSKTCH
So I've got a chance.
Maybe.
YOU KNOW ME. WE'VE FOUGHT EACH OTHER A HUNDRED TIMES, AND YOU'VE SEEN ME FIGHT A THOUSAND MORE.
IN ALL OF THAT...HAVE YOU EVER SEEN ME SURRENDER?
PLEASE. PLEASE.
JUST TALK TO ME. TELL ME WHAT'S GOING ON.
I WON'T FIGHT YOU.
BUT I MIGHT BE ABLE TO HELP.

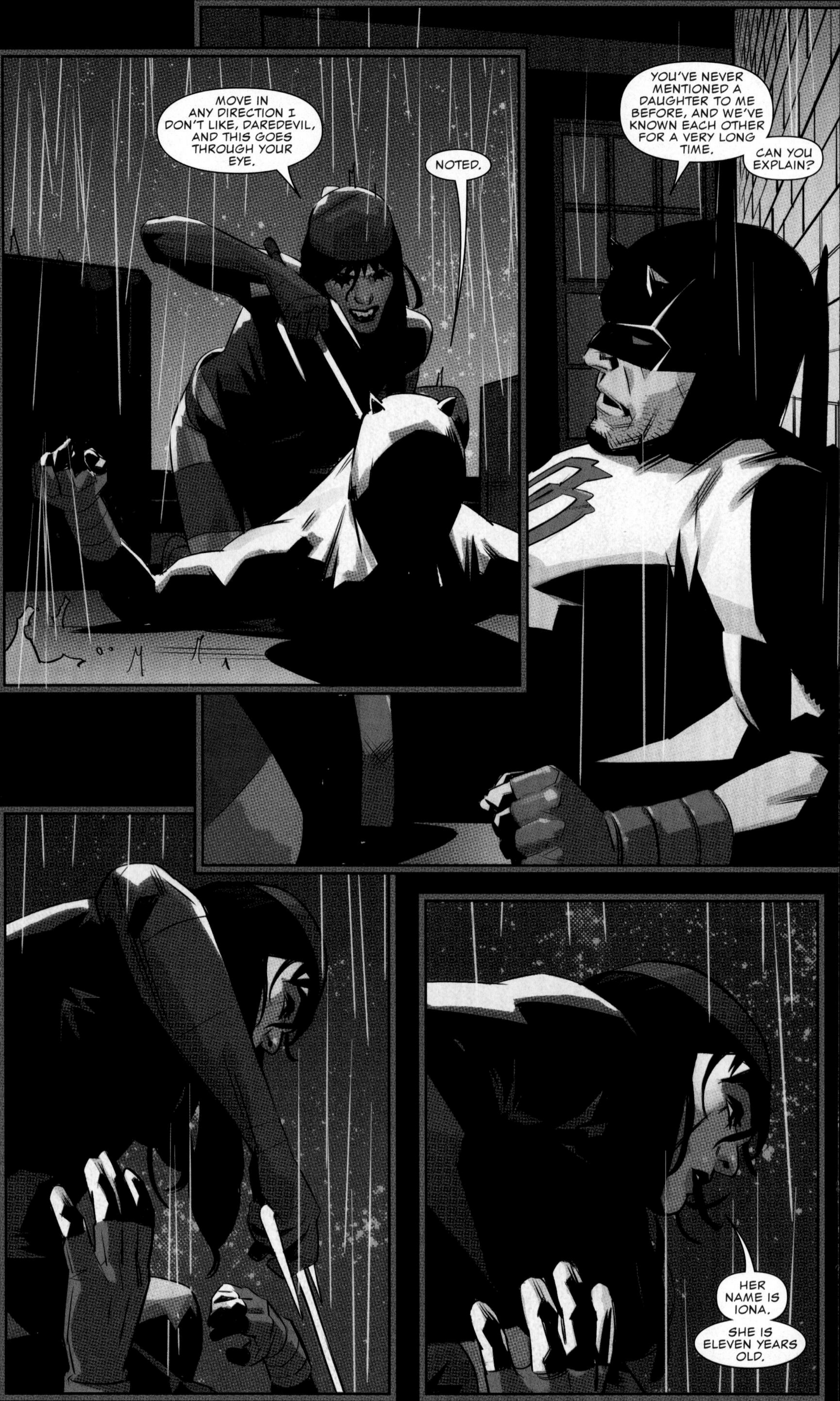
MOVE IN ANY DIRECTION I DON'T LIKE, DAREDEVIL, AND THIS GOES THROUGH YOUR EYE.
NOTED.
YOU'VE NEVER MENTIONED A DAUGHTER TO ME BEFORE, AND WE'VE KNOWN EACH OTHER FOR A VERY LONG TIME.
CAN YOU EXPLAIN?
HER NAME IS IONA.
SHE IS ELEVEN YEARS OLD.

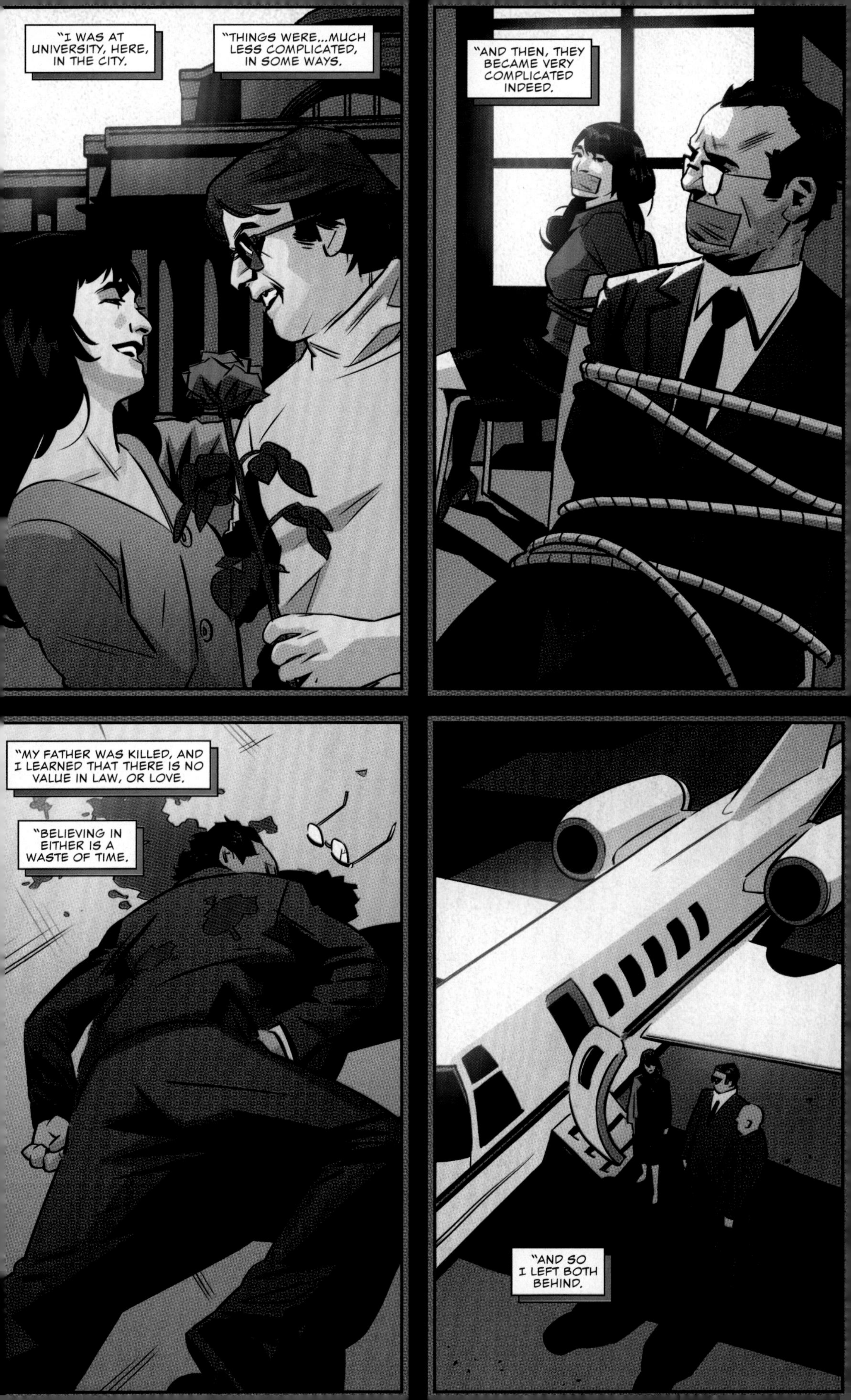
"I WAS AT UNIVERSITY, HERE, IN THE CITY.
"THINGS WERE...MUCH LESS COMPLICATED, IN SOME WAYS.
"AND THEN, THEY BECAME VERY COMPLICATED INDEED.
"MY FATHER WAS KILLED, AND I LEARNED THAT THERE IS NO VALUE IN LAW, OR LOVE.
"BELIEVING IN EITHER IS A WASTE OF TIME.
"AND SO I LEFT BOTH BEHIND.

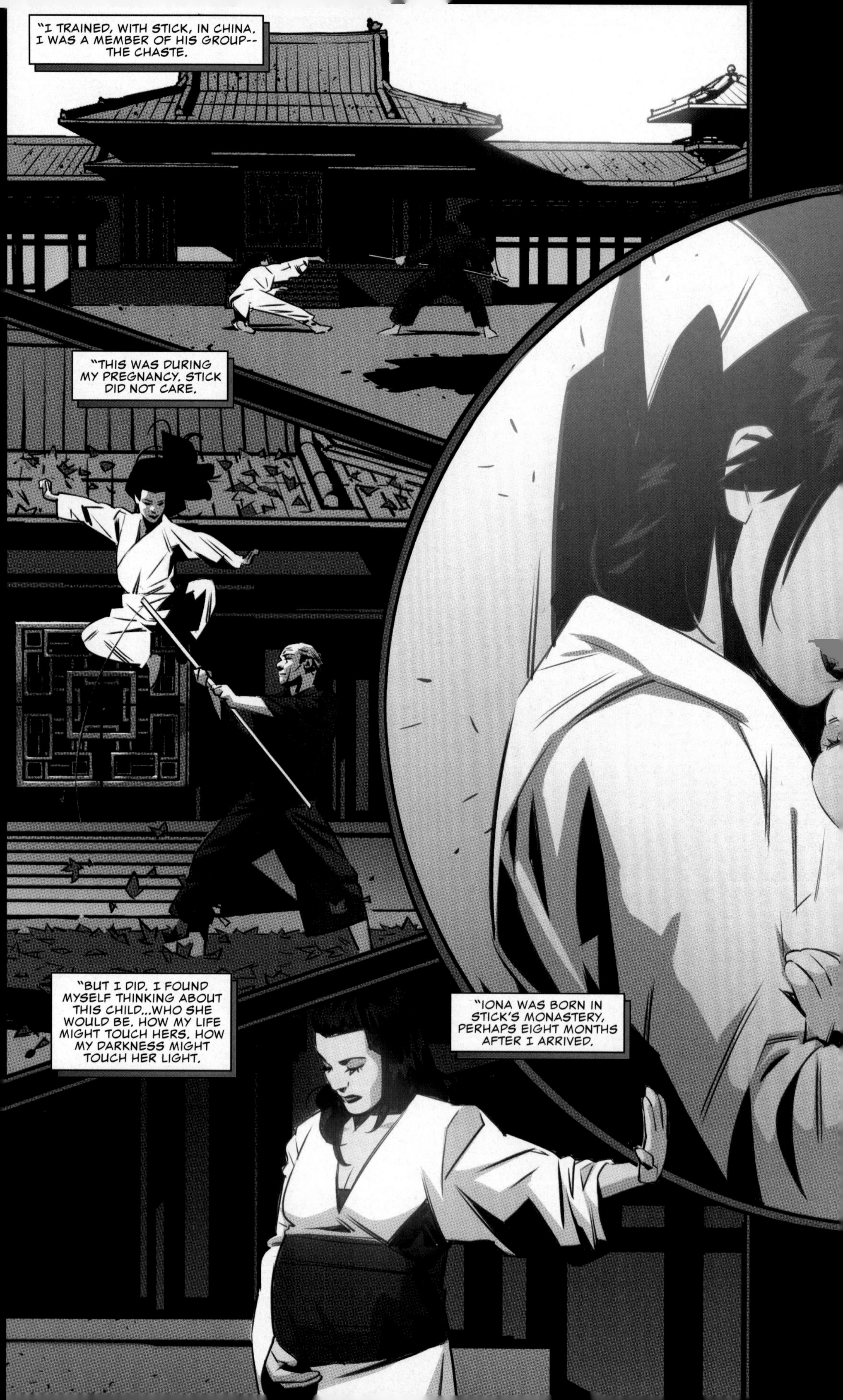

"I TRAINED, WITH STICK, IN CHINA. I WAS A MEMBER OF HIS GROUP-- THE CHASTE.
"THIS WAS DURING MY PREGNANCY. STICK DID NOT CARE.
"BUT I DID. I FOUND MYSELF THINKING ABOUT THIS CHILD...WHO SHE WOULD BE. HOW MY LIFE MIGHT TOUCH HERS. HOW MY DARKNESS MIGHT TOUCH HER LIGHT.
"IONA WAS BORN IN STICK'S MONASTERY, PERHAPS EIGHT MONTHS AFTER I ARRIVED.

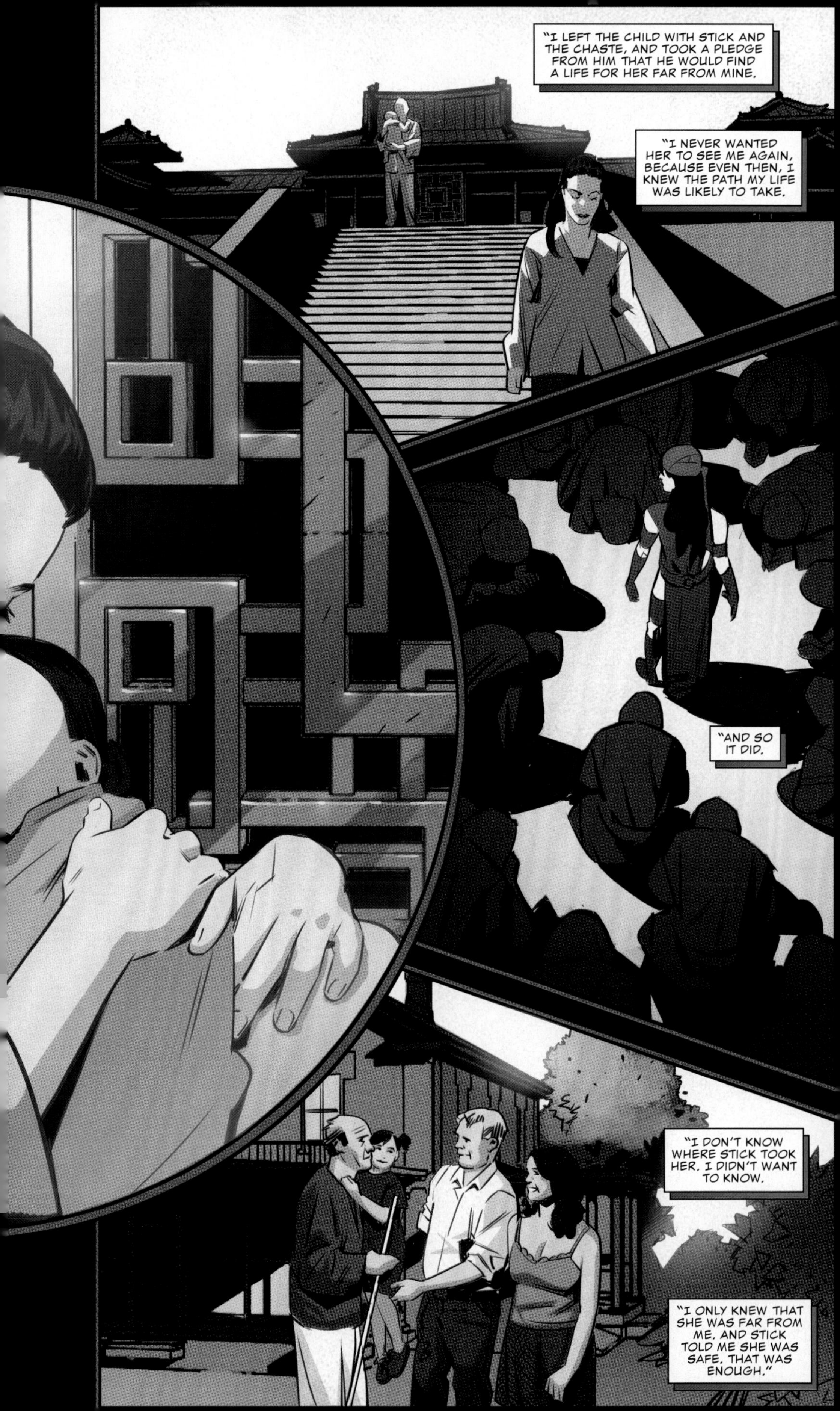
"I LEFT THE CHILD WITH STICK AND THE CHASTE, AND TOOK A PLEDGE FROM HIM THAT HE WOULD FIND A LIFE FOR HER FAR FROM MINE.
"I NEVER WANTED HER TO SEE ME AGAIN, BECAUSE EVEN THEN, I KNEW THE PATH MY LIFE WAS LIKELY TO TAKE.
"AND SO IT DID.
"I DON'T KNOW WHERE STICK TOOK HER. I DIDN'T WANT TO KNOW.
"I ONLY KNEW THAT SHE WAS FAR FROM ME, AND STICK TOLD ME SHE WAS SAFE. THAT WAS ENOUGH."

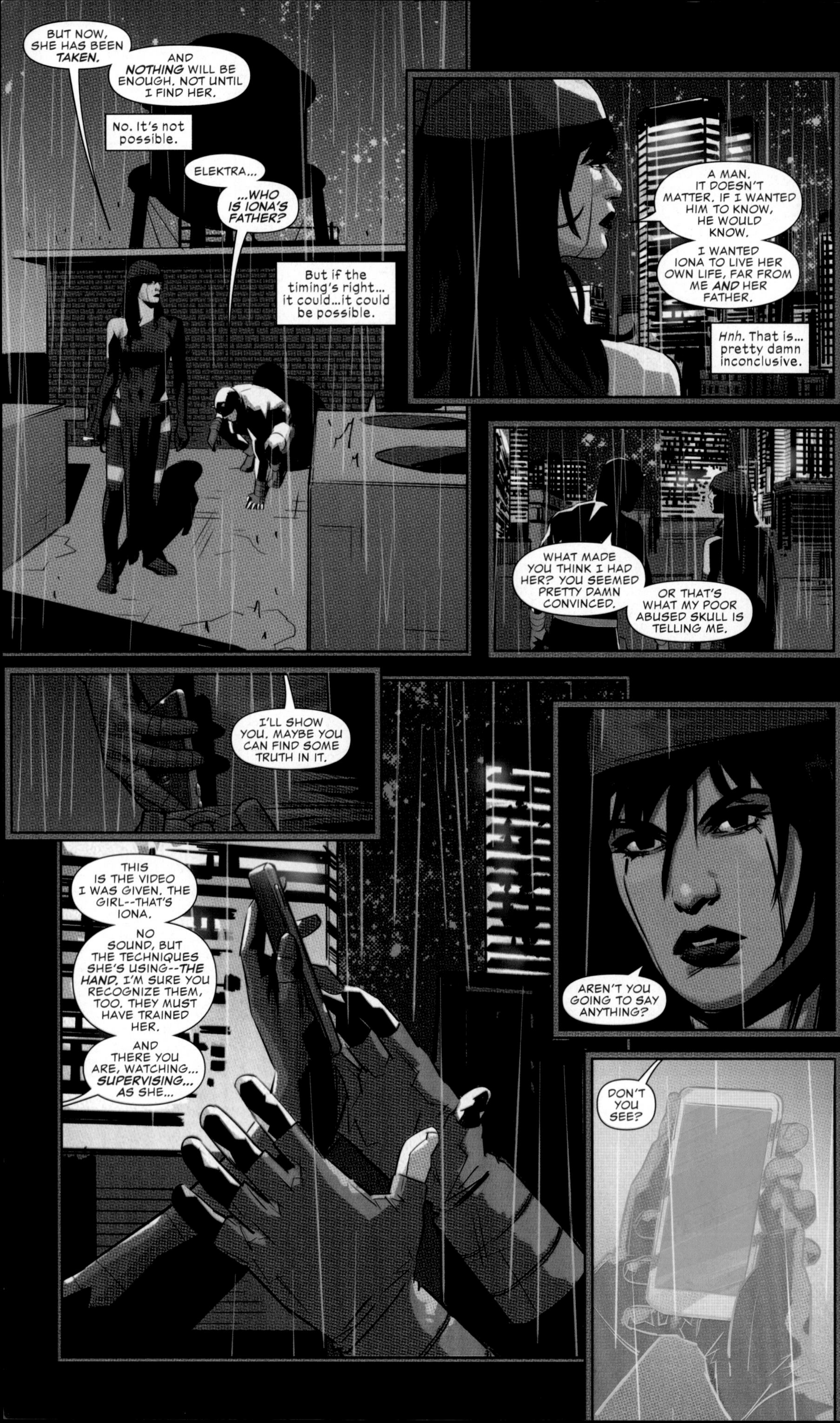
BUT NOW, SHE HAS BEEN TAKEN.
AND NOTHING WILL BE ENOUGH. NOT UNTIL I FIND HER.
No. It's not possible.
ELEKTRA...
...WHO IS IONA'S FATHER?
But if the timing's right... it could...it could be possible.
A MAN. IT DOESN'T MATTER. IF I WANTED HIM TO KNOW, HE WOULD KNOW.
I WANTED IONA TO LIVE HER OWN LIFE, FAR FROM ME AND HER FATHER.
Hnh. That is... pretty damn inconclusive.
WHAT MADE YOU THINK I HAD HER? YOU SEEMED PRETTY DAMN CONVINCED.
OR THAT'S WHAT MY POOR ABUSED SKULL IS TELLING ME.
I'LL SHOW YOU. MAYBE YOU CAN FIND SOME TRUTH IN IT.
THIS IS THE VIDEO I WAS GIVEN. THE GIRL--THAT'S IONA.
NO SOUND, BUT THE TECHNIQUES SHE'S USING--THE HAND. I'M SURE YOU RECOGNIZE THEM, TOO. THEY MUST HAVE TRAINED HER.
AND THERE YOU ARE, WATCHING... SUPERVISING... AS SHE...
AREN'T YOU GOING TO SAY ANYTHING?
DON'T YOU SEE?

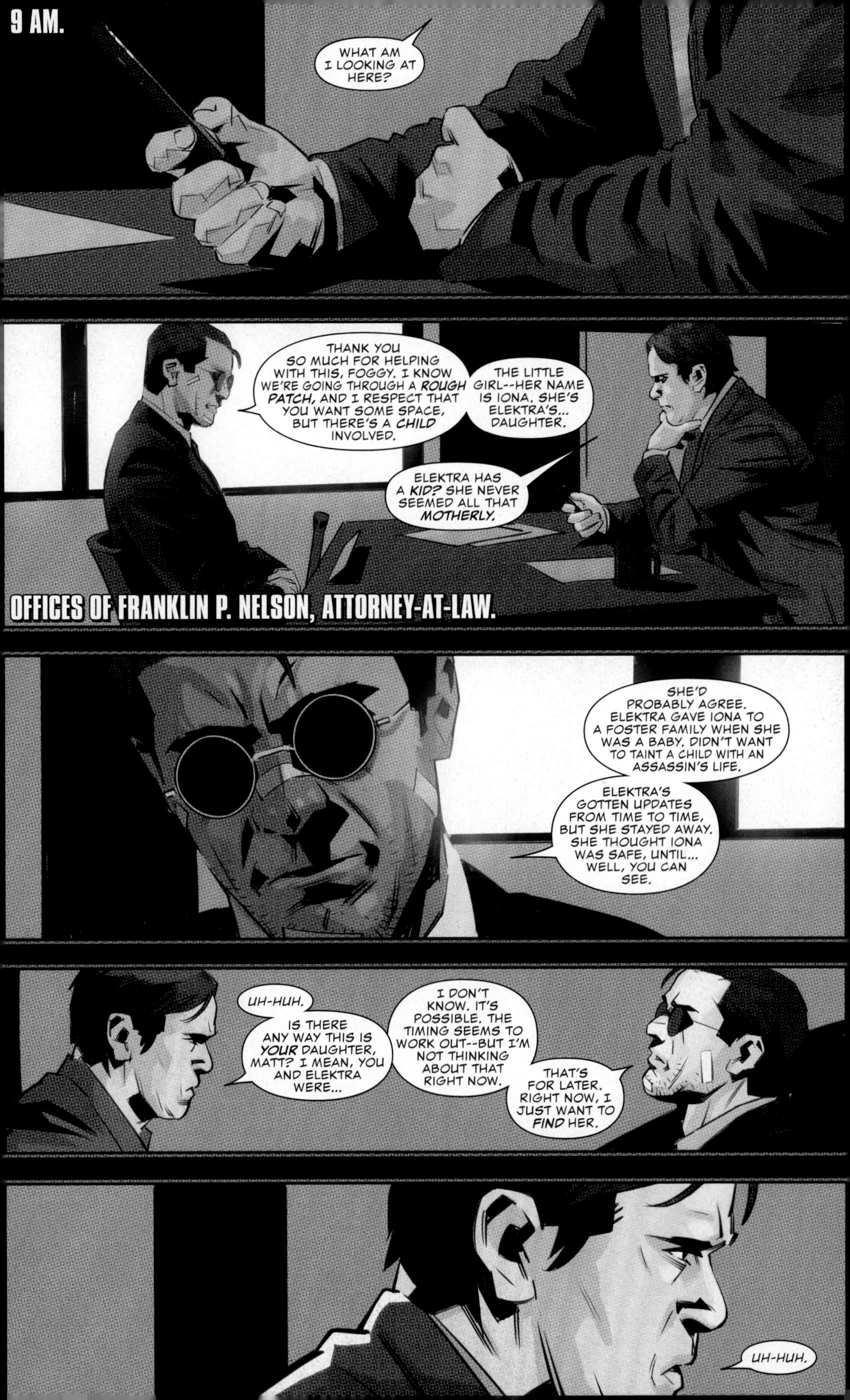

9 AM.
WHAT AM I LOOKING AT HERE?
THANK YOU SO MUCH FOR HELPING WITH THIS, FOGGY. I KNOW WE'RE GOING THROUGH A *ROUGH PATCH,* AND I RESPECT THAT YOU WANT SOME SPACE, BUT THERE'S A *CHILD* INVOLVED.
THE LITTLE GIRL--HER NAME IS IONA. SHE'S ELEKTRA'S... DAUGHTER.
ELEKTRA HAS A *KID?* SHE NEVER SEEMED ALL THAT *MOTHERLY.*
OFFICES OF FRANKLIN P. NELSON, ATTORNEY-AT-LAW.
SHE'D PROBABLY AGREE. ELEKTRA GAVE IONA TO A FOSTER FAMILY WHEN SHE WAS A BABY. DIDN'T WANT TO TAINT A CHILD WITH AN ASSASSIN'S LIFE.
ELEKTRA'S GOTTEN UPDATES FROM TIME TO TIME, BUT SHE STAYED AWAY. SHE THOUGHT IONA WAS SAFE, UNTIL... WELL, YOU CAN SEE.
UH-HUH.
IS THERE ANY WAY THIS IS *YOUR* DAUGHTER, MATT? I MEAN, YOU AND ELEKTRA WERE...
I DON'T KNOW. IT'S POSSIBLE. THE TIMING SEEMS TO WORK OUT--BUT I'M NOT THINKING ABOUT THAT RIGHT NOW.
THAT'S FOR LATER. RIGHT NOW, I JUST WANT TO *FIND* HER.
UH-HUH.

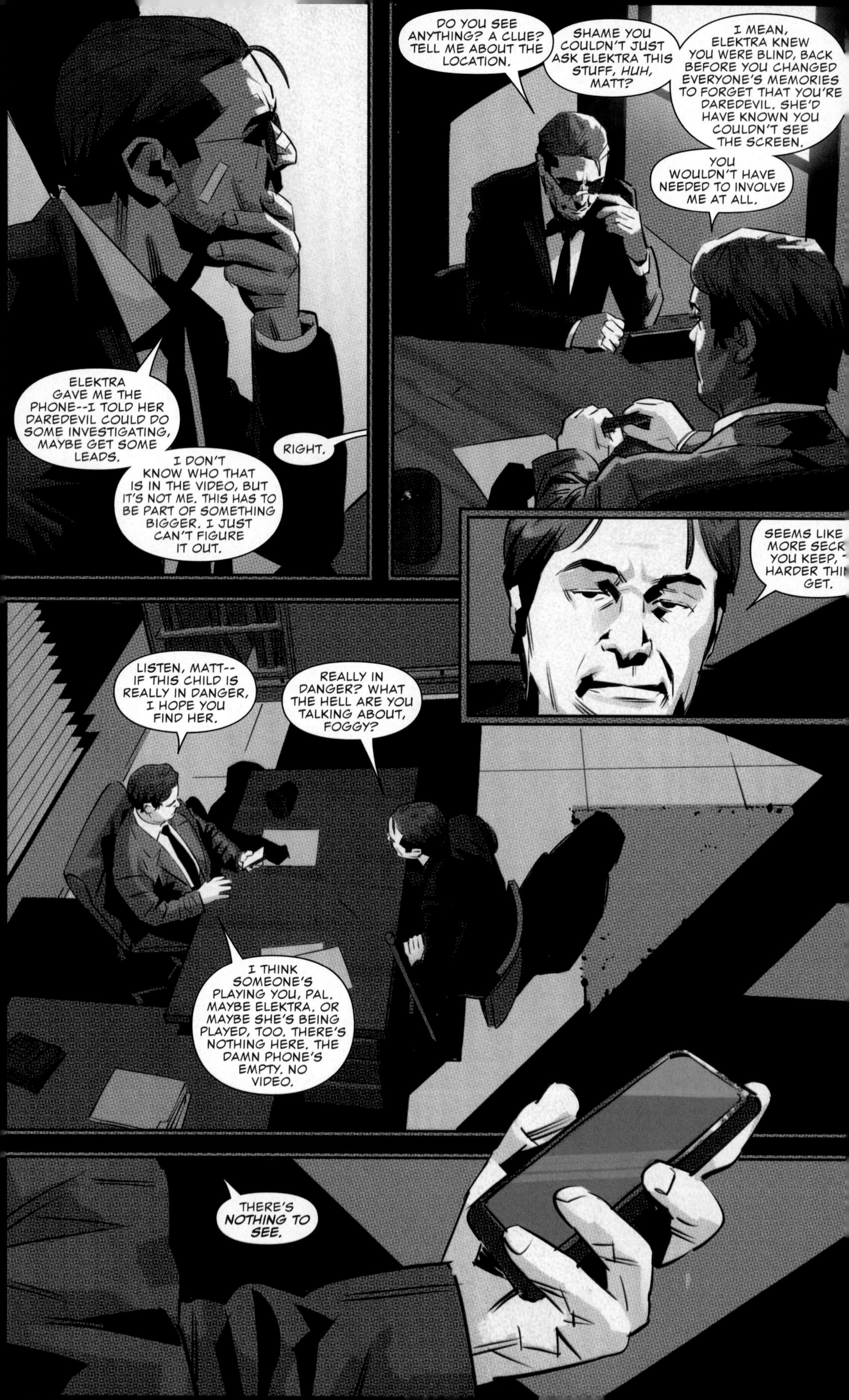
ELEKTRA GAVE ME THE PHONE--I TOLD HER DAREDEVIL COULD DO SOME INVESTIGATING, MAYBE GET SOME LEADS.
RIGHT.
I DON'T KNOW WHO THAT IS IN THE VIDEO, BUT IT'S NOT ME. THIS HAS TO BE PART OF SOMETHING BIGGER. I JUST CAN'T FIGURE IT OUT.
DO YOU SEE ANYTHING? A CLUE? TELL ME ABOUT THE LOCATION.
SHAME YOU COULDN'T JUST ASK ELEKTRA THIS STUFF, *HUH*, MATT?
I MEAN, ELEKTRA KNEW YOU WERE BLIND, BACK BEFORE YOU CHANGED EVERYONE'S MEMORIES TO FORGET THAT YOU'RE DAREDEVIL. SHE'D HAVE KNOWN YOU COULDN'T SEE THE SCREEN.
YOU WOULDN'T HAVE NEEDED TO INVOLVE ME AT ALL.
LISTEN, MATT-- IF THIS CHILD IS REALLY IN DANGER, I HOPE YOU FIND HER.
REALLY IN DANGER? WHAT THE HELL ARE YOU TALKING ABOUT, FOGGY?
I THINK SOMEONE'S PLAYING YOU, PAL. MAYBE ELEKTRA. OR MAYBE SHE'S BEING PLAYED, TOO. THERE'S NOTHING HERE. THE DAMN PHONE'S EMPTY. NO VIDEO.
THERE'S *NOTHING TO SEE.*

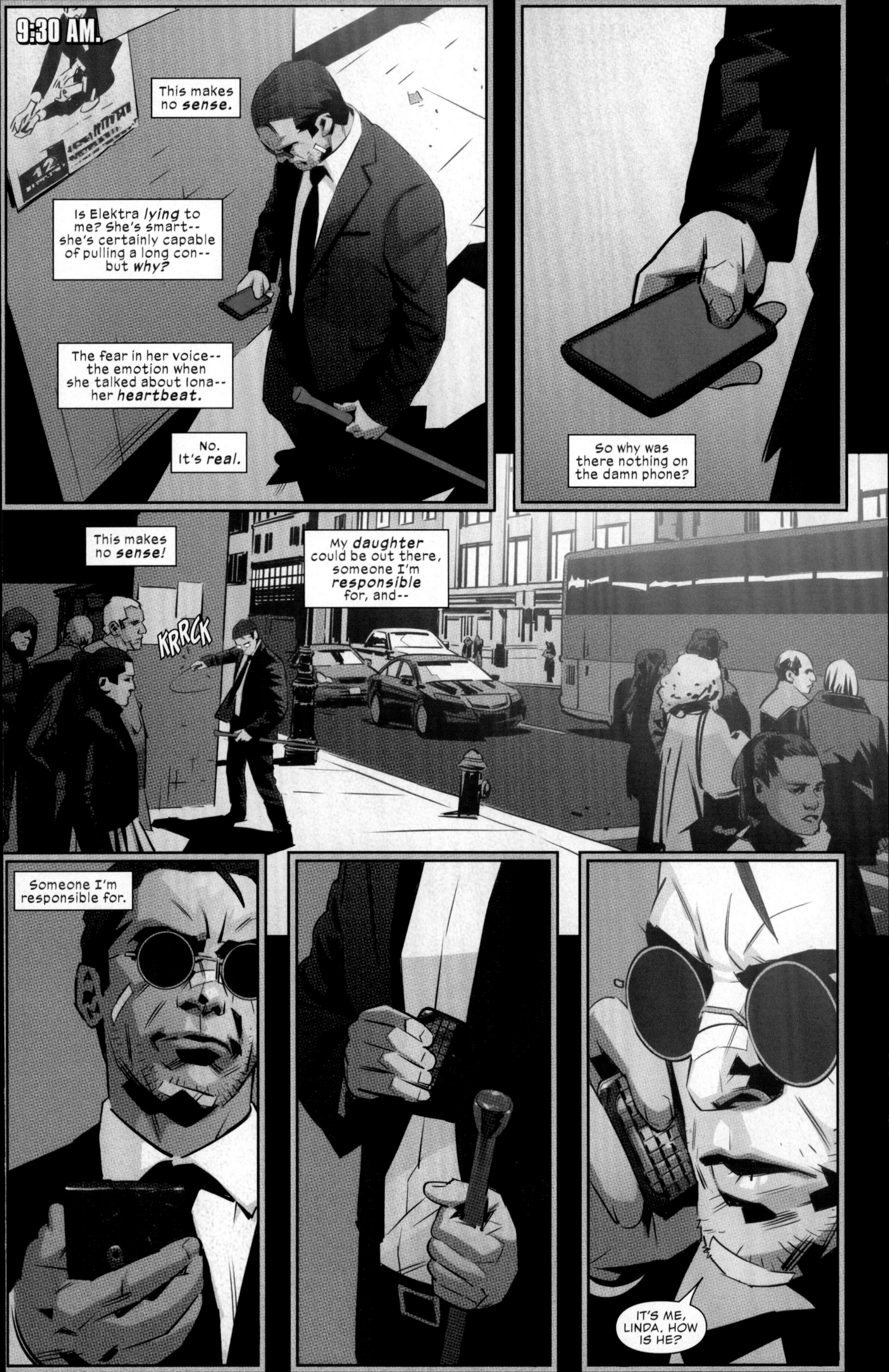
9:30 AM.
This makes no *sense.*
Is Elektra *lying* to me? She's smart-- she's certainly capable of pulling a long con-- but *why?*
The fear in her voice-- the emotion when she talked about Iona-- her *heartbeat.*
No. It's *real.*
So why was there nothing on the damn phone?
This makes no *sense!*
My *daughter* could be out there, someone I'm *responsible* for, and--
KRRCK
Someone I'm responsible for.
IT'S ME, LINDA. HOW IS HE?

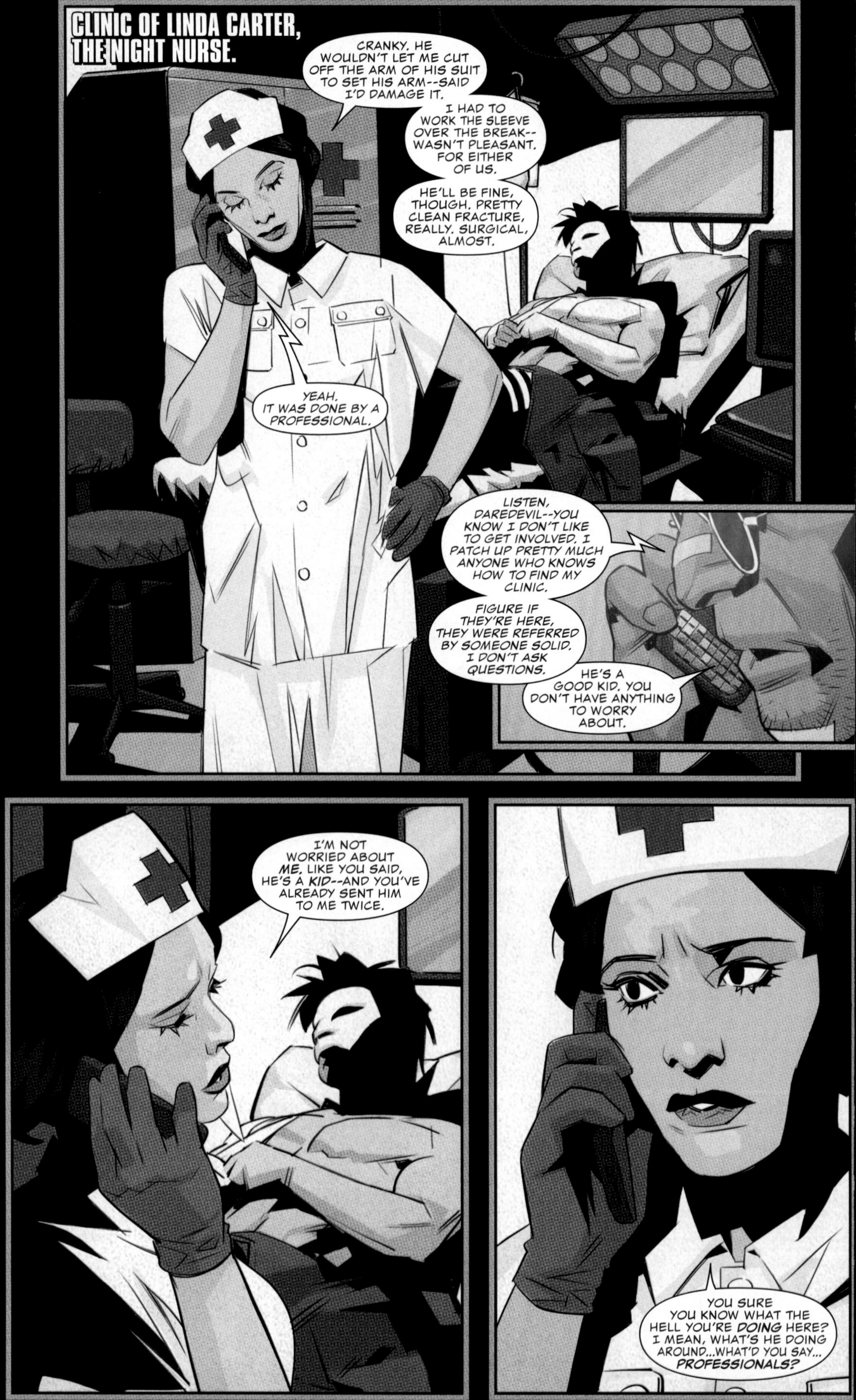
CLINIC OF LINDA CARTER, THE NIGHT NURSE.
CRANKY. HE WOULDN'T LET ME CUT OFF THE ARM OF HIS SUIT TO SET HIS ARM--SAID I'D DAMAGE IT.
I HAD TO WORK THE SLEEVE OVER THE BREAK--WASN'T PLEASANT. FOR EITHER OF US.
HE'LL BE FINE, THOUGH. PRETTY CLEAN FRACTURE, REALLY. SURGICAL, ALMOST.
YEAH. IT WAS DONE BY A PROFESSIONAL.
LISTEN, DAREDEVIL--YOU KNOW I DON'T LIKE TO GET INVOLVED. I PATCH UP PRETTY MUCH ANYONE WHO KNOWS HOW TO FIND MY CLINIC.
FIGURE IF THEY'RE HERE, THEY WERE REFERRED BY SOMEONE SOLID. I DON'T ASK QUESTIONS.
HE'S A GOOD KID. YOU DON'T HAVE ANYTHING TO WORRY ABOUT.
I'M NOT WORRIED ABOUT ME. LIKE YOU SAID, HE'S A KID--AND YOU'VE ALREADY SENT HIM TO ME TWICE.
YOU SURE YOU KNOW WHAT THE HELL YOU'RE DOING HERE? I MEAN, WHAT'S HE DOING AROUND...WHAT'D YOU SAY... PROFESSIONALS?

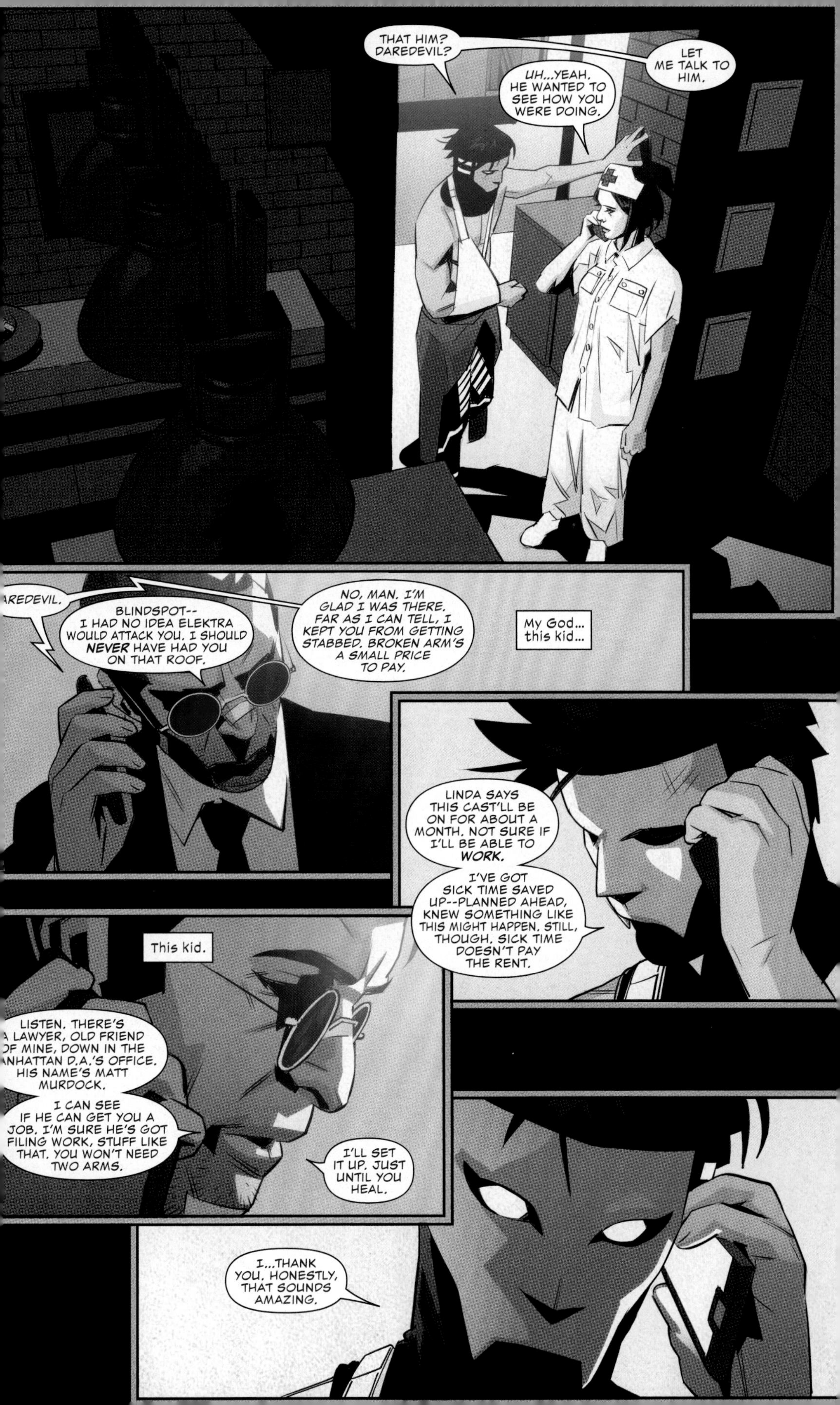
THAT HIM? DAREDEVIL?
UH...YEAH. HE WANTED TO SEE HOW YOU WERE DOING.
LET ME TALK TO HIM.
AREDEVIL.
BLINDSPOT-- I HAD NO IDEA ELEKTRA WOULD ATTACK YOU. I SHOULD NEVER HAVE HAD YOU ON THAT ROOF.
NO, MAN. I'M GLAD I WAS THERE. FAR AS I CAN TELL, I KEPT YOU FROM GETTING STABBED. BROKEN ARM'S A SMALL PRICE TO PAY.
My God... this kid...
LINDA SAYS THIS CAST'LL BE ON FOR ABOUT A MONTH. NOT SURE IF I'LL BE ABLE TO WORK.
I'VE GOT SICK TIME SAVED UP--PLANNED AHEAD, KNEW SOMETHING LIKE THIS MIGHT HAPPEN. STILL, THOUGH. SICK TIME DOESN'T PAY THE RENT.
This kid.
LISTEN. THERE'S A LAWYER, OLD FRIEND OF MINE, DOWN IN THE ANHATTAN D.A.'S OFFICE. HIS NAME'S MATT MURDOCK.
I CAN SEE IF HE CAN GET YOU A JOB. I'M SURE HE'S GOT FILING WORK, STUFF LIKE THAT. YOU WON'T NEED TWO ARMS.
I'LL SET IT UP. JUST UNTIL YOU HEAL.
I...THANK YOU. HONESTLY, THAT SOUNDS AMAZING.

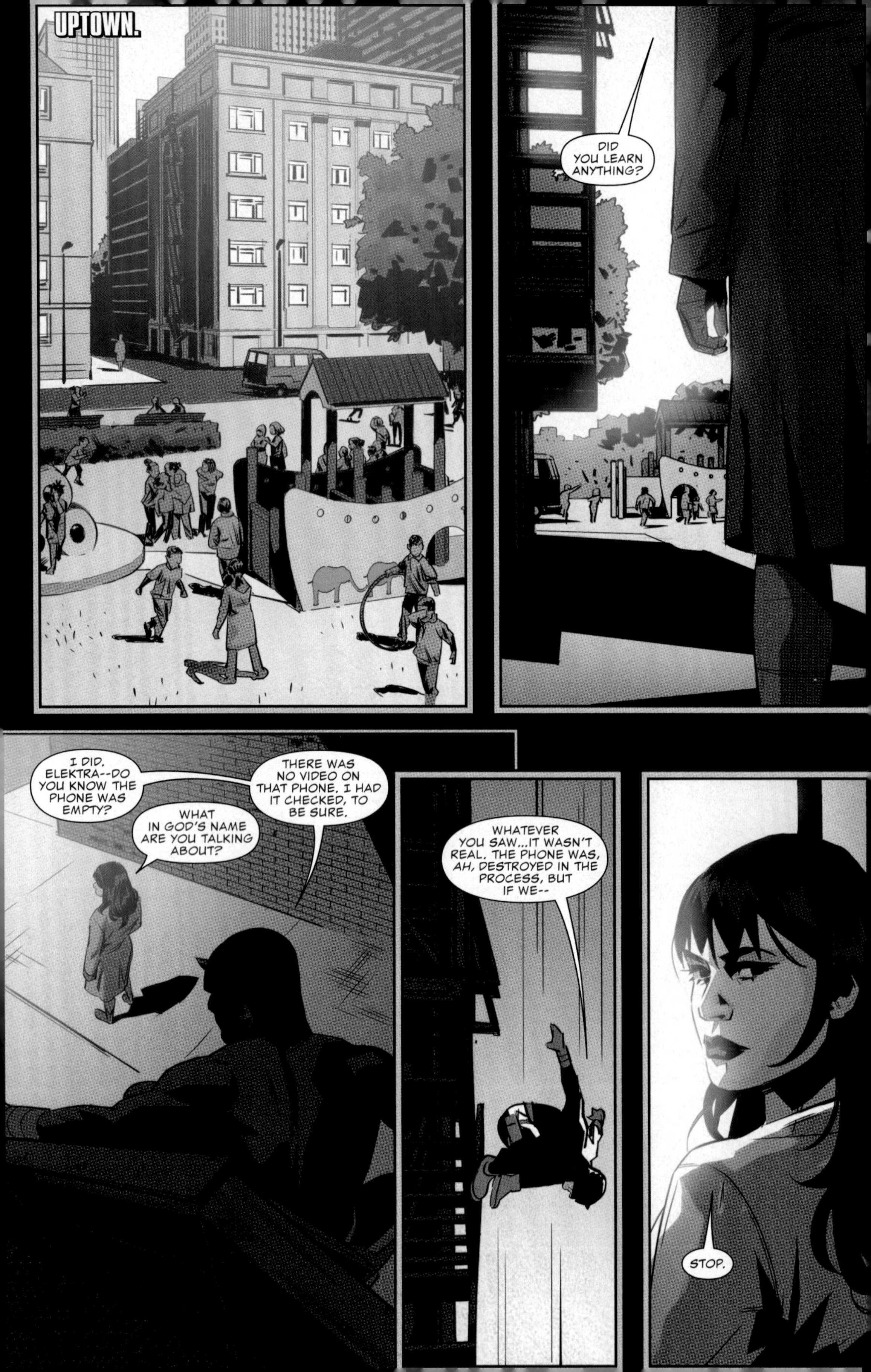
UPTOWN.
DID YOU LEARN ANYTHING?
I DID. ELEKTRA--DO YOU KNOW THE PHONE WAS EMPTY?
WHAT IN GOD'S NAME ARE YOU TALKING ABOUT?
THERE WAS NO VIDEO ON THAT PHONE. I HAD IT CHECKED, TO BE SURE.
WHATEVER YOU SAW...IT WASN'T REAL. THE PHONE WAS, AH, DESTROYED IN THE PROCESS, BUT IF WE--
STOP.

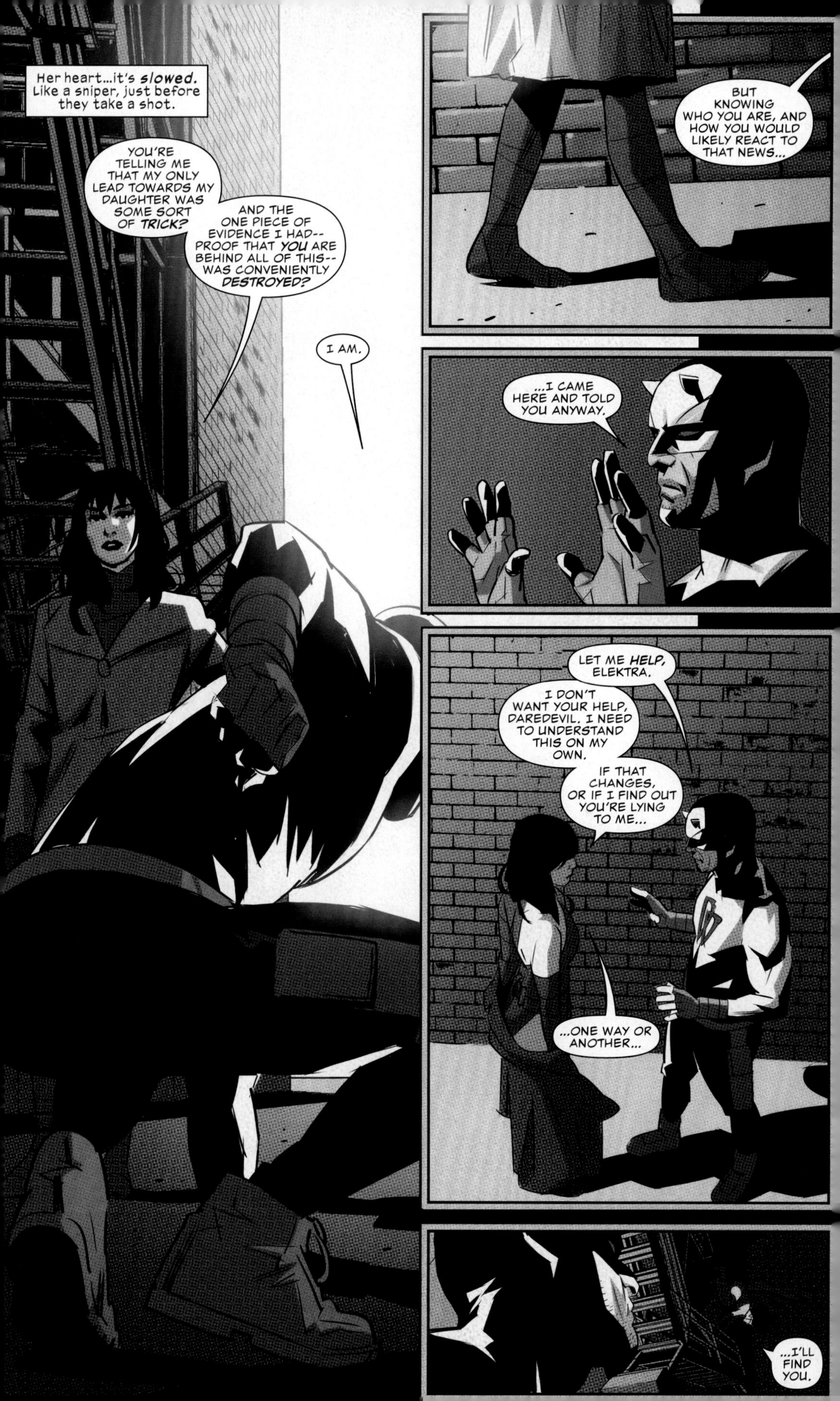
Her heart...it's *slowed.* Like a sniper, just before they take a shot.
YOU'RE TELLING ME THAT MY ONLY LEAD TOWARDS MY DAUGHTER WAS SOME SORT OF ***TRICK?***
AND THE ONE PIECE OF EVIDENCE I HAD-- PROOF THAT ***YOU*** ARE BEHIND ALL OF THIS-- WAS CONVENIENTLY ***DESTROYED?***
I AM.
BUT KNOWING WHO YOU ARE, AND HOW YOU WOULD LIKELY REACT TO THAT NEWS...
...I CAME HERE AND TOLD YOU ANYWAY.
LET ME ***HELP,*** ELEKTRA.
I DON'T WANT YOUR HELP, DAREDEVIL. I NEED TO UNDERSTAND THIS ON MY OWN.
IF THAT CHANGES, OR IF I FIND OUT YOU'RE LYING TO ME...
...ONE WAY OR ANOTHER...
...I'LL FIND YOU.

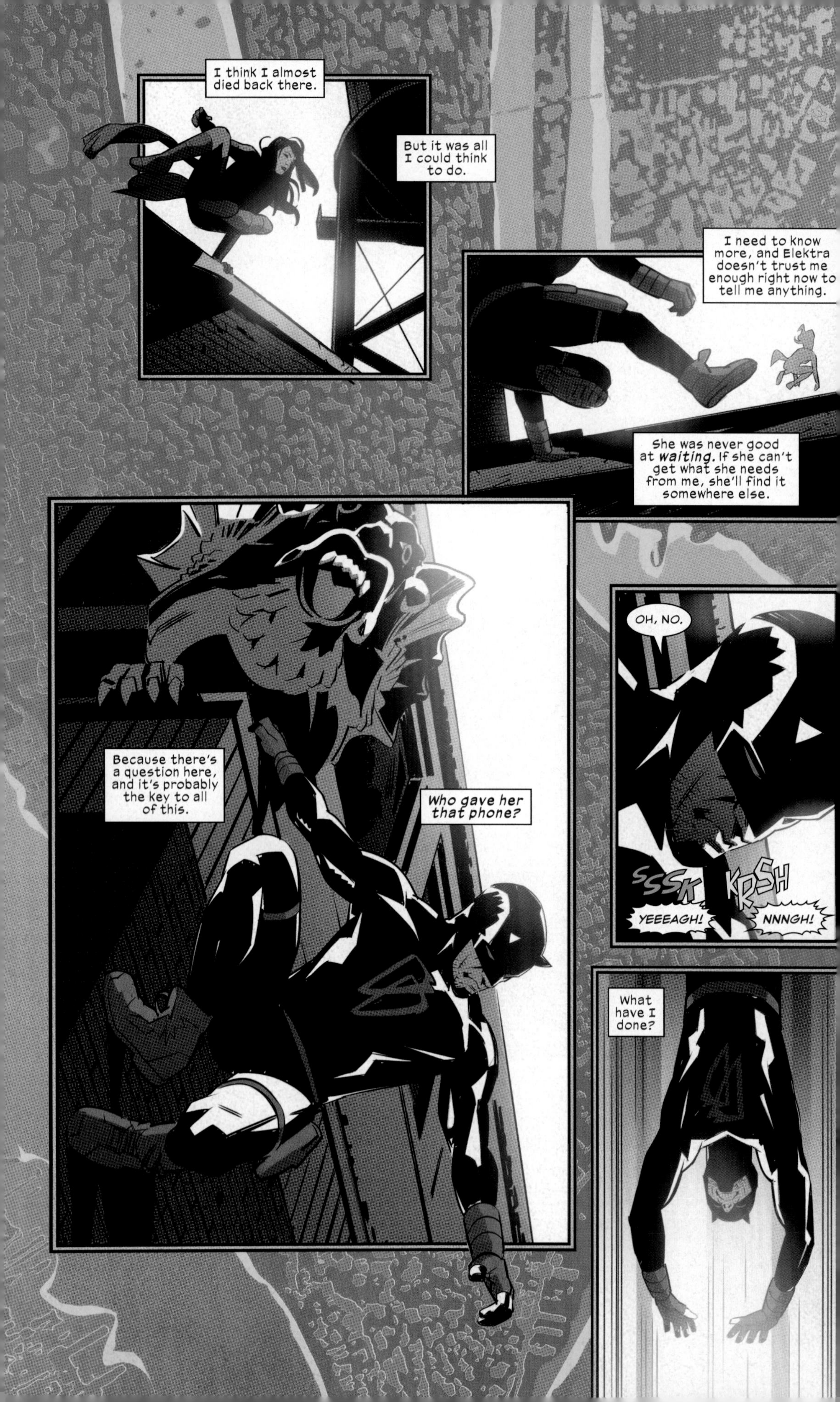
I think I almost died back there.
But it was all I could think to do.
I need to know more, and Elektra doesn't trust me enough right now to tell me anything.
She was never good at *waiting.* If she can't get what she needs from me, she'll find it somewhere else.
Because there's a question here, and it's probably the key to all of this.
Who gave her that phone?
OH, NO.
SSSK
KRSH
YEEEAGH!
NNNGH!
What have I done?

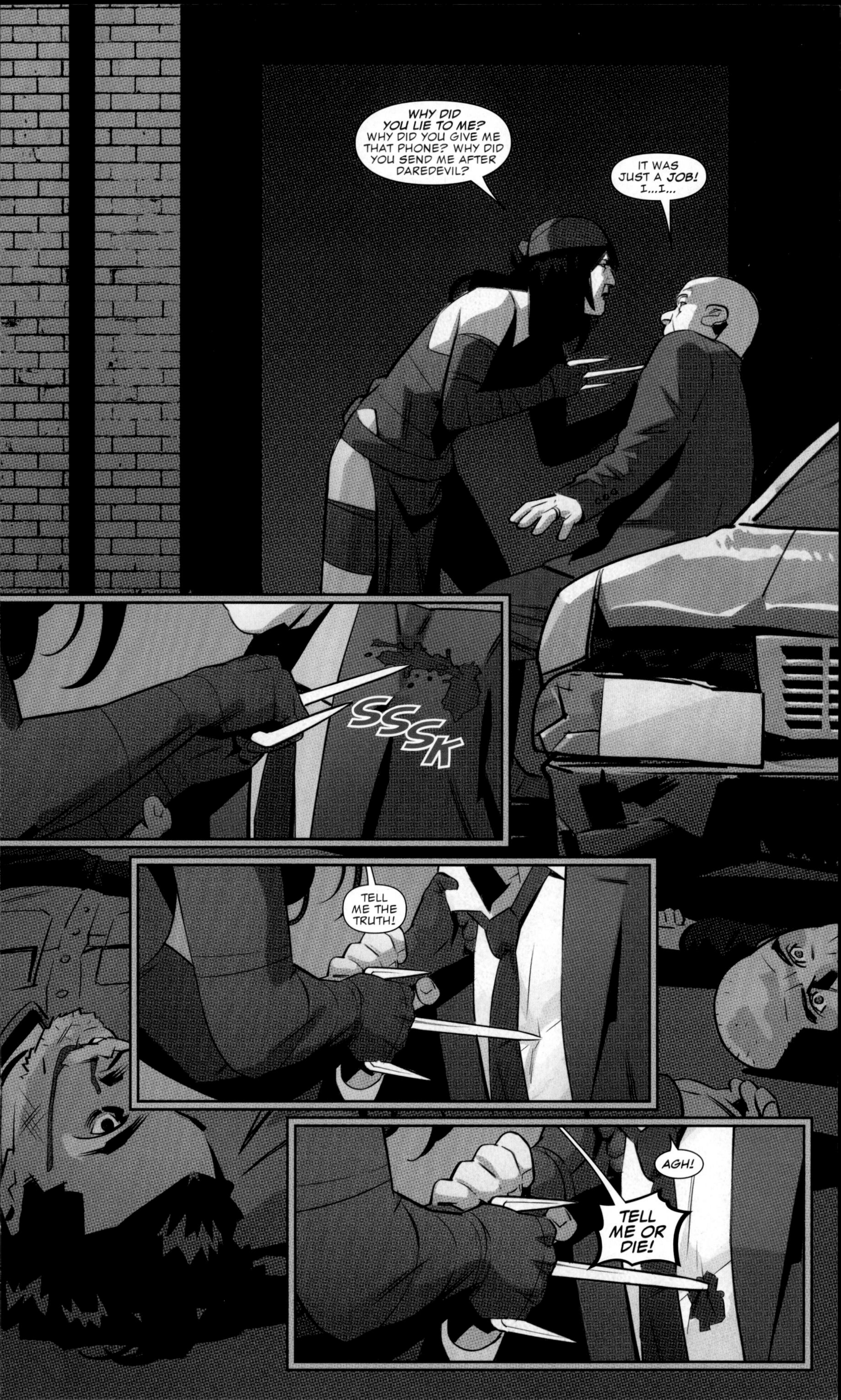
WHY DID YOU LIE TO ME? WHY DID YOU GIVE ME THAT PHONE? WHY DID YOU SEND ME AFTER DAREDEVIL?
IT WAS JUST A JOB! I...I...
SSSK
TELL ME THE TRUTH!
AGH!
TELL ME OR DIE!

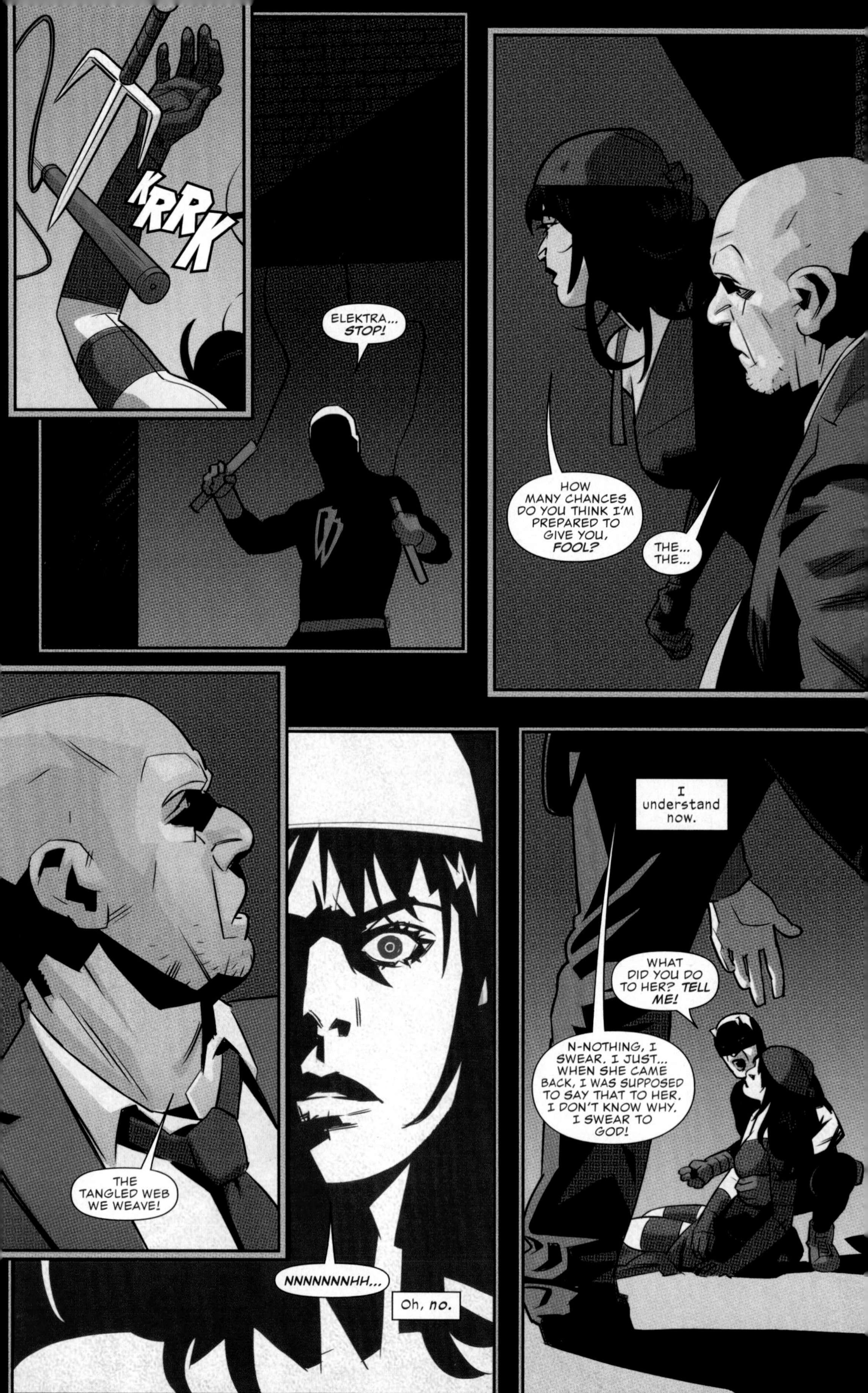
KRRK
ELEKTRA... STOP!
HOW MANY CHANCES DO YOU THINK I'M PREPARED TO GIVE YOU, FOOL?
THE... THE...
THE TANGLED WEB WE WEAVE!
NNNNNNNHH...
Oh, no.
I understand now.
WHAT DID YOU DO TO HER? TELL ME!
N-NOTHING, I SWEAR. I JUST... WHEN SHE CAME BACK, I WAS SUPPOSED TO SAY THAT TO HER. I DON'T KNOW WHY. I SWEAR TO GOD!

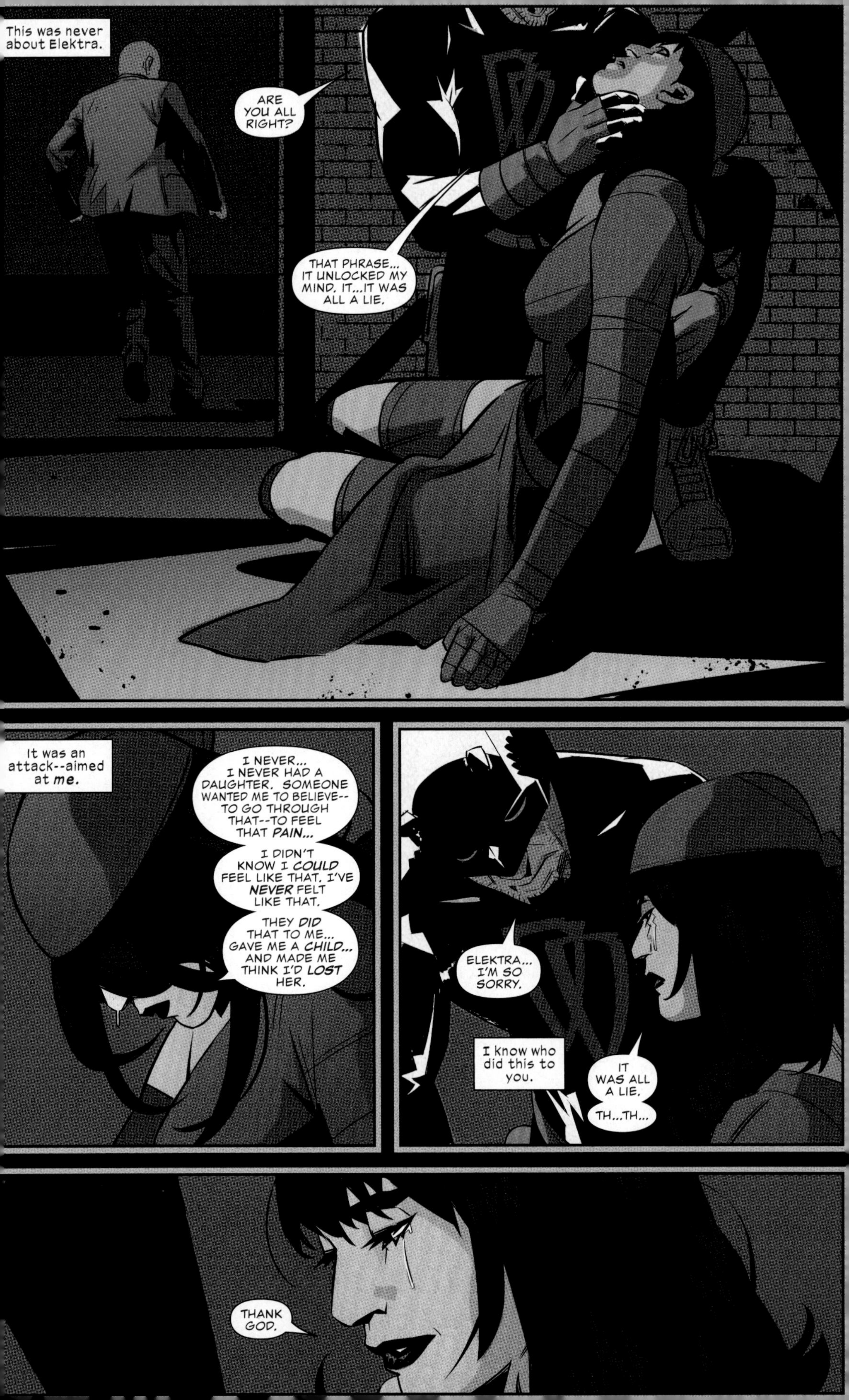
This was never about Elektra.
ARE YOU ALL RIGHT?
THAT PHRASE... IT UNLOCKED MY MIND. IT...IT WAS ALL A LIE.
It was an attack--aimed at *me.*
I NEVER... I NEVER HAD A DAUGHTER. SOMEONE WANTED ME TO BELIEVE-- TO GO THROUGH THAT--TO FEEL THAT *PAIN...*
I DIDN'T KNOW I *COULD* FEEL LIKE THAT. I'VE *NEVER* FELT LIKE THAT.
THEY *DID* THAT TO ME... GAVE ME A *CHILD...* AND MADE ME THINK I'D *LOST* HER.
ELEKTRA... I'M SO SORRY.
I know who did this to you.
IT WAS ALL A LIE.
TH...TH...
THANK GOD.

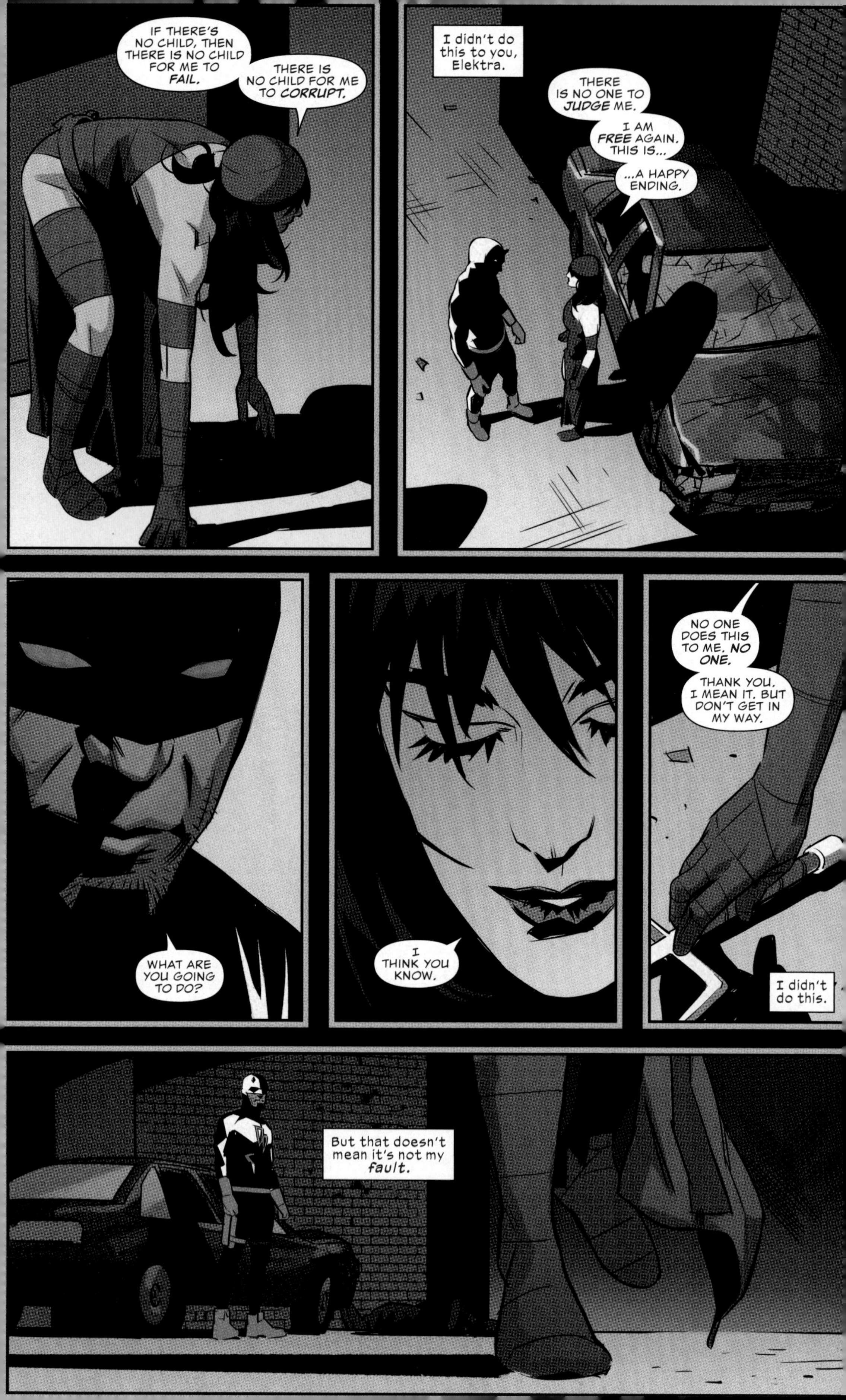

IF THERE'S NO CHILD, THEN THERE IS NO CHILD FOR ME TO *FAIL.*
THERE IS NO CHILD FOR ME TO *CORRUPT.*
I didn't do this to you, Elektra.
THERE IS NO ONE TO *JUDGE* ME.
I AM *FREE* AGAIN. THIS IS...
...A HAPPY ENDING.
WHAT ARE YOU GOING TO DO?
I THINK YOU KNOW.
NO ONE DOES THIS TO ME. *NO ONE.*
THANK YOU. I MEAN IT. BUT DON'T GET IN MY WAY.
I didn't do this.
But that doesn't mean it's not my *fault.*

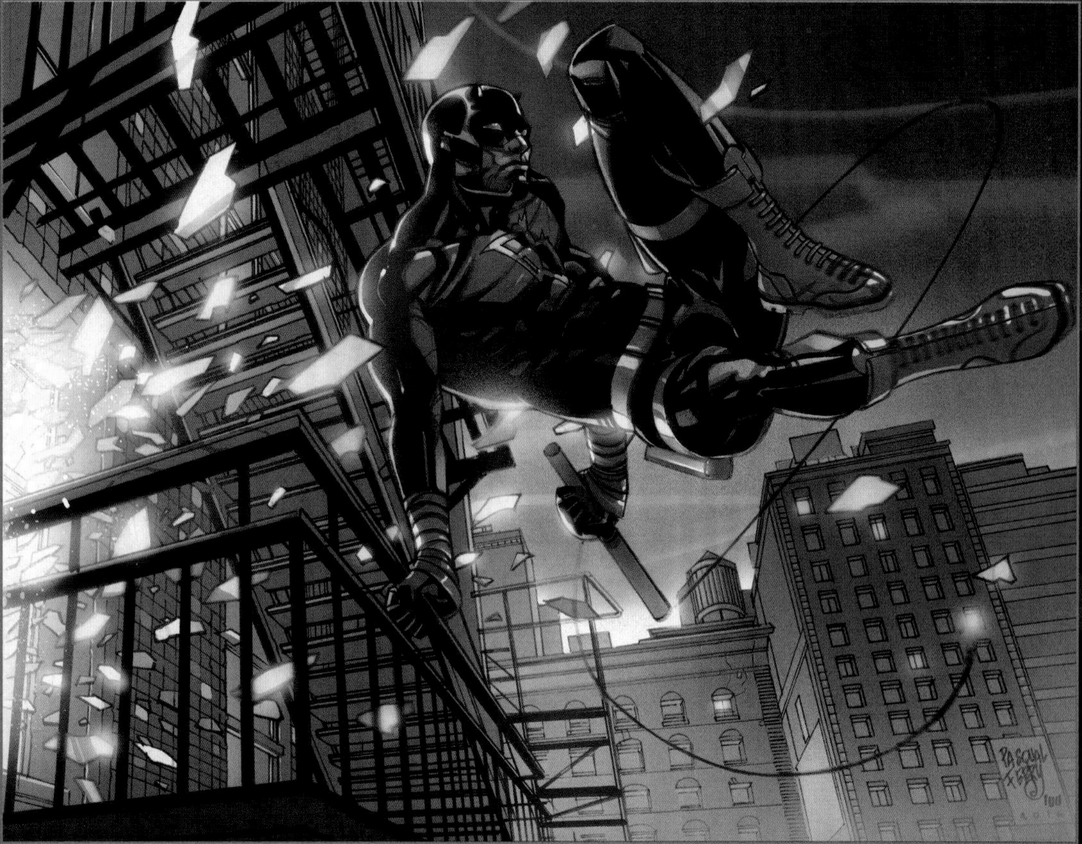

PASQUAL FERRY & FRANK D'ARMATA
No. 6 CIVIL WAR VARIANT

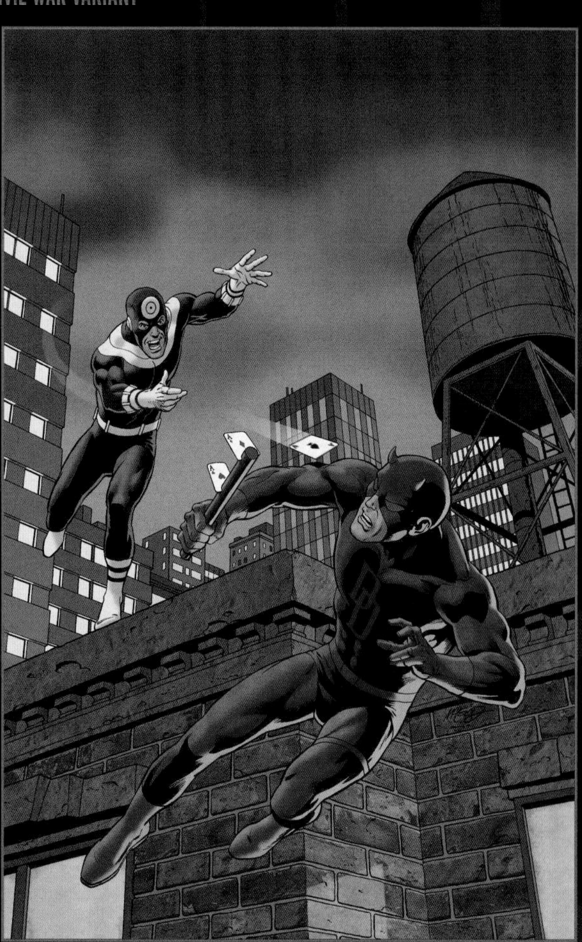

BOB McLEOD
No. 6 VARIANT

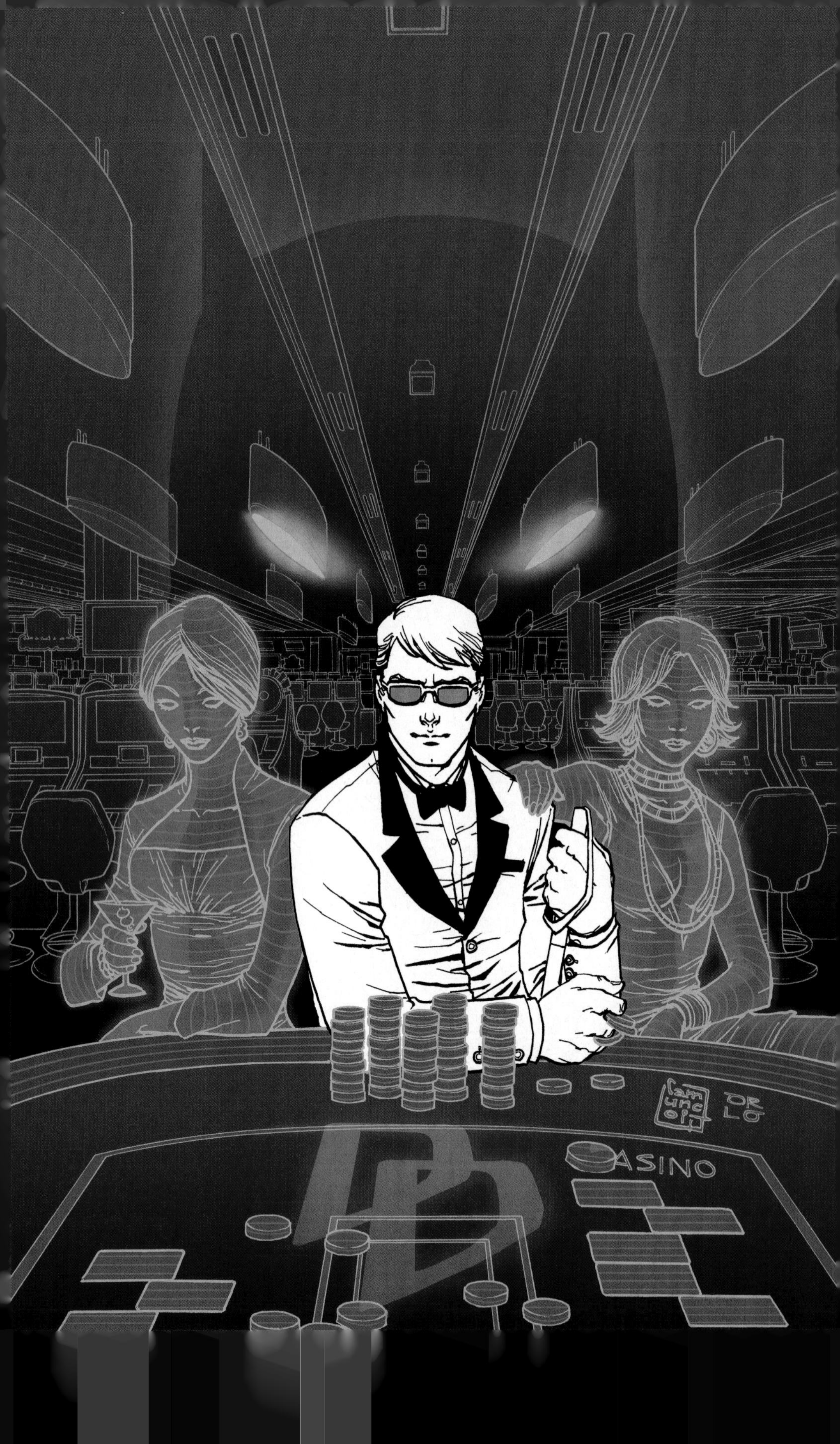
ASINO

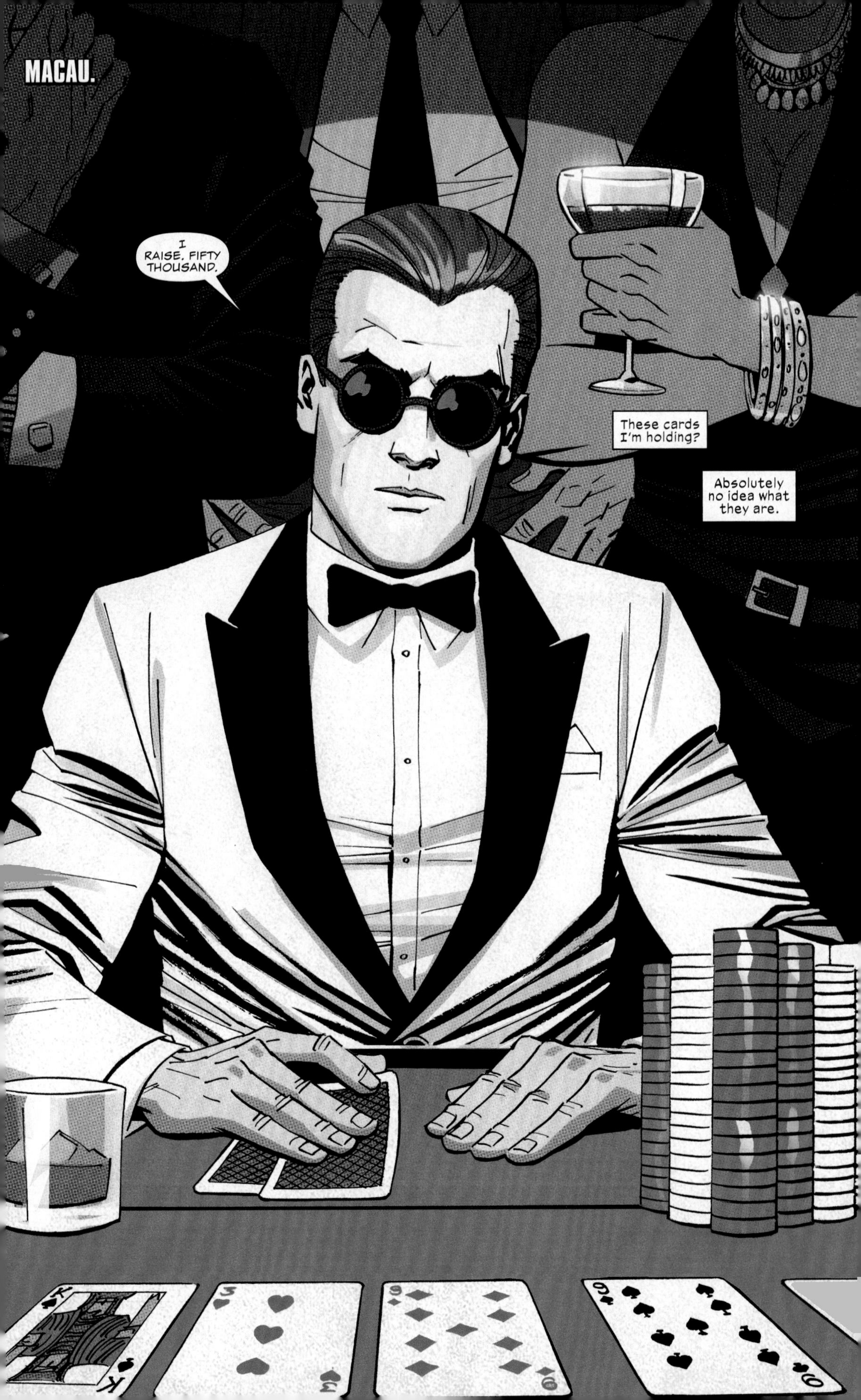
MACAU.
I RAISE. FIFTY THOUSAND.
These cards I'm holding?
Absolutely no idea what they are.

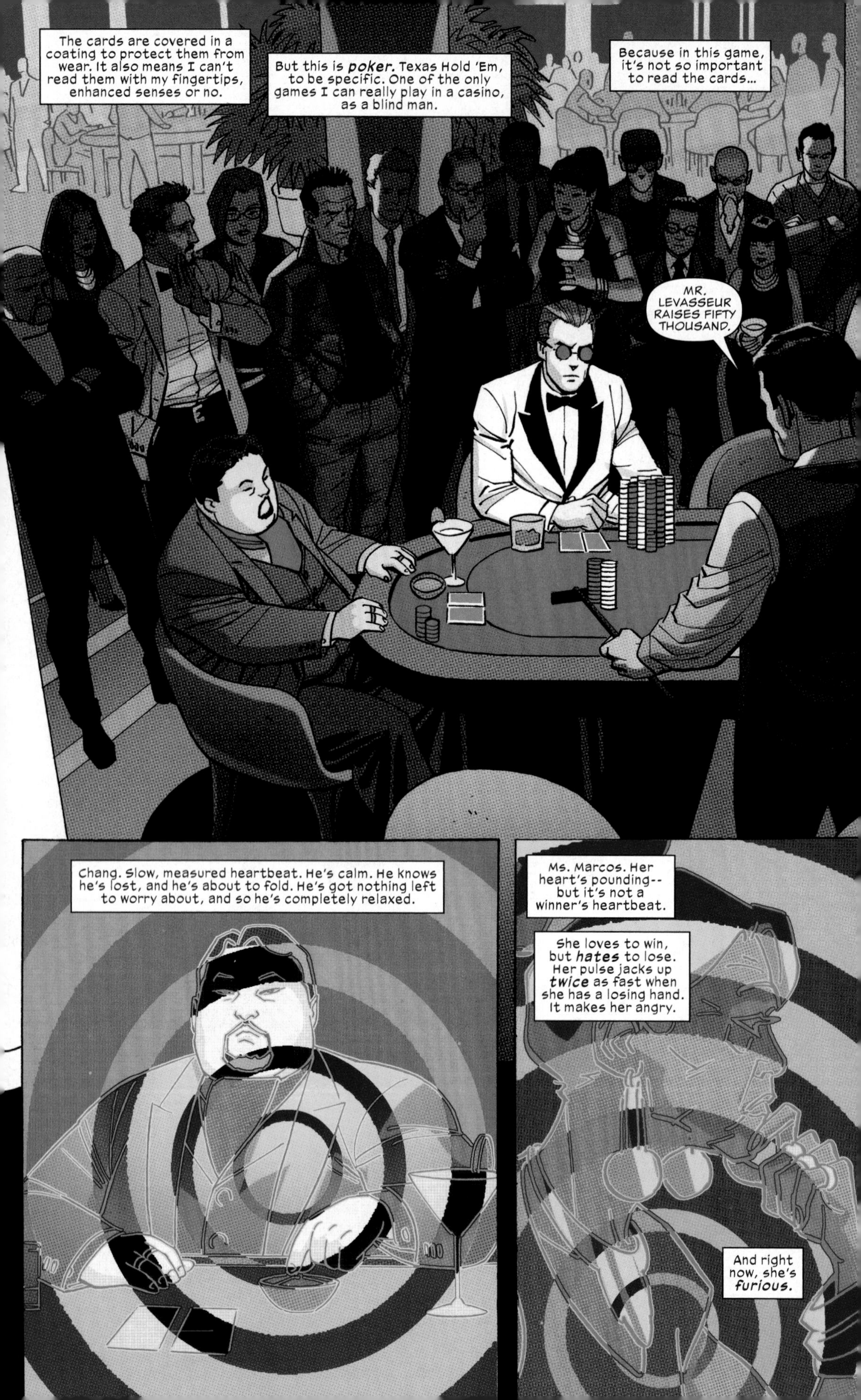
The cards are covered in a coating to protect them from wear. It also means I can't read them with my fingertips, enhanced senses or no.
But this is *poker.* Texas Hold 'Em, to be specific. One of the only games I can really play in a casino, as a blind man.
Because in this game, it's not so important to read the cards...
MR. LEVASSEUR RAISES FIFTY THOUSAND.
Chang. Slow, measured heartbeat. He's calm. He knows he's lost, and he's about to fold. He's got nothing left to worry about, and so he's completely relaxed.
Ms. Marcos. Her heart's pounding-- but it's not a winner's heartbeat.
She loves to win, but *hates* to lose. Her pulse jacks up *twice* as fast when she has a losing hand. It makes her angry.
And right now, she's *furious.*

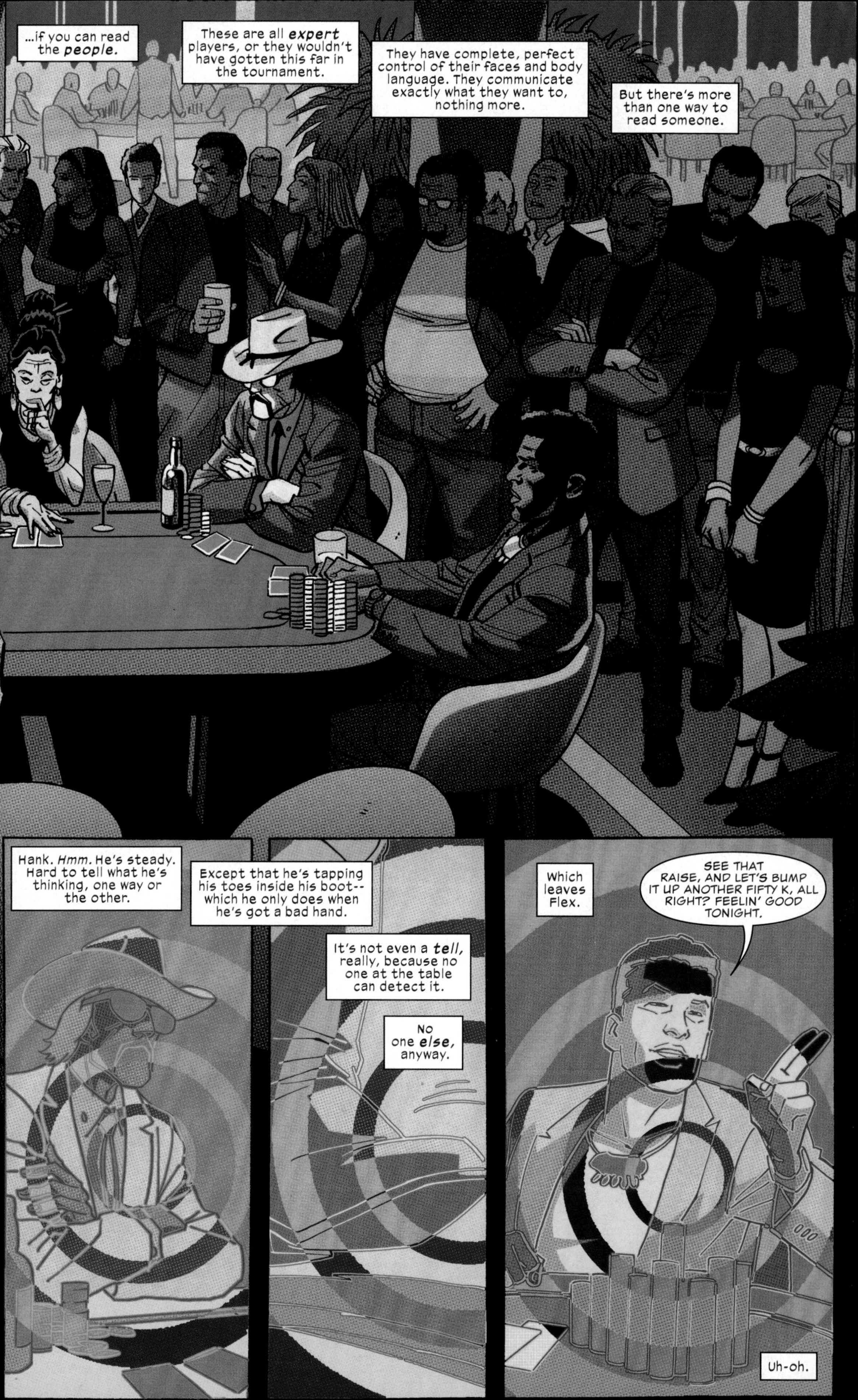

...if you can read the *people.*
These are all *expert* players, or they wouldn't have gotten this far in the tournament.
They have complete, perfect control of their faces and body language. They communicate exactly what they want to, nothing more.
But there's more than one way to read someone.
Hank. *Hmm.* He's steady. Hard to tell what he's thinking, one way or the other.
Except that he's tapping his toes inside his boot--which he only does when he's got a bad hand.
It's not even a *tell,* really, because no one at the table can detect it.
No one *else,* anyway.
Which leaves Flex.
SEE THAT RAISE, AND LET'S BUMP IT UP ANOTHER FIFTY K, ALL RIGHT? FEELIN' GOOD TONIGHT.
Uh-oh.

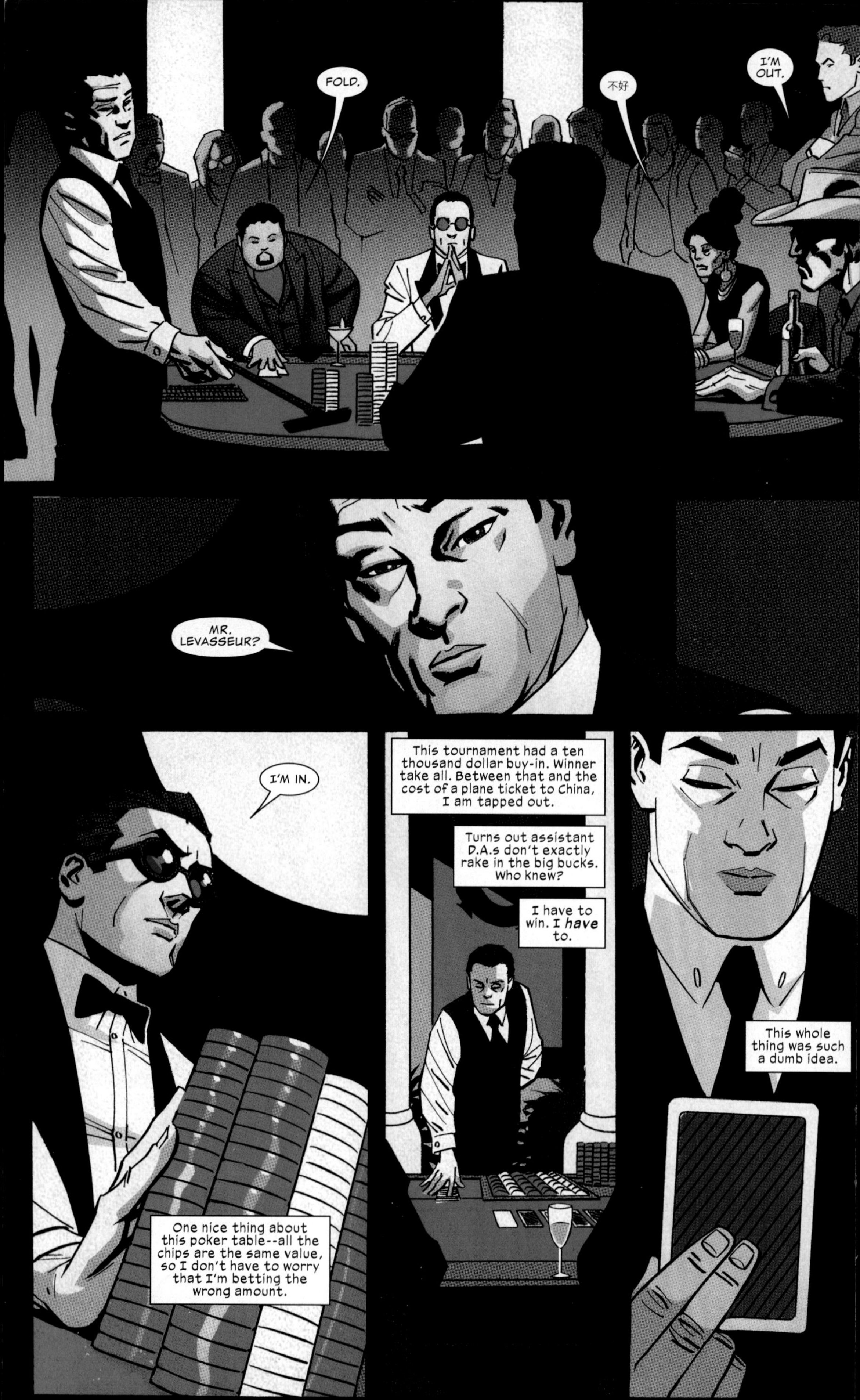
FOLD.
不好
I'M OUT.
MR. LEVASSEUR?
I'M IN.
One nice thing about this poker table--all the chips are the same value, so I don't have to worry that I'm betting the wrong amount.
This tournament had a ten thousand dollar buy-in. Winner take all. Between that and the cost of a plane ticket to China, I am tapped out.
Turns out assistant D.A.s don't exactly rake in the big bucks. Who knew?
I have to win. I *have* to.
This whole thing was such a dumb idea.

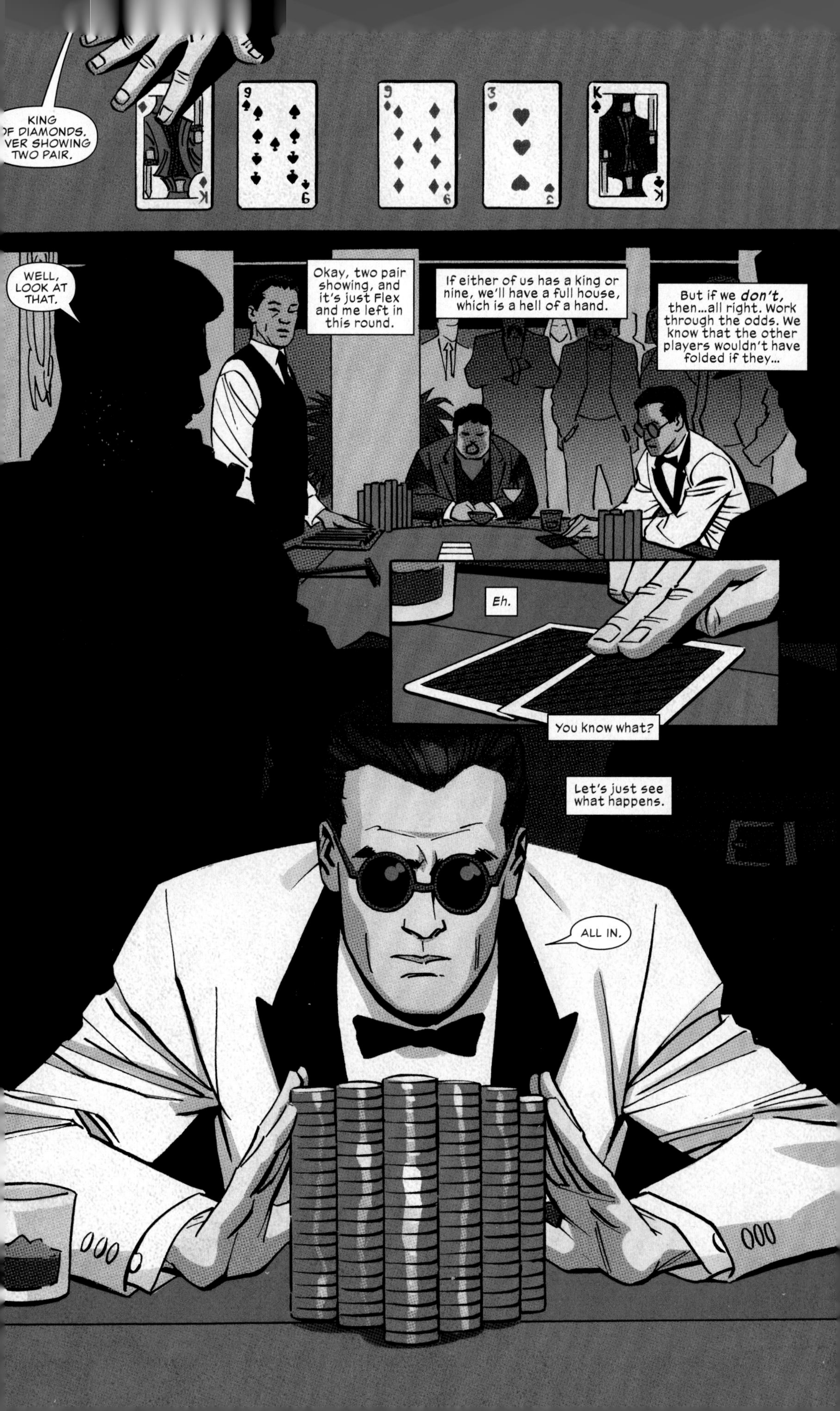
KING
OF DIAMONDS.
...VER SHOWING
TWO PAIR.
WELL,
LOOK AT
THAT.
Okay, two pair showing, and it's just Flex and me left in this round.
If either of us has a king or nine, we'll have a full house, which is a hell of a hand.
But if we *don't*, then...all right. Work through the odds. We know that the other players wouldn't have folded if they...
Eh.
You know what?
Let's just see what happens.
ALL IN.

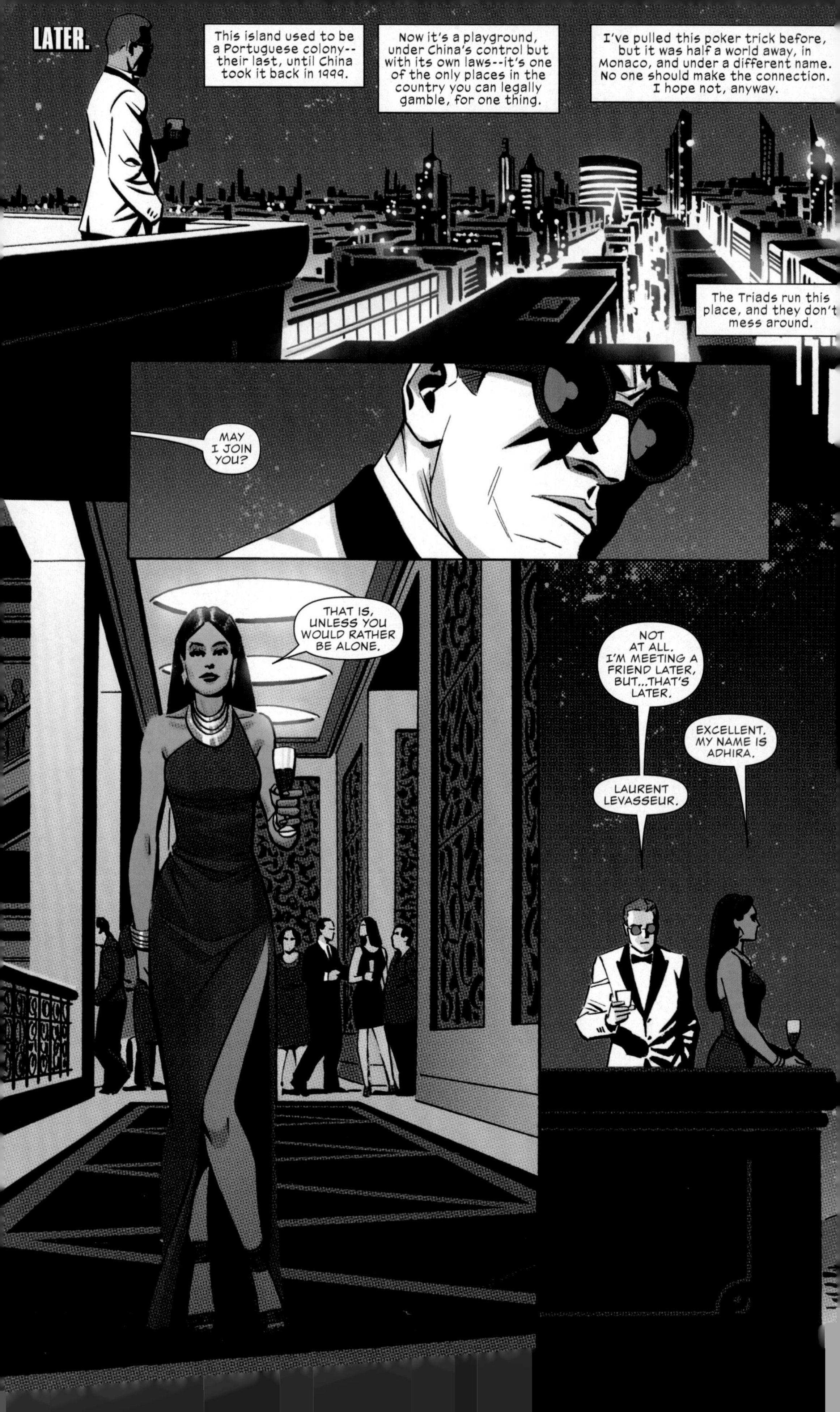
LATER.
This island used to be a Portuguese colony--their last, until China took it back in 1999.
Now it's a playground, under China's control but with its own laws--it's one of the only places in the country you can legally gamble, for one thing.
I've pulled this poker trick before, but it was half a world away, in Monaco, and under a different name. No one should make the connection. I hope not, anyway.
The Triads run this place, and they don't mess around.
MAY I JOIN YOU?
THAT IS, UNLESS YOU WOULD RATHER BE ALONE.
NOT AT ALL. I'M MEETING A FRIEND LATER, BUT...THAT'S LATER.
EXCELLENT. MY NAME IS ADHIRA.
LAURENT LEVASSEUR.

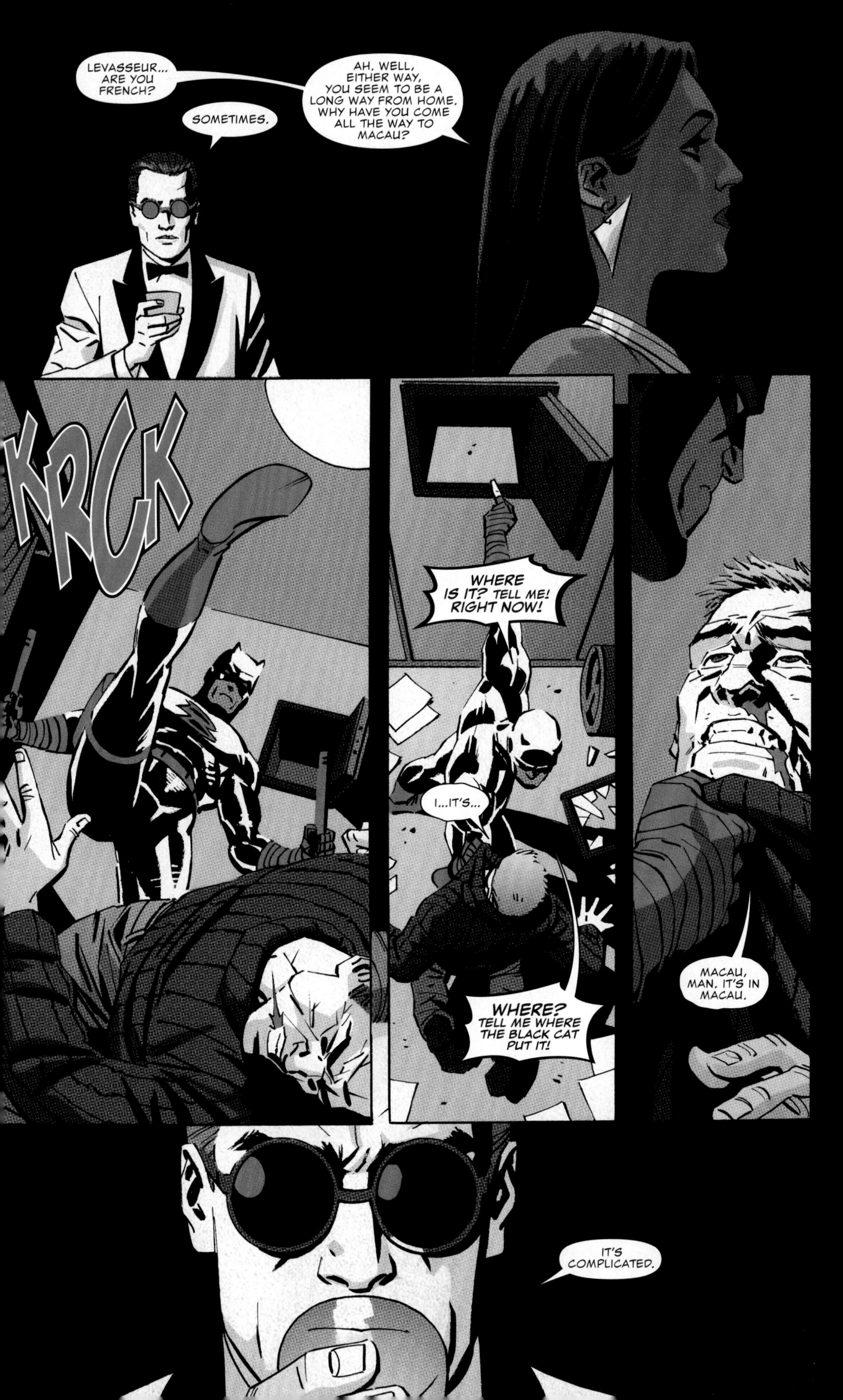
LEVASSEUR... ARE YOU FRENCH?
SOMETIMES.
AH, WELL, EITHER WAY, YOU SEEM TO BE A LONG WAY FROM HOME. WHY HAVE YOU COME ALL THE WAY TO MACAU?
KRCK
WHERE IS IT? TELL ME! RIGHT NOW!
I...IT'S...
WHERE? TELL ME WHERE THE BLACK CAT PUT IT!
MACAU, MAN. IT'S IN MACAU.
IT'S COMPLICATED.

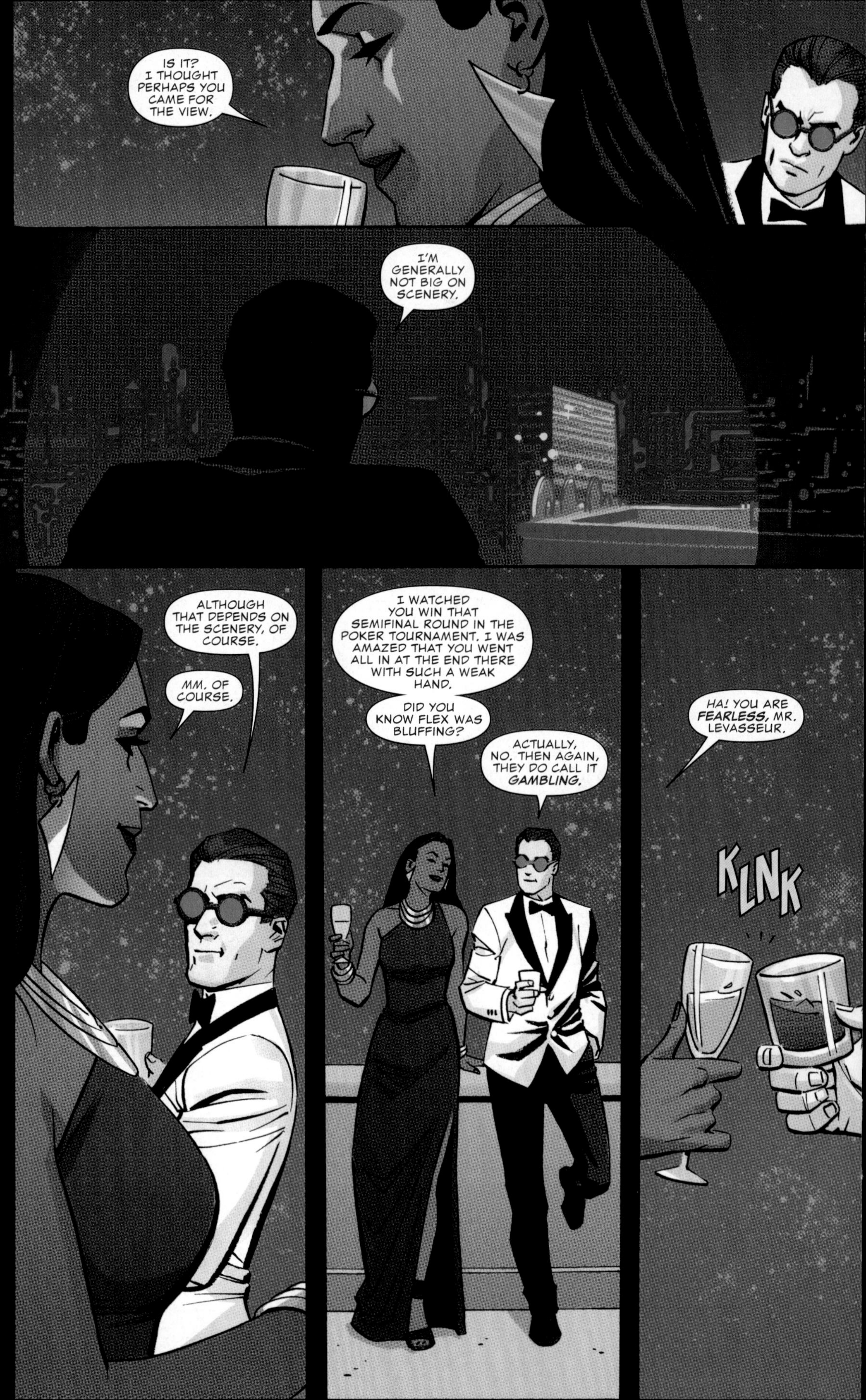
IS IT? I THOUGHT PERHAPS YOU CAME FOR THE VIEW.
I'M GENERALLY NOT BIG ON SCENERY.
ALTHOUGH THAT DEPENDS ON THE SCENERY, OF COURSE.
MM. OF COURSE.
I WATCHED YOU WIN THAT SEMIFINAL ROUND IN THE POKER TOURNAMENT. I WAS AMAZED THAT YOU WENT ALL IN AT THE END THERE WITH SUCH A WEAK HAND.
DID YOU KNOW FLEX WAS BLUFFING?
ACTUALLY, NO. THEN AGAIN, THEY DO CALL IT GAMBLING.
HA! YOU ARE FEARLESS, MR. LEVASSEUR.
KLNK

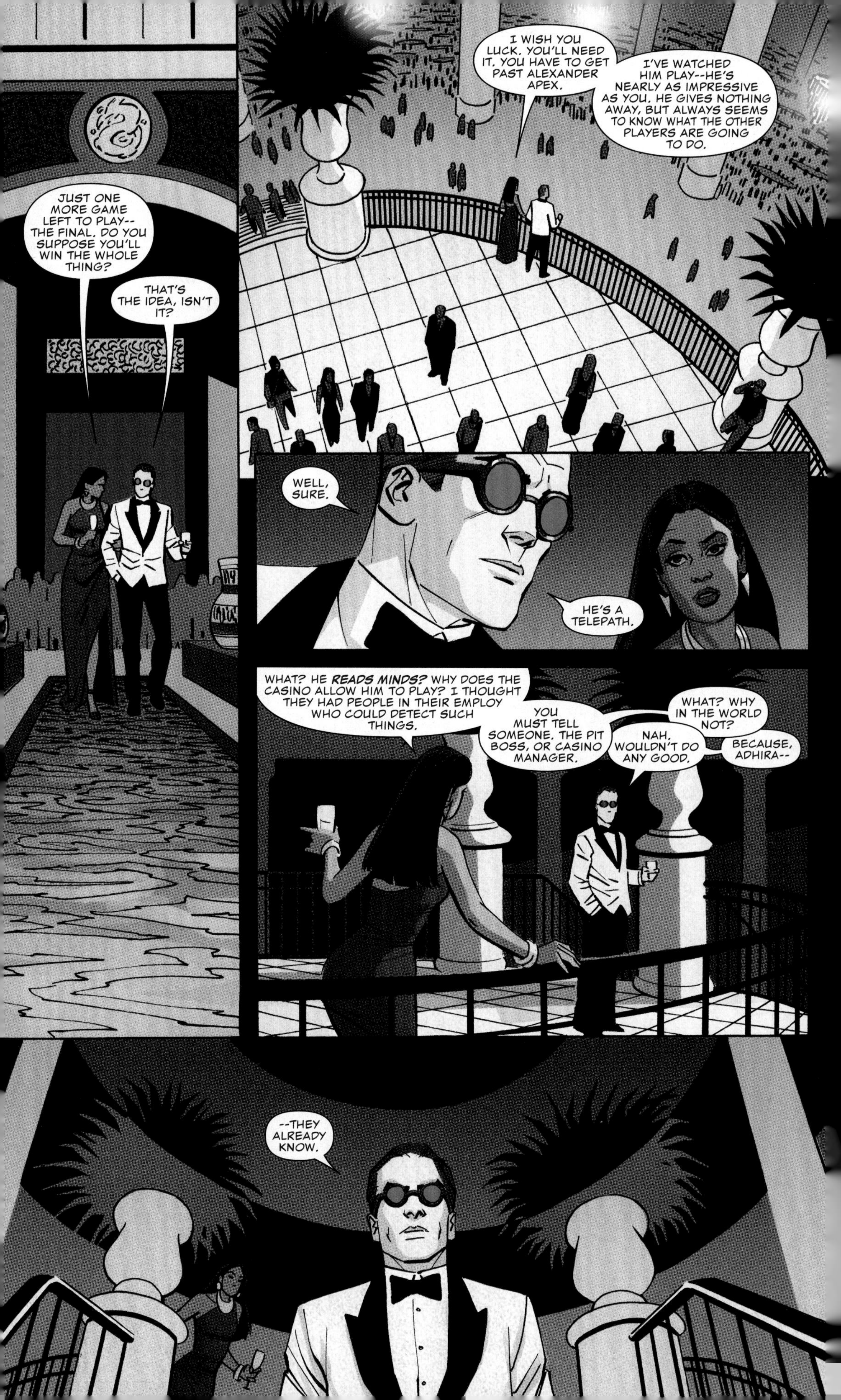
JUST ONE MORE GAME LEFT TO PLAY-- THE FINAL. DO YOU SUPPOSE YOU'LL WIN THE WHOLE THING?
THAT'S THE IDEA, ISN'T IT?
I WISH YOU LUCK. YOU'LL NEED IT. YOU HAVE TO GET PAST ALEXANDER APEX.
I'VE WATCHED HIM PLAY--HE'S NEARLY AS IMPRESSIVE AS YOU. HE GIVES NOTHING AWAY, BUT ALWAYS SEEMS TO KNOW WHAT THE OTHER PLAYERS ARE GOING TO DO.
WELL, SURE.
HE'S A TELEPATH.
WHAT? HE READS MINDS? WHY DOES THE CASINO ALLOW HIM TO PLAY? I THOUGHT THEY HAD PEOPLE IN THEIR EMPLOY WHO COULD DETECT SUCH THINGS.
YOU MUST TELL SOMEONE. THE PIT BOSS, OR CASINO MANAGER.
NAH. WOULDN'T DO ANY GOOD.
WHAT? WHY IN THE WORLD NOT?
BECAUSE, ADHIRA--
--THEY ALREADY KNOW.

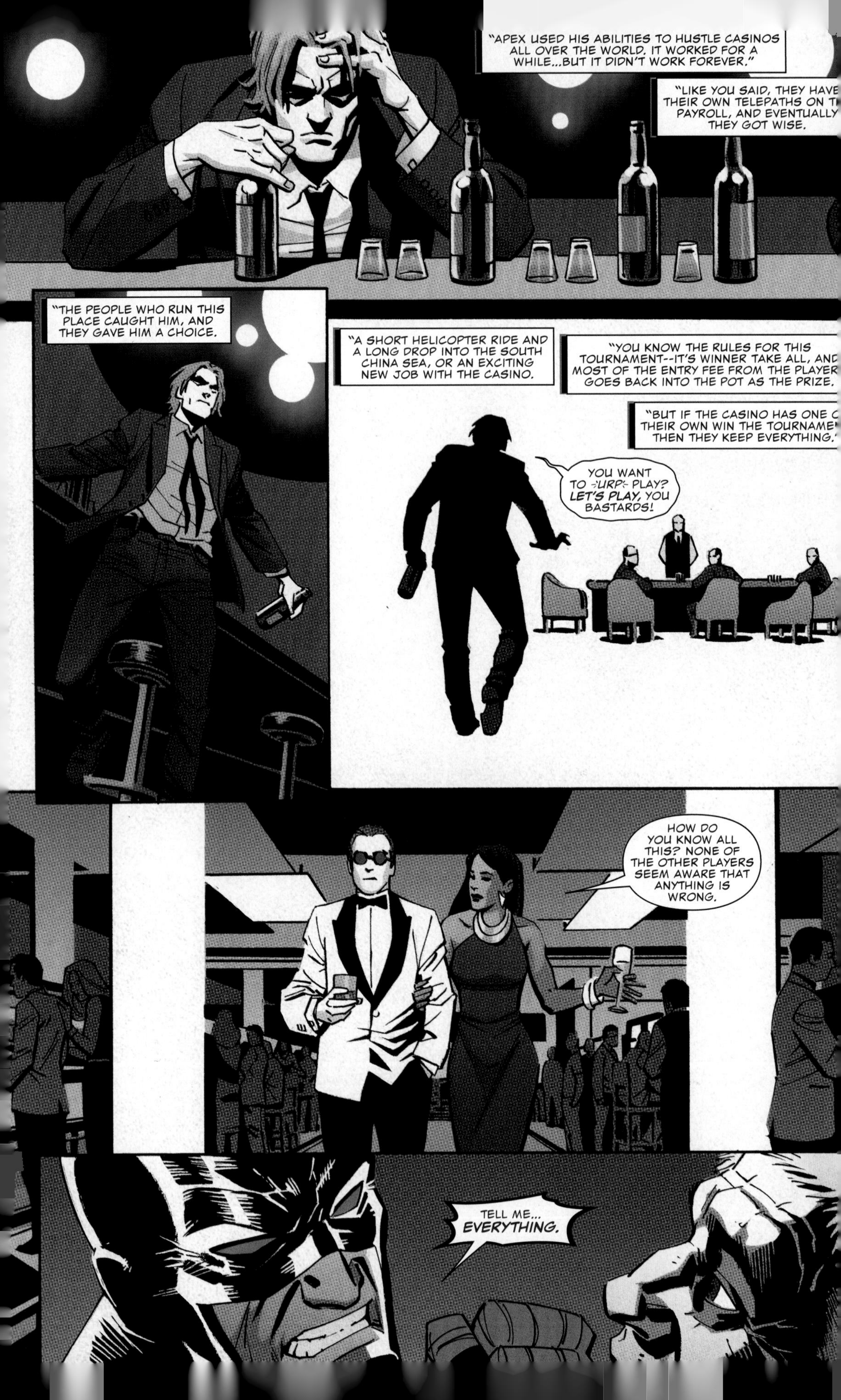

"APEX USED HIS ABILITIES TO HUSTLE CASINOS ALL OVER THE WORLD. IT WORKED FOR A WHILE...BUT IT DIDN'T WORK FOREVER."
"LIKE YOU SAID, THEY HAVE THEIR OWN TELEPATHS ON T PAYROLL, AND EVENTUALLY THEY GOT WISE.
"THE PEOPLE WHO RUN THIS PLACE CAUGHT HIM, AND THEY GAVE HIM A CHOICE.
"A SHORT HELICOPTER RIDE AND A LONG DROP INTO THE SOUTH CHINA SEA, OR AN EXCITING NEW JOB WITH THE CASINO.
"YOU KNOW THE RULES FOR THIS TOURNAMENT--IT'S WINNER TAKE ALL, AND MOST OF THE ENTRY FEE FROM THE PLAYER GOES BACK INTO THE POT AS THE PRIZE.
"BUT IF THE CASINO HAS ONE O THEIR OWN WIN THE TOURNAME THEN THEY KEEP EVERYTHING."
YOU WANT TO *URP* PLAY? LET'S PLAY, YOU BASTARDS!
HOW DO YOU KNOW ALL THIS? NONE OF THE OTHER PLAYERS SEEM AWARE THAT ANYTHING IS WRONG.
TELL ME... EVERYTHING.

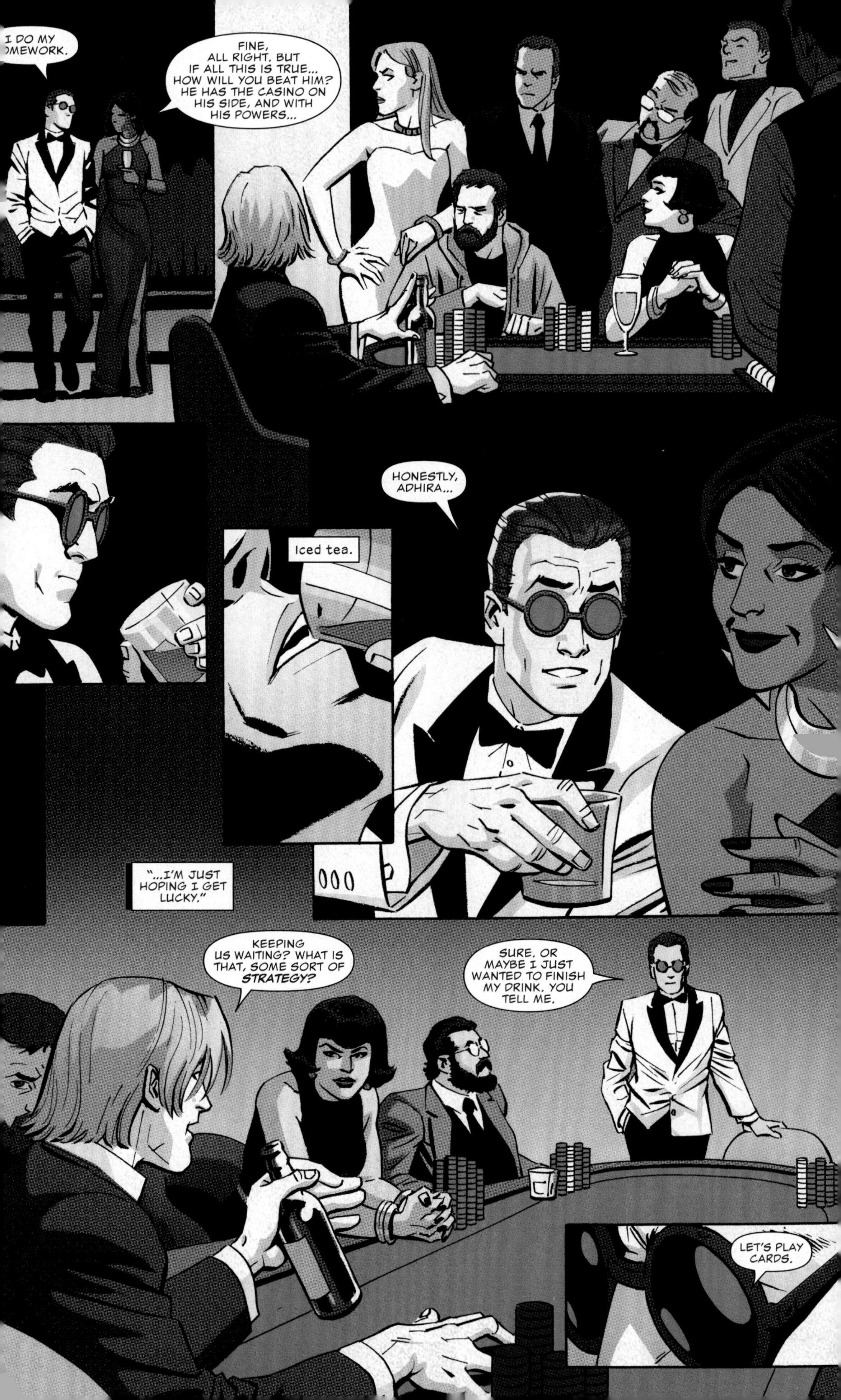

I DO MY
OMEWORK.
FINE, ALL RIGHT. BUT IF ALL THIS IS TRUE... HOW WILL YOU BEAT HIM? HE HAS THE CASINO ON HIS SIDE, AND WITH HIS POWERS...
HONESTLY, ADHIRA...
Iced tea.
"...I'M JUST HOPING I GET LUCKY."
KEEPING US WAITING? WHAT IS THAT, SOME SORT OF *STRATEGY?*
SURE, OR MAYBE I JUST WANTED TO FINISH MY DRINK. YOU TELL ME.
LET'S PLAY CARDS.

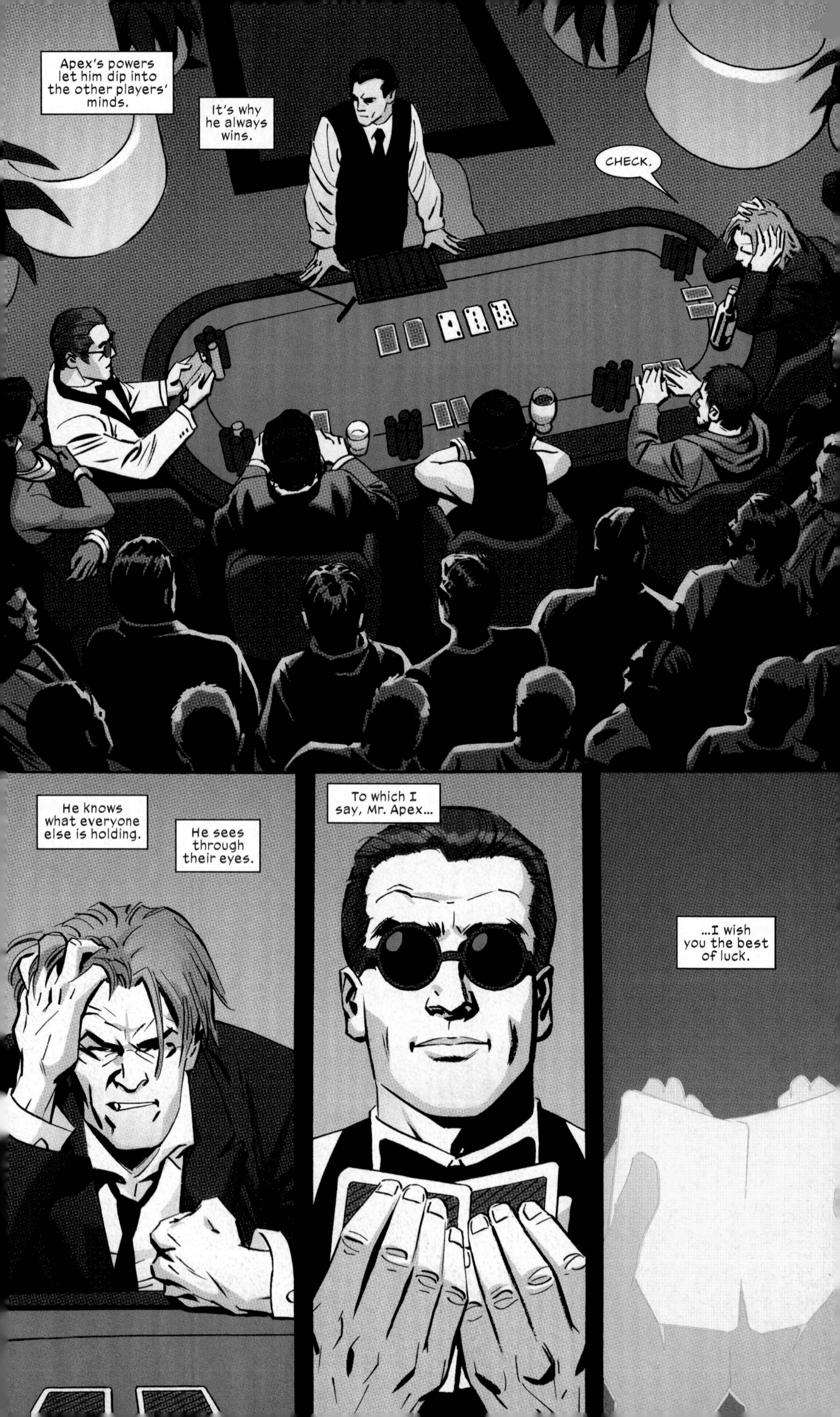
Apex's powers let him dip into the other players' minds.
It's why he always wins.
CHECK.
He knows what everyone else is holding.
He sees through their eyes.
To which I say, Mr. Apex...
...I wish you the best of luck.

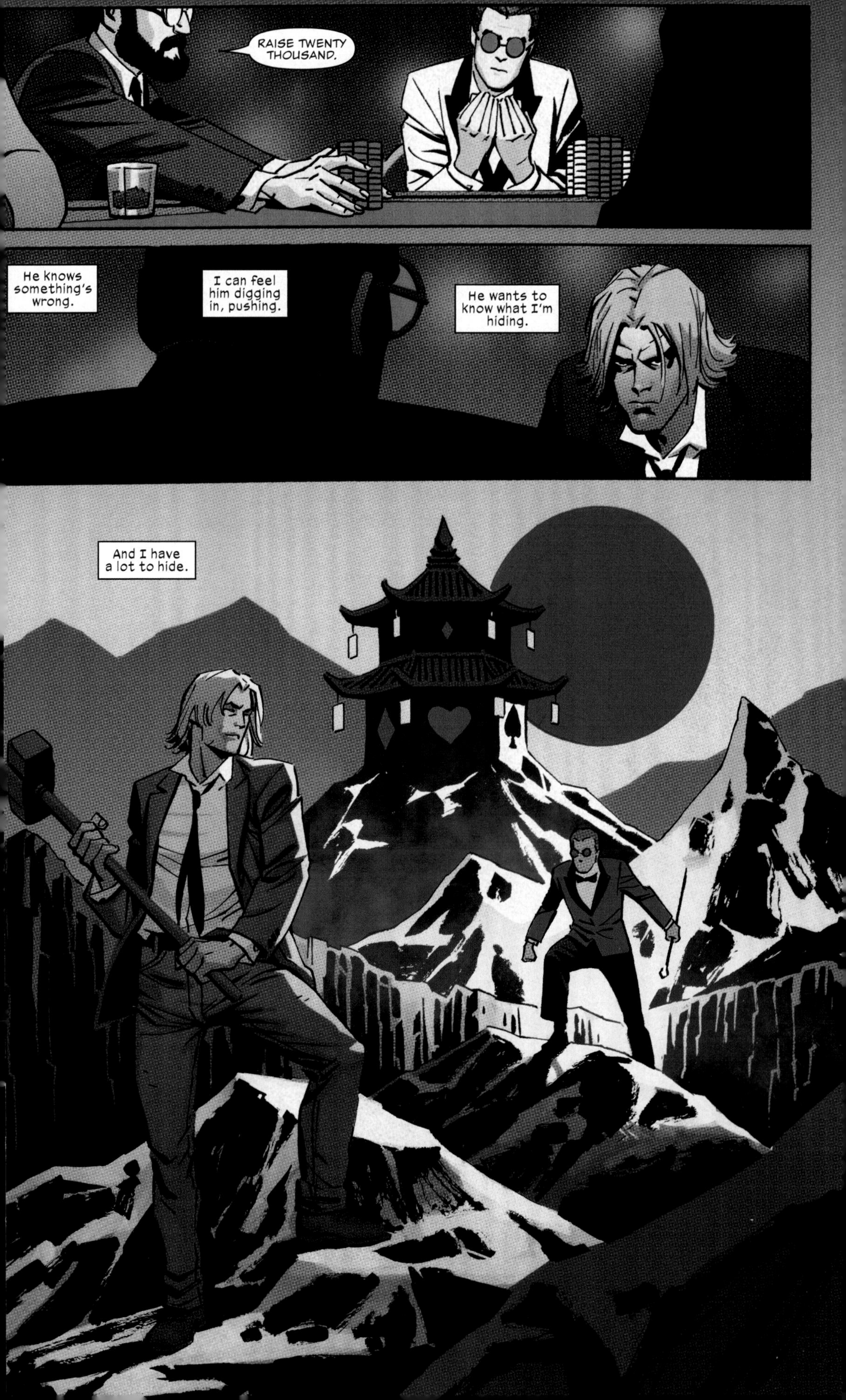
RAISE TWENTY THOUSAND.
He knows something's wrong.
I can feel him digging in, pushing.
He wants to know what I'm hiding.
And I have a lot to hide.

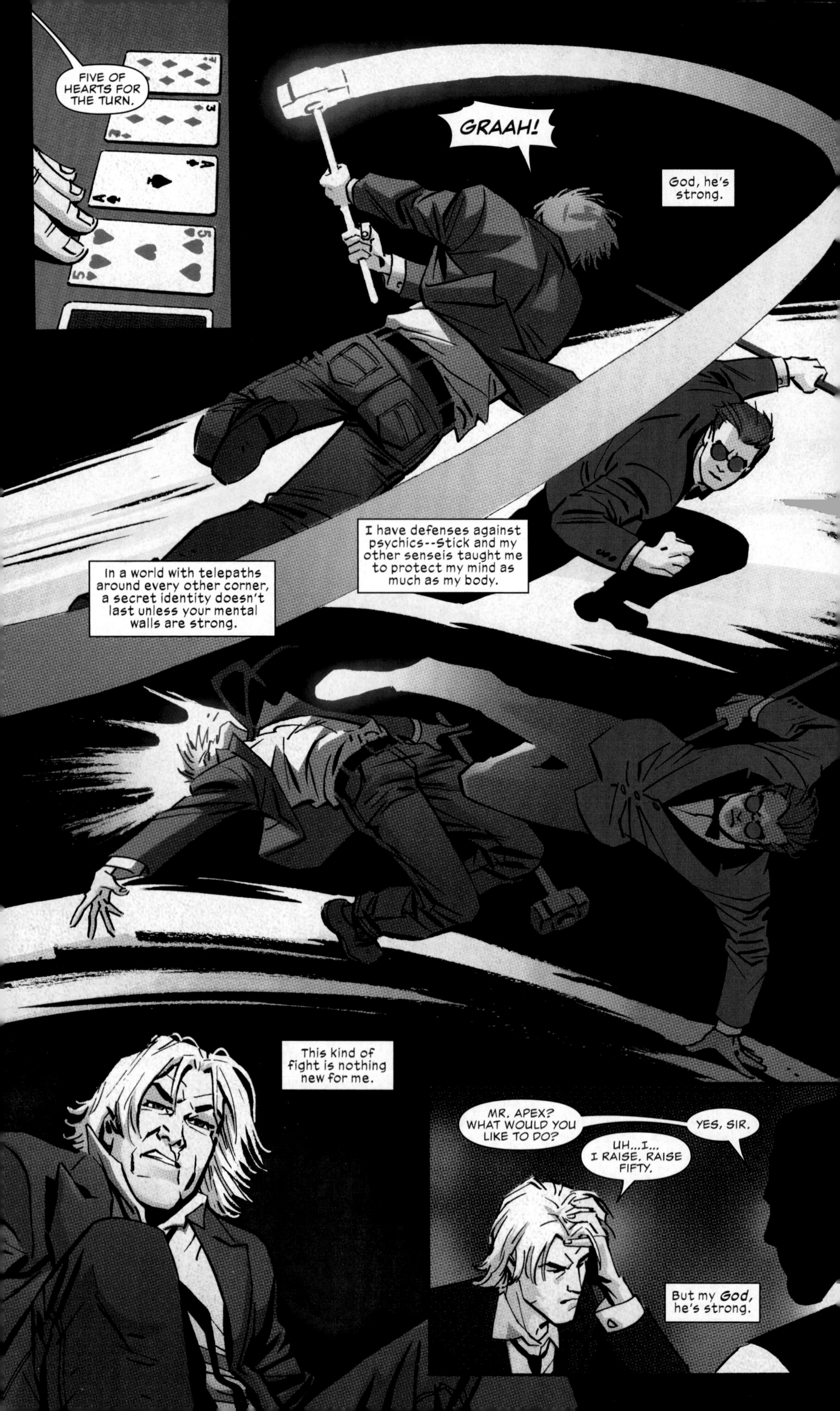

FIVE OF HEARTS FOR THE TURN.
GRAAH!
God, he's strong.
In a world with telepaths around every other corner, a secret identity doesn't last unless your mental walls are strong.
I have defenses against psychics--Stick and my other senseis taught me to protect my mind as much as my body.
This kind of fight is nothing new for me.
MR. APEX? WHAT WOULD YOU LIKE TO DO?
UH...I... I RAISE. RAISE FIFTY.
YES, SIR.
But my God, he's strong.

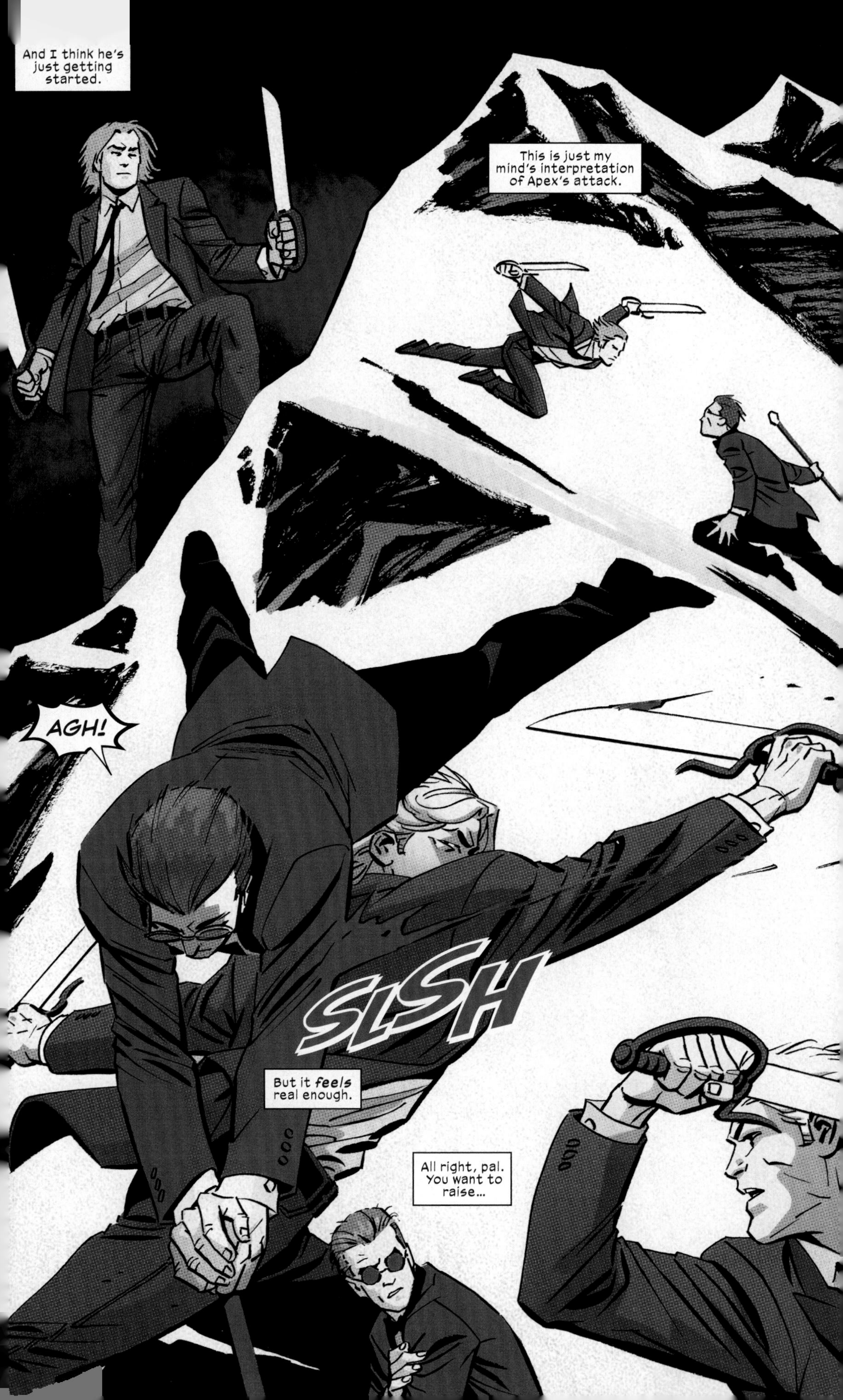
And I think he's just getting started.
This is just my mind's interpretation of Apex's attack.
AGH!
SLSH
But it *feels* real enough.
All right, pal. You want to raise...

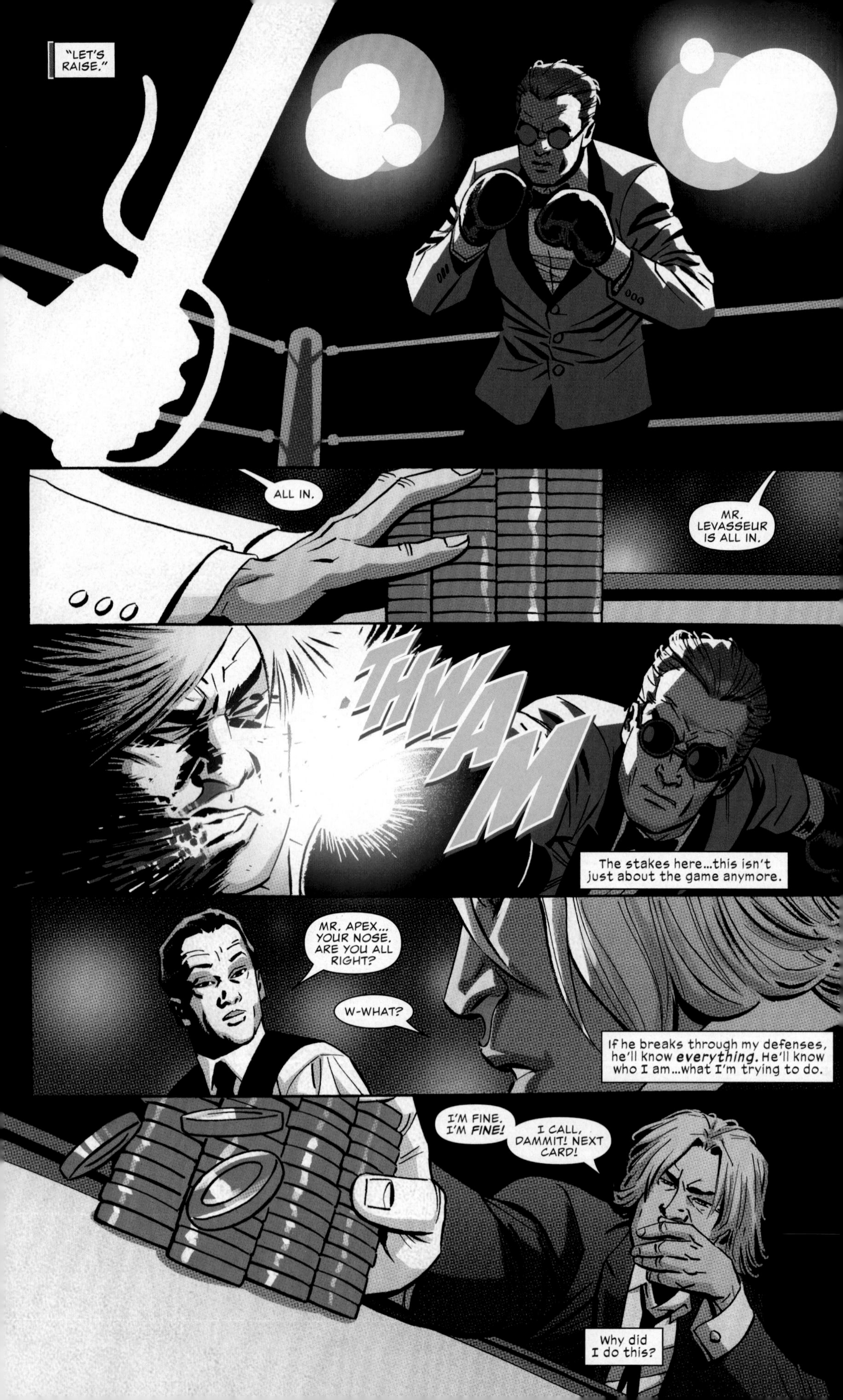
"LET'S RAISE."
ALL IN.
MR. LEVASSEUR IS ALL IN.
THWAM
The stakes here...this isn't just about the game anymore.
MR. APEX... YOUR NOSE. ARE YOU ALL RIGHT?
W-WHAT?
If he breaks through my defenses, he'll know *everything.* He'll know who I am...what I'm trying to do.
I'M FINE. I'M *FINE!*
I CALL, DAMMIT! NEXT CARD!
Why did I do this?

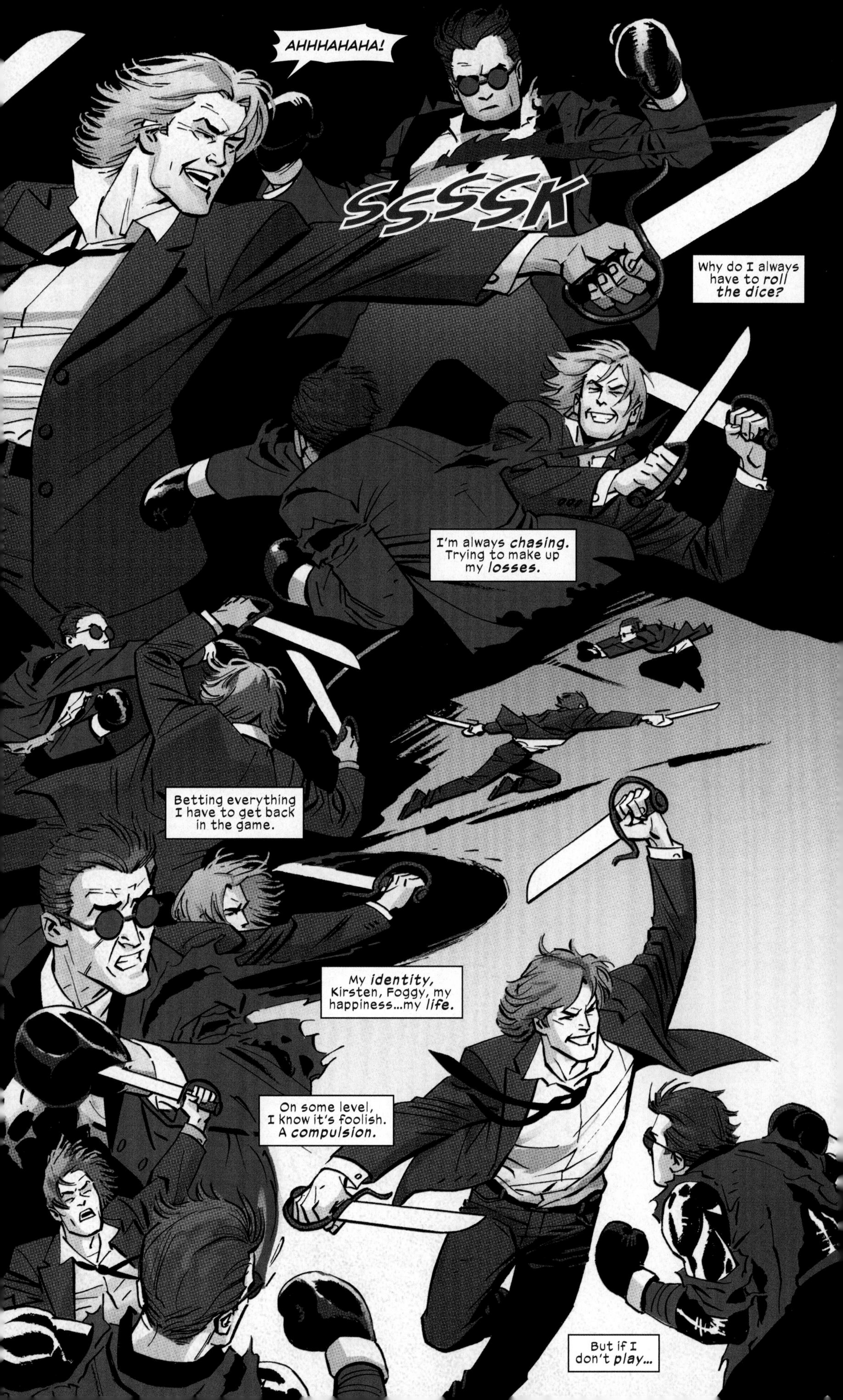
AHHHAHAHA!
SSSSK
Why do I always have to *roll the dice?*
I'm always *chasing.* Trying to make up my *losses.*
Betting everything I have to get back in the game.
My *identity,* Kirsten, Foggy, my happiness...my *life.*
On some level, I know it's foolish. A *compulsion.*
But if I don't *play...*

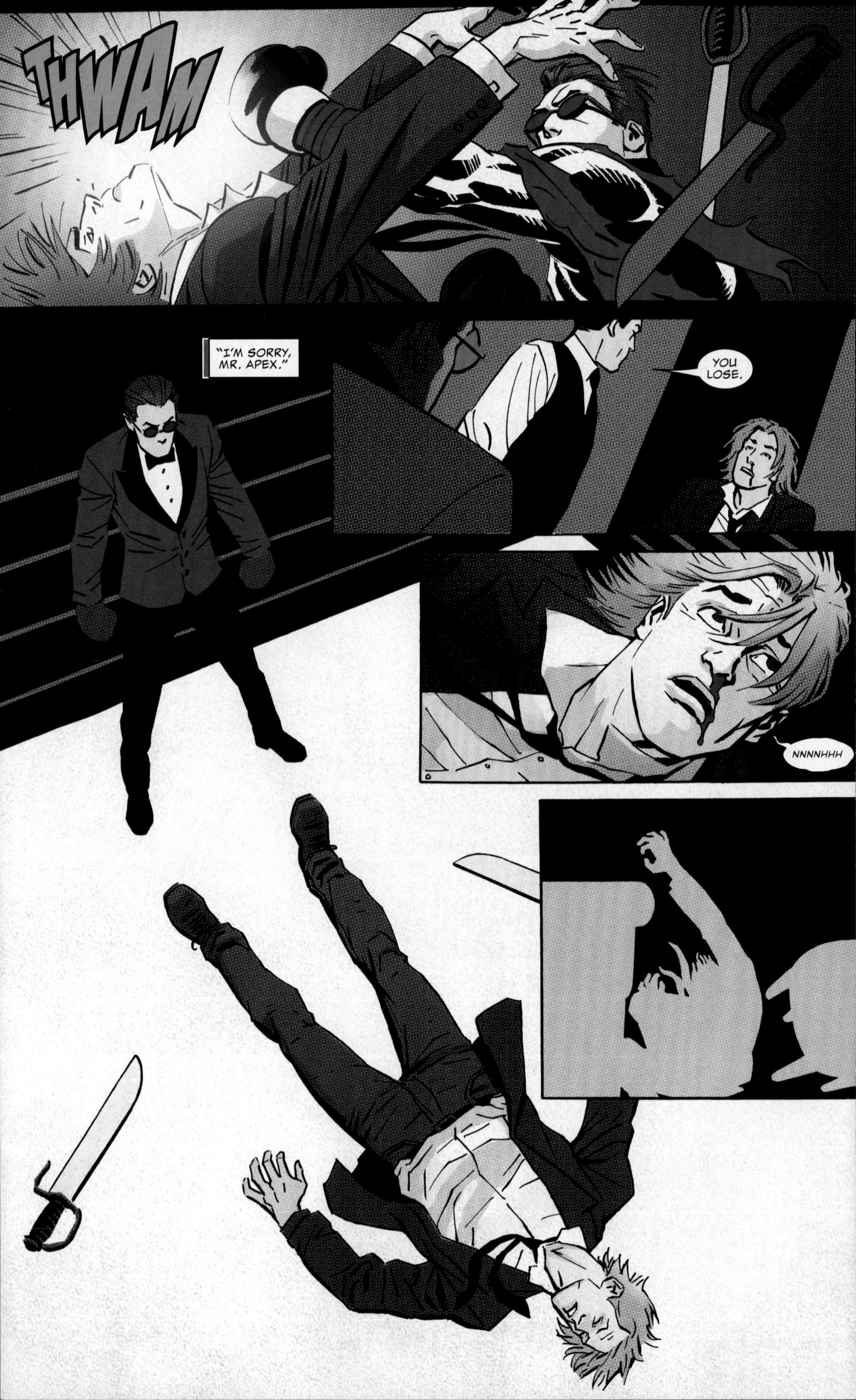
THWAM
"I'M SORRY, MR. APEX."
YOU LOSE.
NNNNHHH

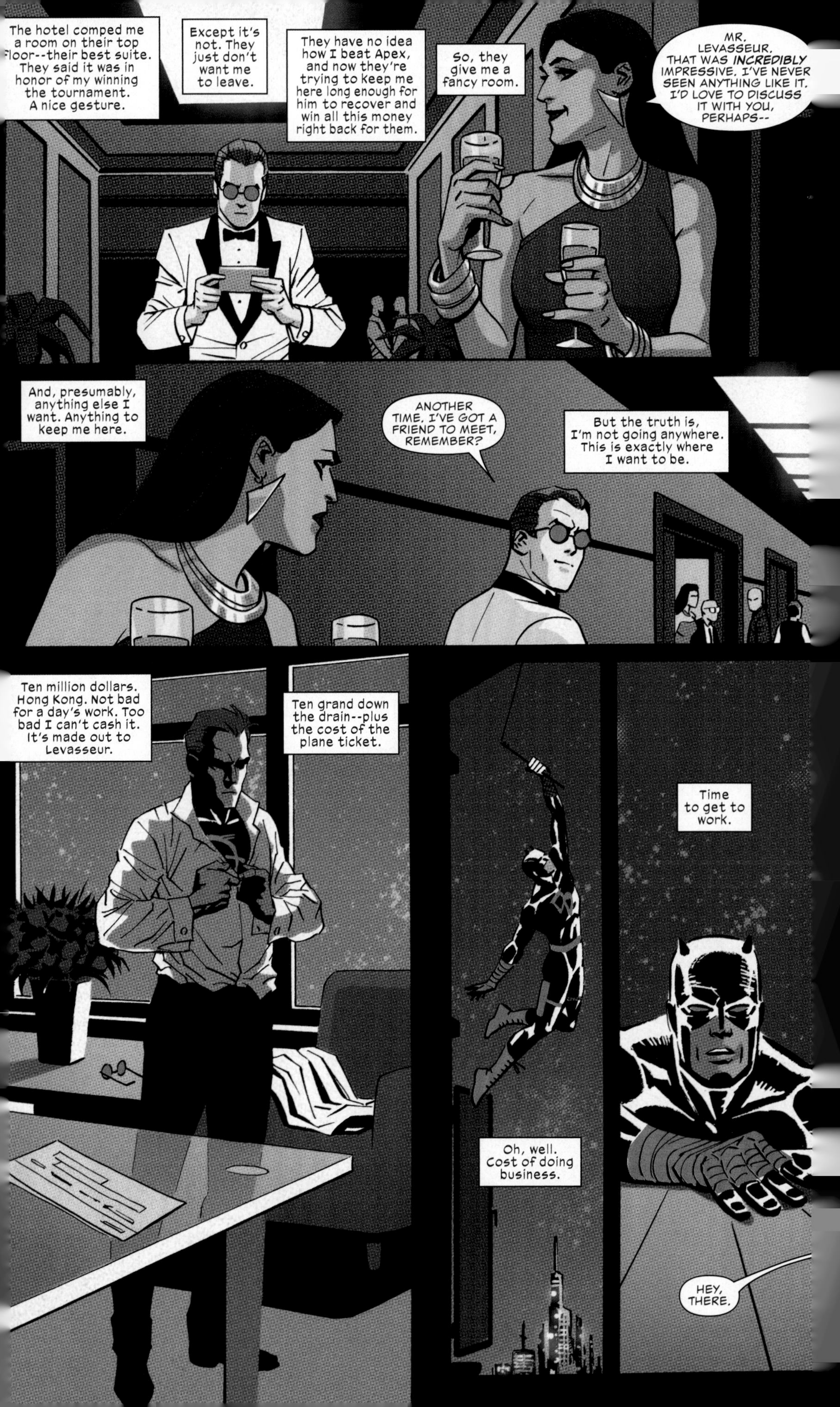
The hotel comped me a room on their top floor--their best suite. They said it was in honor of my winning the tournament. A nice gesture.
Except it's not. They just don't want me to leave.
They have no idea how I beat Apex, and now they're trying to keep me here long enough for him to recover and win all this money right back for them.
So, they give me a fancy room.
MR. LEVASSEUR. THAT WAS INCREDIBLY IMPRESSIVE. I'VE NEVER SEEN ANYTHING LIKE IT. I'D LOVE TO DISCUSS IT WITH YOU, PERHAPS--
And, presumably, anything else I want. Anything to keep me here.
ANOTHER TIME. I'VE GOT A FRIEND TO MEET, REMEMBER?
But the truth is, I'm not going anywhere. This is exactly where I want to be.
Ten million dollars. Hong Kong. Not bad for a day's work. Too bad I can't cash it. It's made out to Levasseur.
Ten grand down the drain--plus the cost of the plane ticket.
Oh, well. Cost of doing business.
Time to get to work.
HEY, THERE.

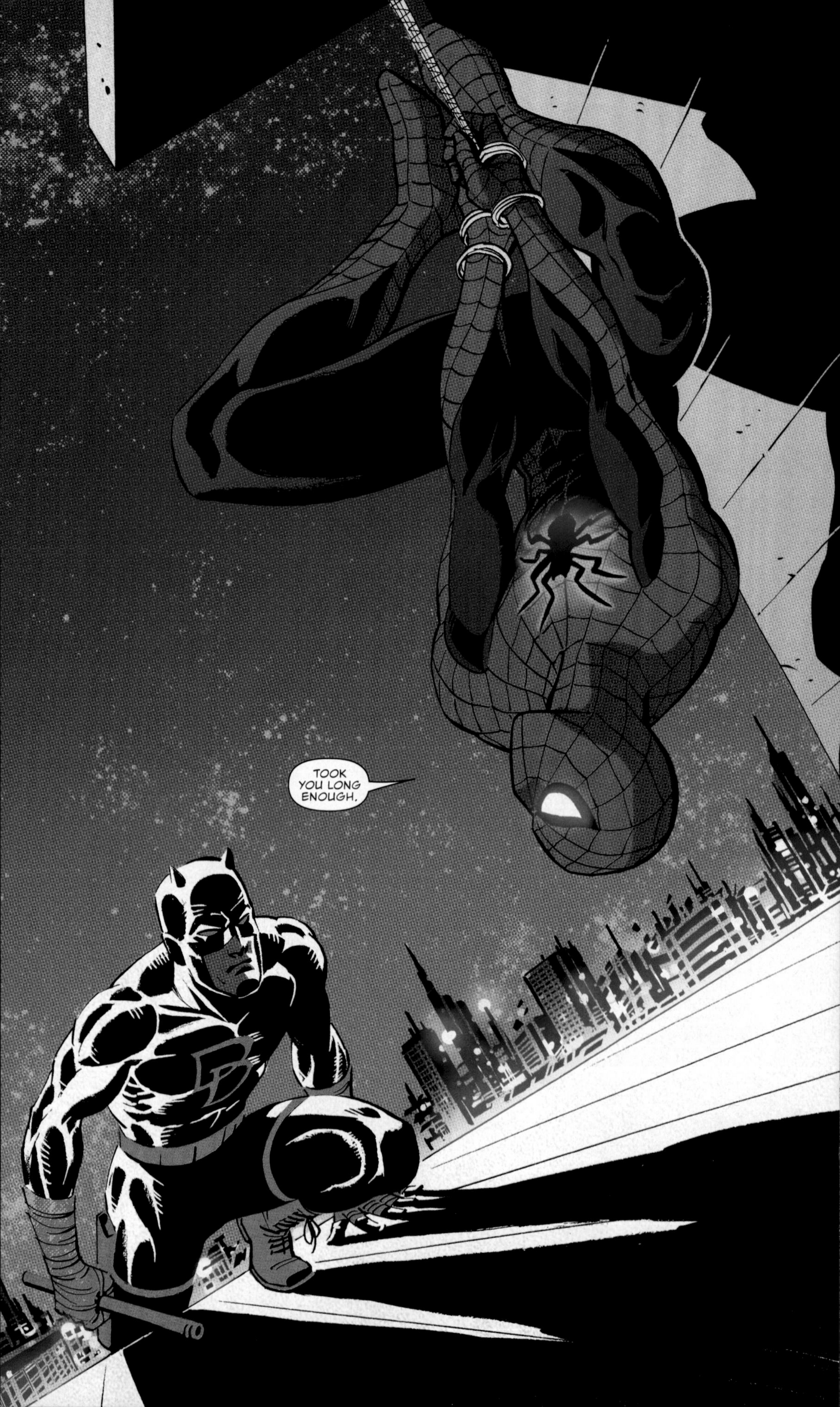
TOOK YOU LONG ENOUGH.

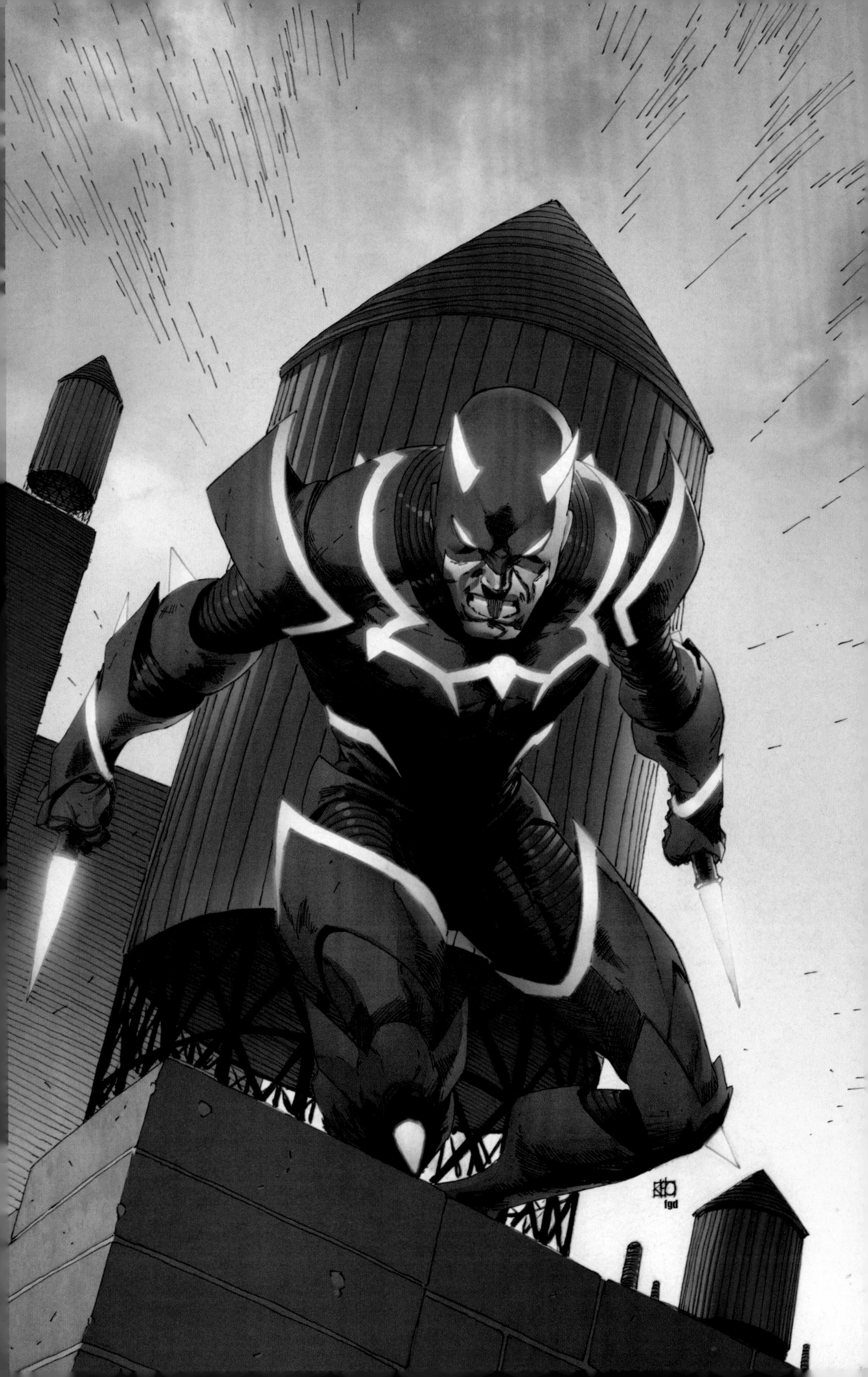
fgd

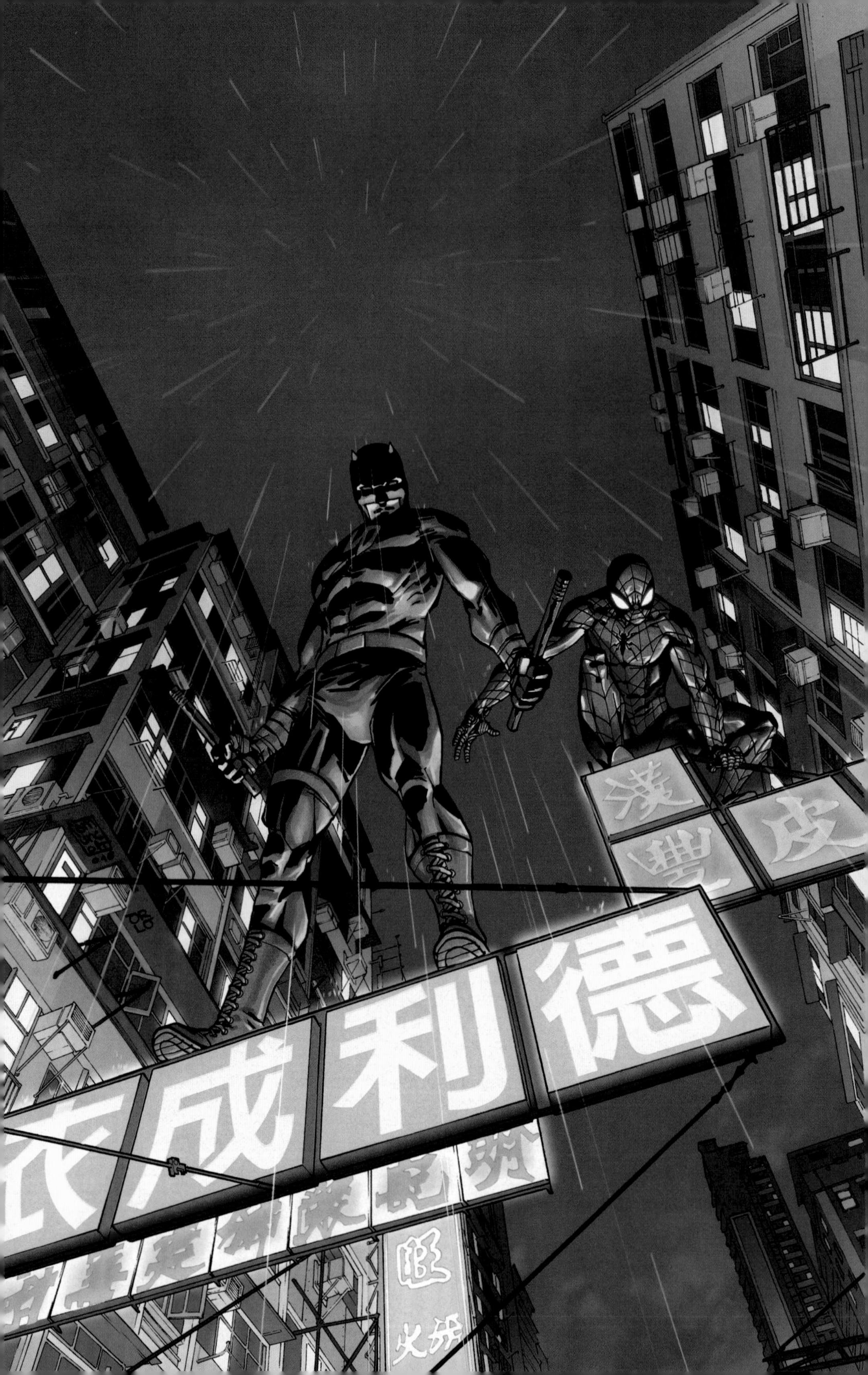
成利德

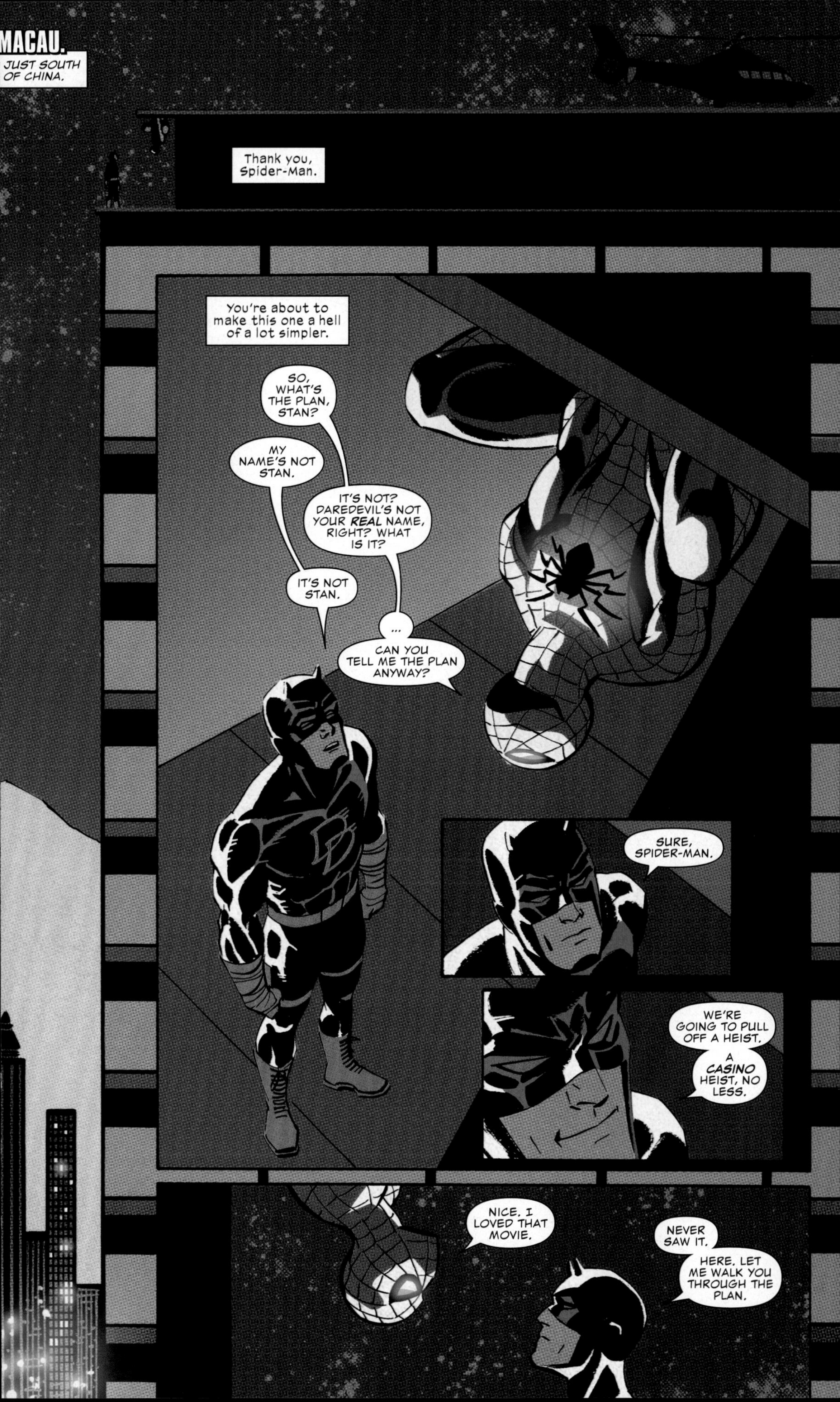
MACAU.
JUST SOUTH OF CHINA.
Thank you, Spider-Man.
You're about to make this one a hell of a lot simpler.
SO, WHAT'S THE PLAN, STAN?
MY NAME'S NOT STAN.
IT'S NOT? DAREDEVIL'S NOT YOUR REAL NAME, RIGHT? WHAT IS IT?
IT'S NOT STAN.
...
CAN YOU TELL ME THE PLAN ANYWAY?
SURE, SPIDER-MAN.
WE'RE GOING TO PULL OFF A HEIST.
A CASINO HEIST, NO LESS.
NICE. I LOVED THAT MOVIE.
NEVER SAW IT.
HERE, LET ME WALK YOU THROUGH THE PLAN.

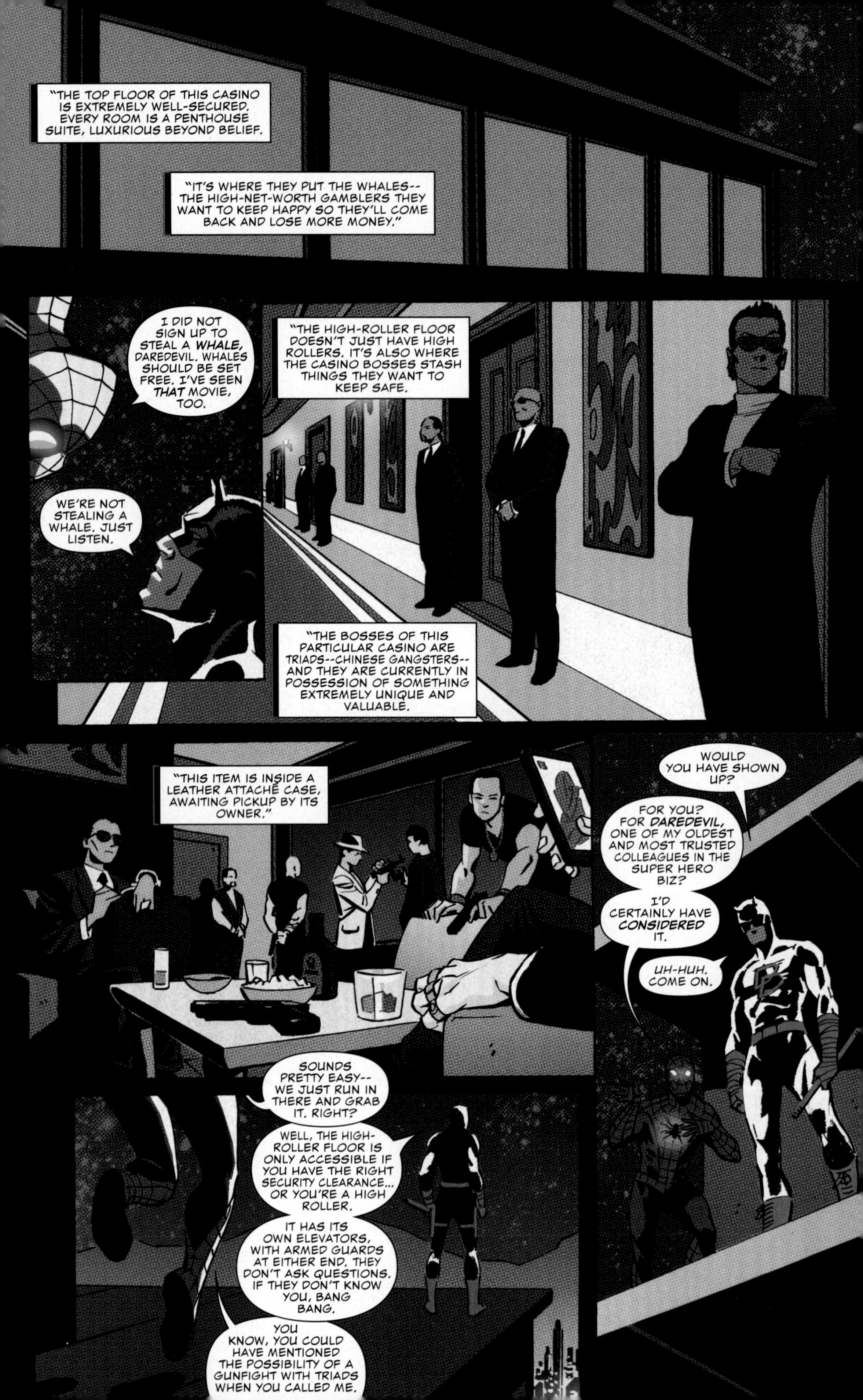
"THE TOP FLOOR OF THIS CASINO IS EXTREMELY WELL-SECURED. EVERY ROOM IS A PENTHOUSE SUITE, LUXURIOUS BEYOND BELIEF.
"IT'S WHERE THEY PUT THE WHALES-- THE HIGH-NET-WORTH GAMBLERS THEY WANT TO KEEP HAPPY SO THEY'LL COME BACK AND LOSE MORE MONEY."
I DID NOT SIGN UP TO STEAL A WHALE, DAREDEVIL. WHALES SHOULD BE SET FREE. I'VE SEEN THAT MOVIE, TOO.
WE'RE NOT STEALING A WHALE. JUST LISTEN.
"THE HIGH-ROLLER FLOOR DOESN'T JUST HAVE HIGH ROLLERS. IT'S ALSO WHERE THE CASINO BOSSES STASH THINGS THEY WANT TO KEEP SAFE.
"THE BOSSES OF THIS PARTICULAR CASINO ARE TRIADS--CHINESE GANGSTERS-- AND THEY ARE CURRENTLY IN POSSESSION OF SOMETHING EXTREMELY UNIQUE AND VALUABLE.
"THIS ITEM IS INSIDE A LEATHER ATTACHÉ CASE, AWAITING PICKUP BY ITS OWNER."
SOUNDS PRETTY EASY-- WE JUST RUN IN THERE AND GRAB IT, RIGHT?
WELL, THE HIGH-ROLLER FLOOR IS ONLY ACCESSIBLE IF YOU HAVE THE RIGHT SECURITY CLEARANCE... OR YOU'RE A HIGH ROLLER.
IT HAS ITS OWN ELEVATORS, WITH ARMED GUARDS AT EITHER END. THEY DON'T ASK QUESTIONS. IF THEY DON'T KNOW YOU, BANG BANG.
YOU KNOW, YOU COULD HAVE MENTIONED THE POSSIBILITY OF A GUNFIGHT WITH TRIADS WHEN YOU CALLED ME.
WOULD YOU HAVE SHOWN UP?
FOR YOU? FOR DAREDEVIL, ONE OF MY OLDEST AND MOST TRUSTED COLLEAGUES IN THE SUPER HERO BIZ?
I'D CERTAINLY HAVE CONSIDERED IT.
UH-HUH. COME ON.

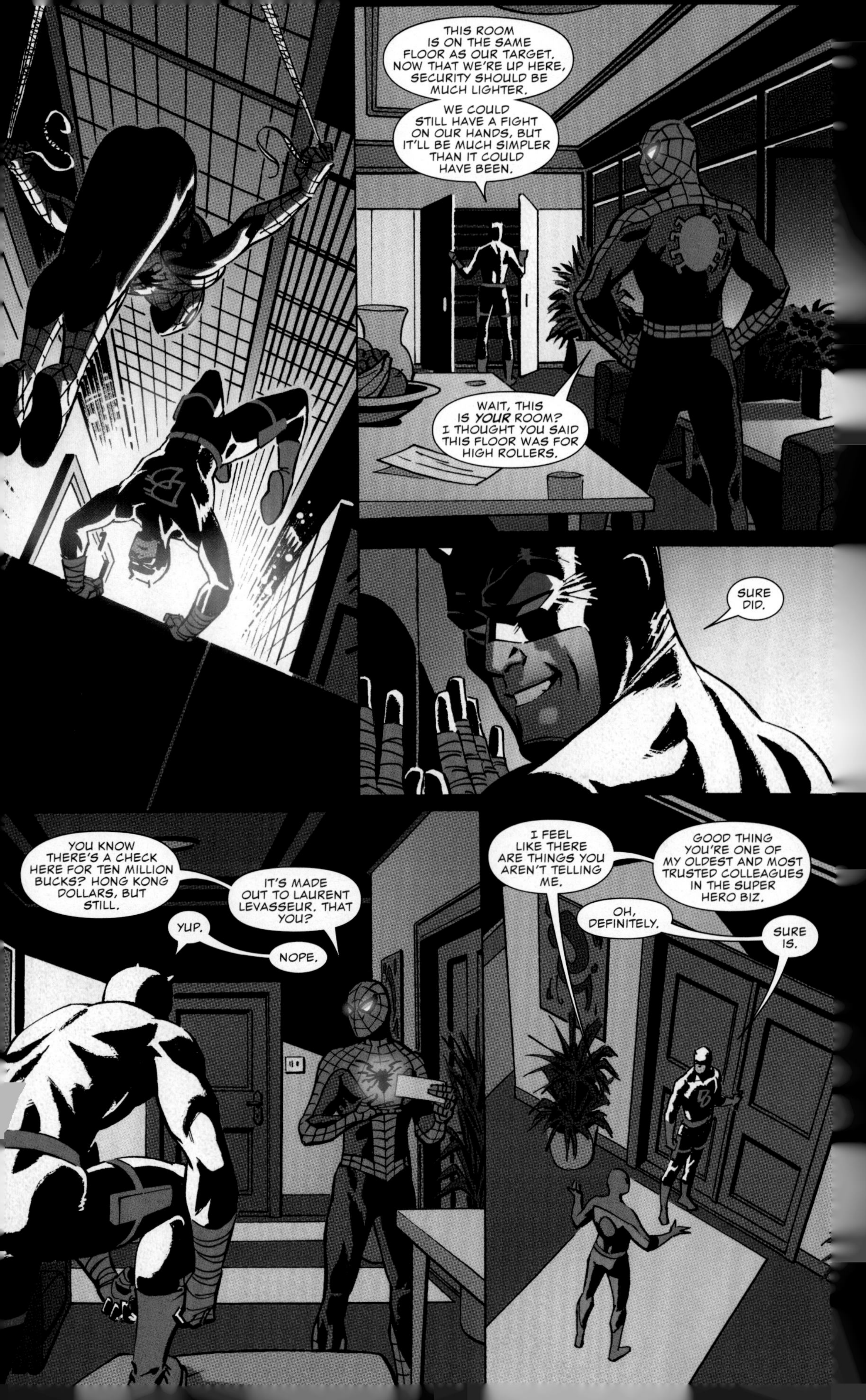
THIS ROOM IS ON THE SAME FLOOR AS OUR TARGET. NOW THAT WE'RE UP HERE, SECURITY SHOULD BE MUCH LIGHTER.
WE COULD STILL HAVE A FIGHT ON OUR HANDS, BUT IT'LL BE MUCH SIMPLER THAN IT COULD HAVE BEEN.
WAIT, THIS IS *YOUR* ROOM? I THOUGHT YOU SAID THIS FLOOR WAS FOR HIGH ROLLERS.
SURE DID.
YOU KNOW THERE'S A CHECK HERE FOR TEN MILLION BUCKS? HONG KONG DOLLARS, BUT STILL.
IT'S MADE OUT TO LAURENT LEVASSEUR. THAT YOU?
YUP.
NOPE.
I FEEL LIKE THERE ARE THINGS YOU AREN'T TELLING ME.
GOOD THING YOU'RE ONE OF MY OLDEST AND MOST TRUSTED COLLEAGUES IN THE SUPER HERO BIZ.
OH, DEFINITELY.
SURE IS.

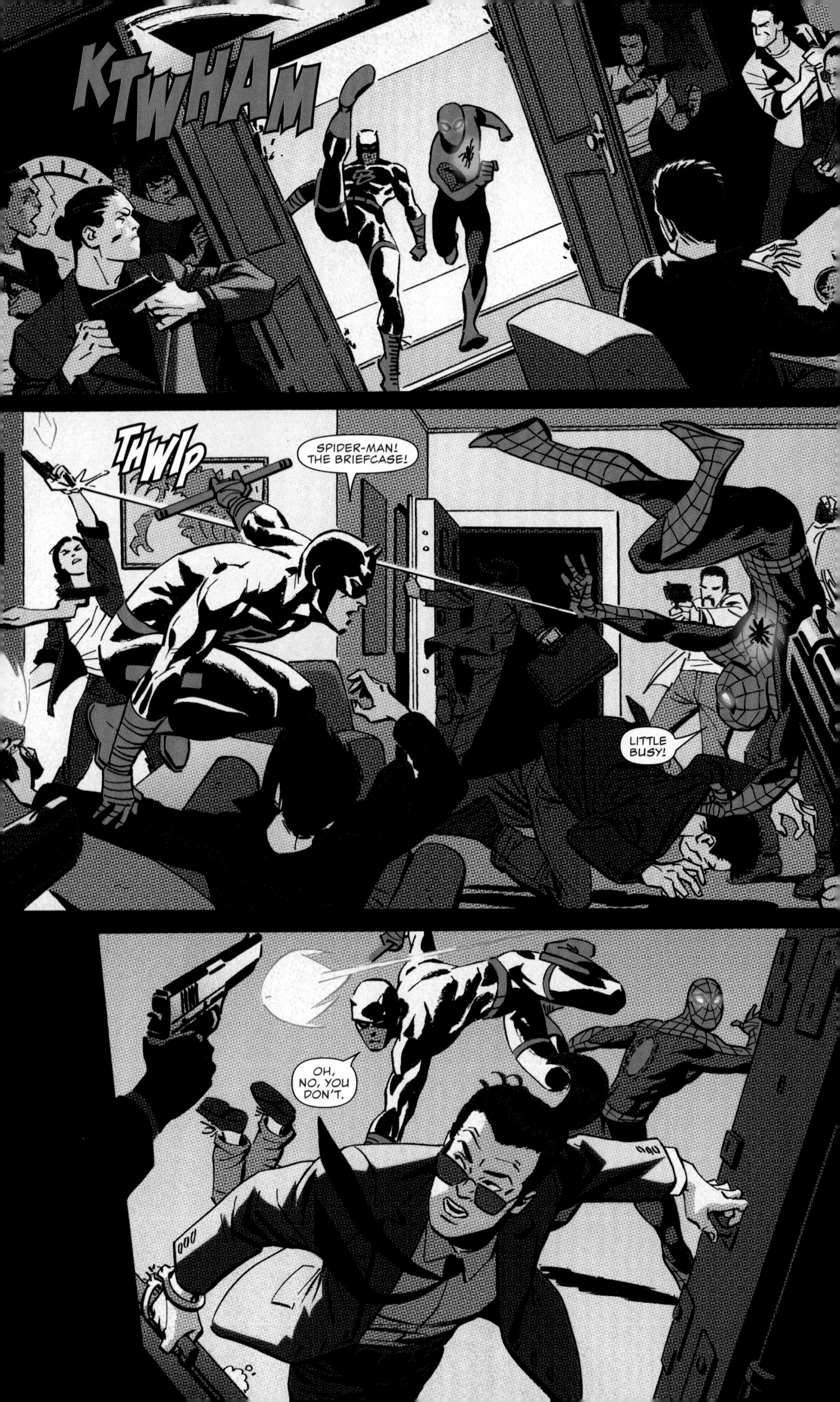
KTWHAM
THWIP
SPIDER-MAN! THE BRIEFCASE!
LITTLE BUSY!
OH, NO, YOU DON'T.

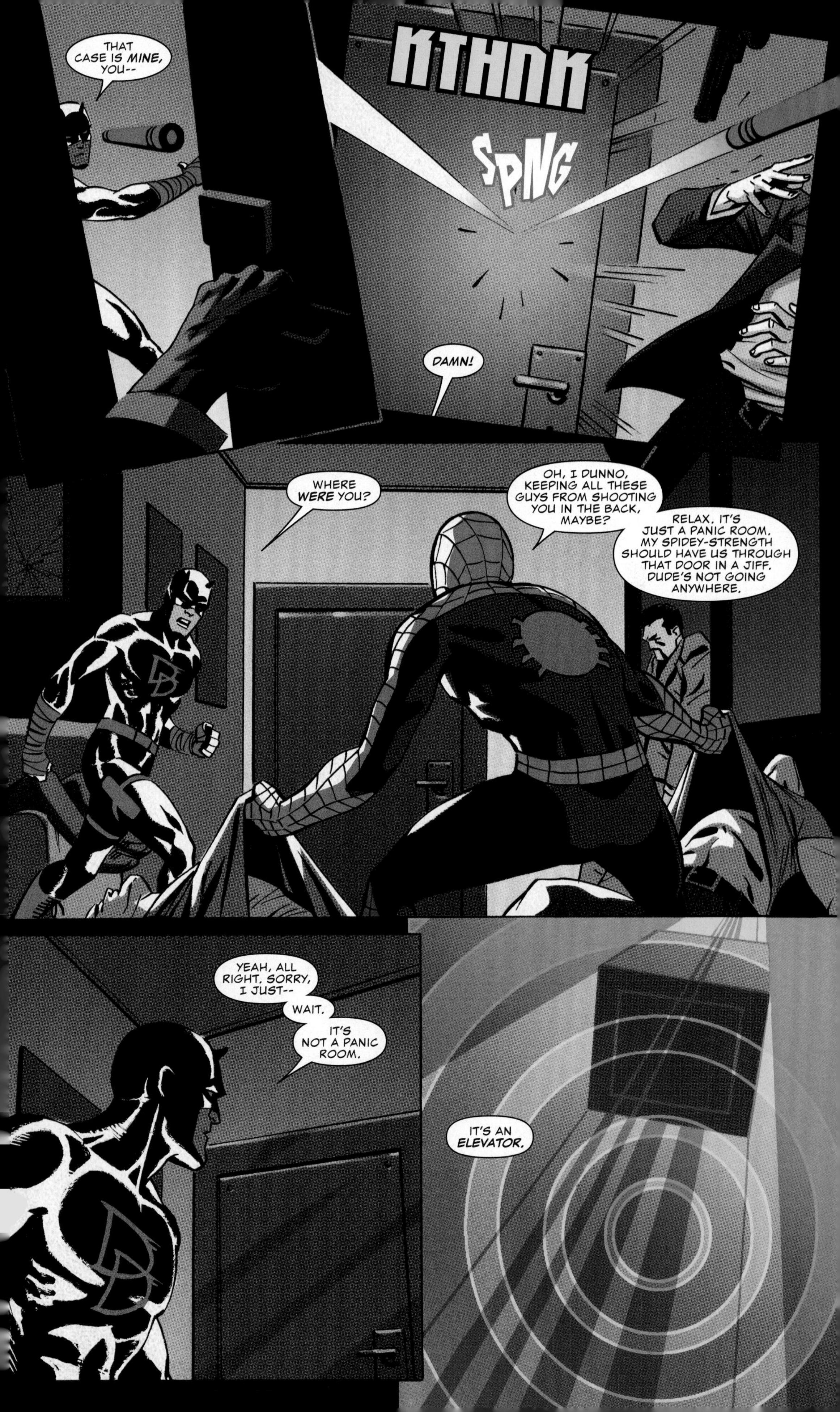
THAT CASE IS MINE, YOU--
KTHNK
SPNG
DAMN!
WHERE WERE YOU?
OH, I DUNNO, KEEPING ALL THESE GUYS FROM SHOOTING YOU IN THE BACK, MAYBE?
RELAX. IT'S JUST A PANIC ROOM. MY SPIDEY-STRENGTH SHOULD HAVE US THROUGH THAT DOOR IN A JIFF. DUDE'S NOT GOING ANYWHERE.
YEAH, ALL RIGHT. SORRY, I JUST--
WAIT.
IT'S NOT A PANIC ROOM.
IT'S AN ELEVATOR.

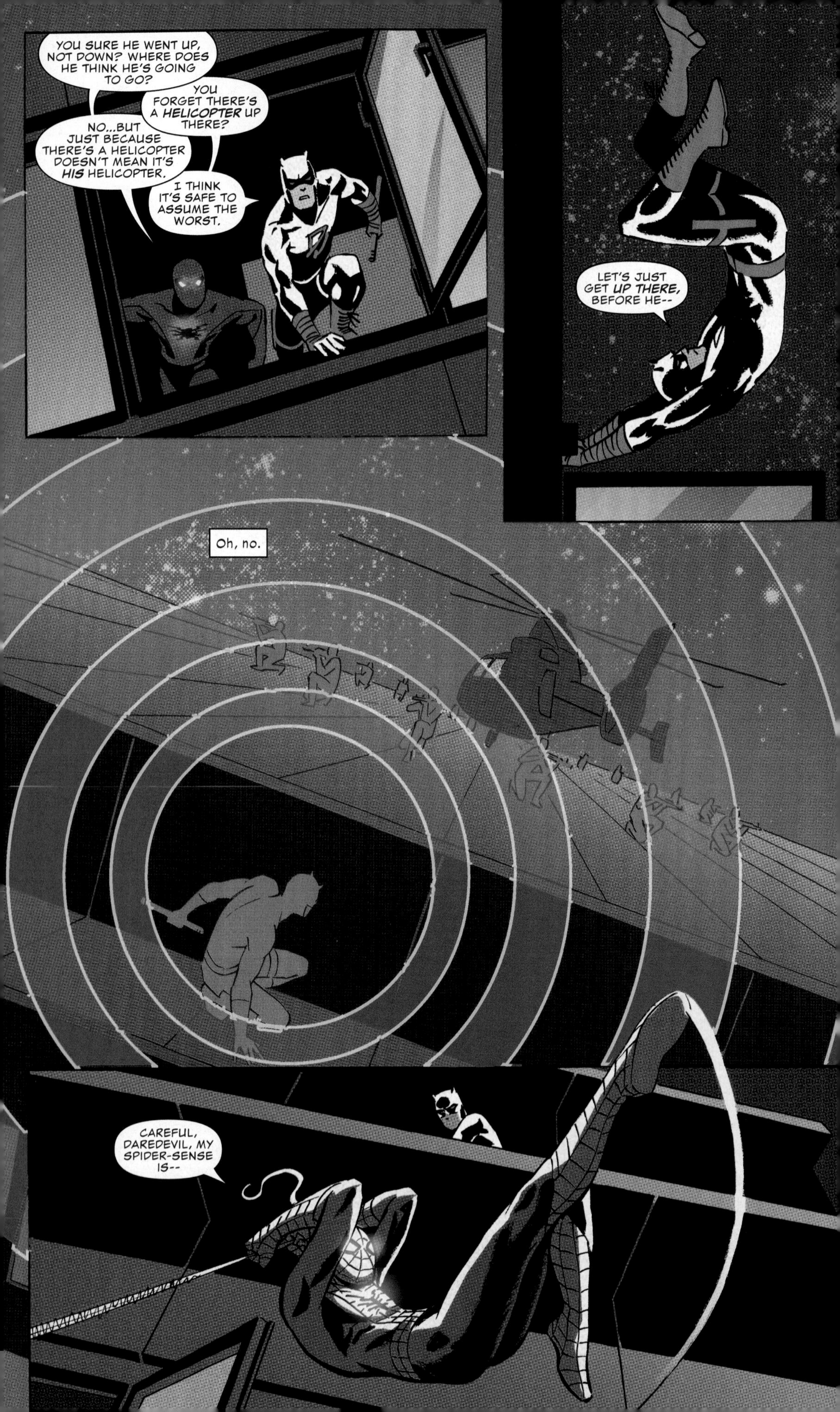
YOU SURE HE WENT UP, NOT DOWN? WHERE DOES HE THINK HE'S GOING TO GO?
YOU FORGET THERE'S A HELICOPTER UP THERE?
NO...BUT JUST BECAUSE THERE'S A HELICOPTER DOESN'T MEAN IT'S HIS HELICOPTER.
I THINK IT'S SAFE TO ASSUME THE WORST.
LET'S JUST GET UP THERE, BEFORE HE--
Oh, no.
CAREFUL, DAREDEVIL, MY SPIDER-SENSE IS--

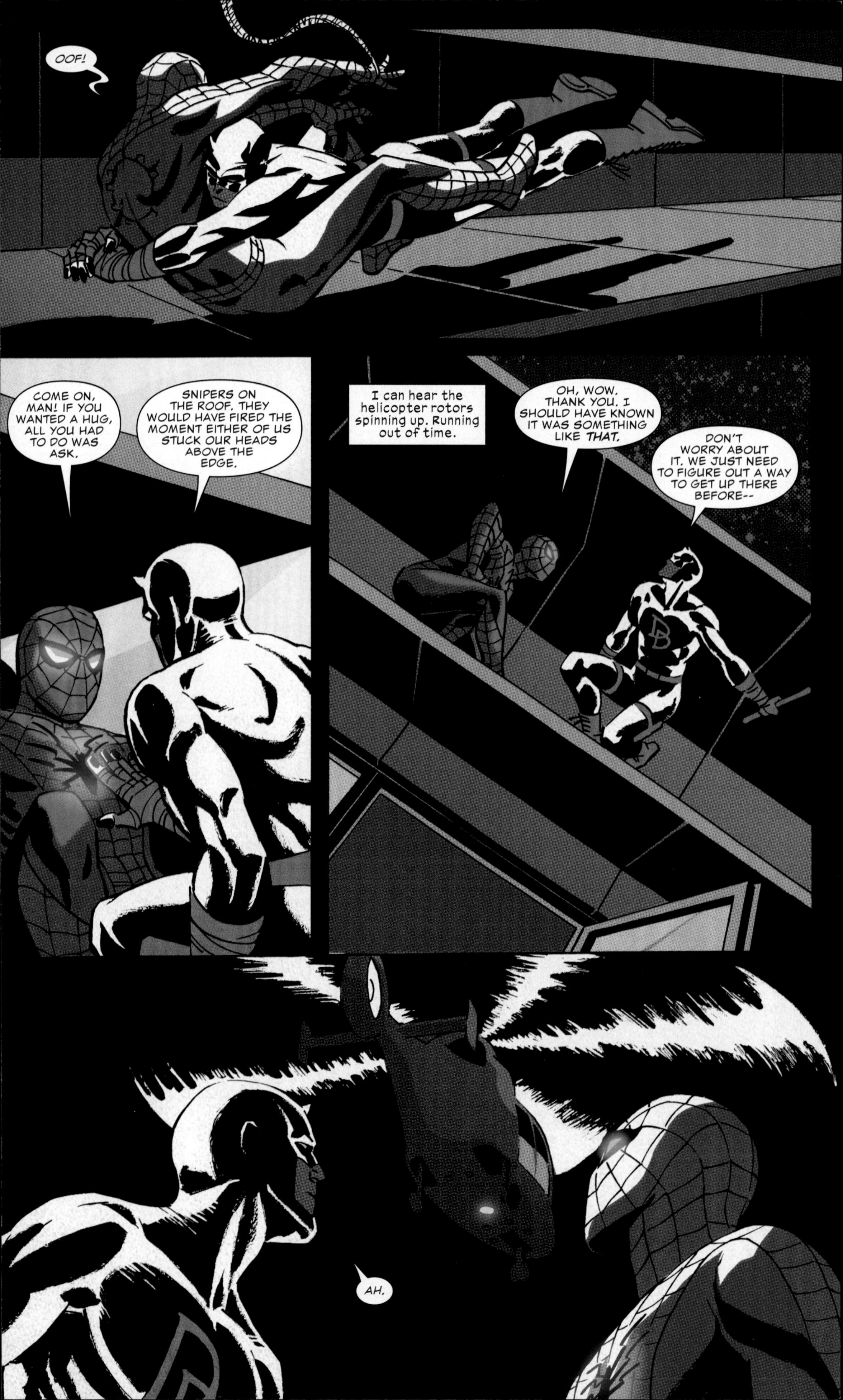
OOF!
COME ON, MAN! IF YOU WANTED A HUG, ALL YOU HAD TO DO WAS ASK.
SNIPERS ON THE ROOF. THEY WOULD HAVE FIRED THE MOMENT EITHER OF US STUCK OUR HEADS ABOVE THE EDGE.
I can hear the helicopter rotors spinning up. Running out of time.
OH, WOW. THANK YOU. I SHOULD HAVE KNOWN IT WAS SOMETHING LIKE *THAT.*
DON'T WORRY ABOUT IT. WE JUST NEED TO FIGURE OUT A WAY TO GET UP THERE BEFORE--
AH.

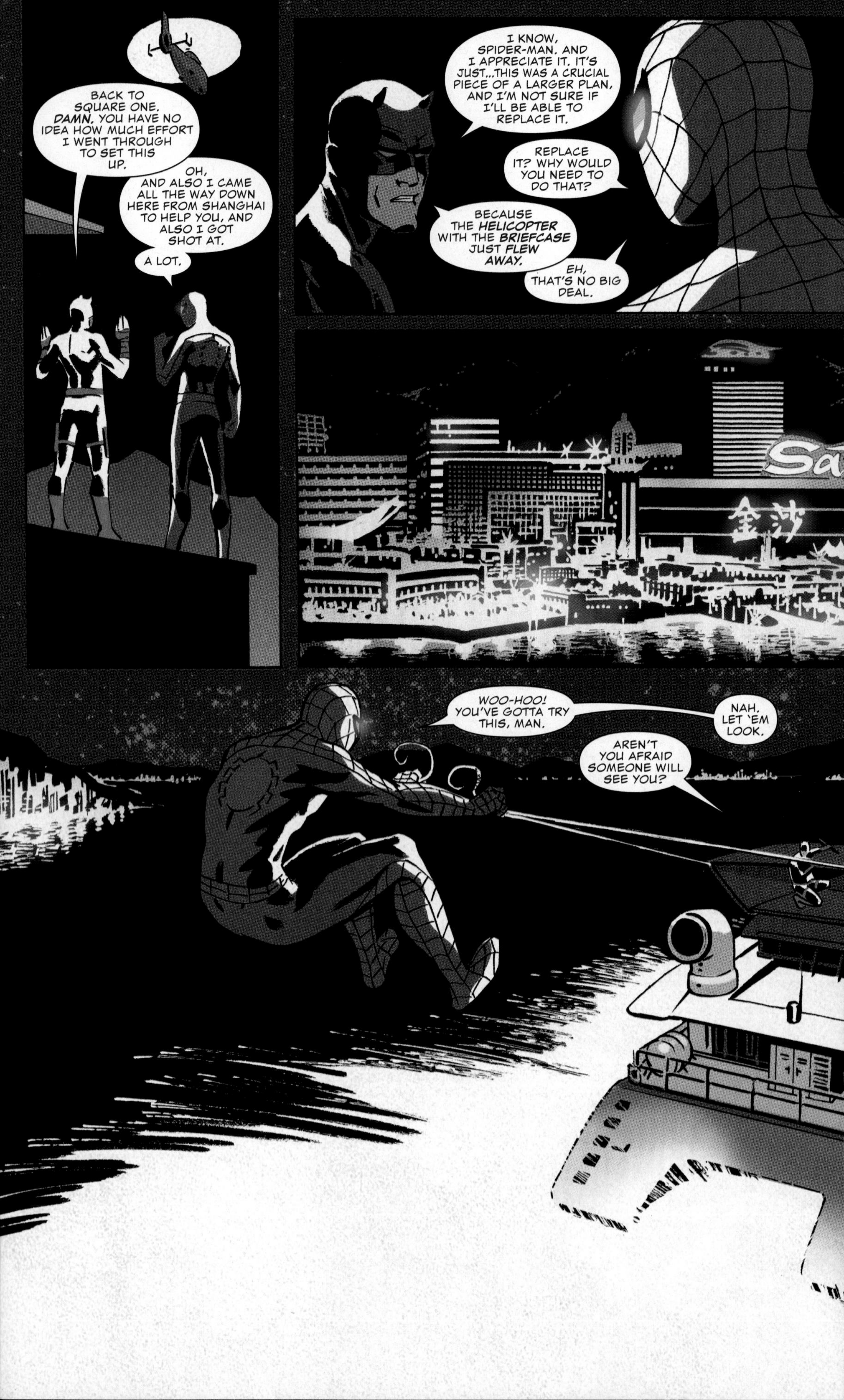

BACK TO SQUARE ONE. DAMN. YOU HAVE NO IDEA HOW MUCH EFFORT I WENT THROUGH TO SET THIS UP.
OH, AND ALSO I CAME ALL THE WAY DOWN HERE FROM SHANGHAI TO HELP YOU, AND ALSO I GOT SHOT AT.
A LOT.
I KNOW, SPIDER-MAN, AND I APPRECIATE IT. IT'S JUST...THIS WAS A CRUCIAL PIECE OF A LARGER PLAN, AND I'M NOT SURE IF I'LL BE ABLE TO REPLACE IT.
REPLACE IT? WHY WOULD YOU NEED TO DO THAT?
BECAUSE THE HELICOPTER WITH THE BRIEFCASE JUST FLEW AWAY.
EH, THAT'S NO BIG DEAL.
金沙
WOO-HOO! YOU'VE GOTTA TRY THIS, MAN.
AREN'T YOU AFRAID SOMEONE WILL SEE YOU?
NAH, LET 'EM LOOK.

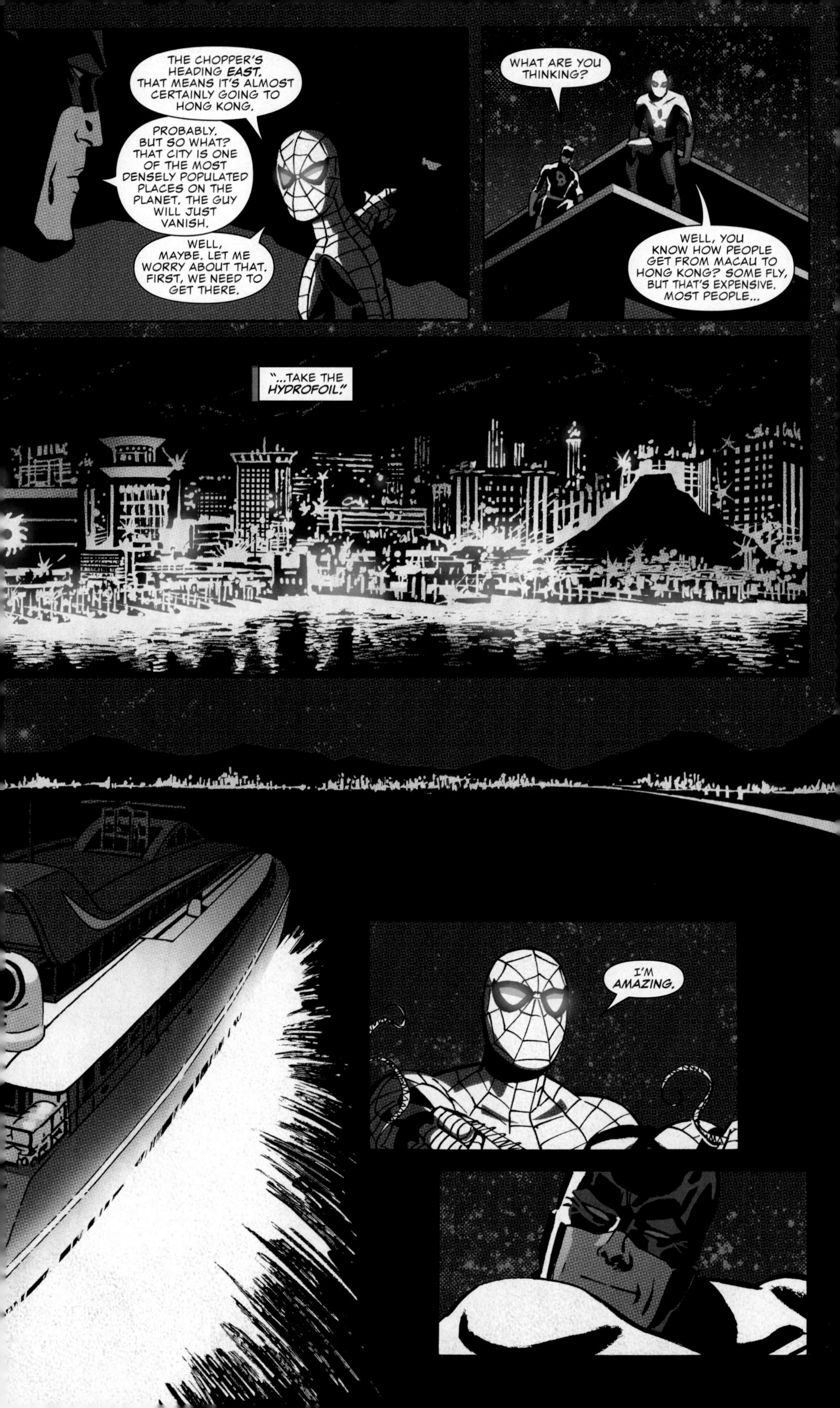
THE CHOPPER'S HEADING EAST. THAT MEANS IT'S ALMOST CERTAINLY GOING TO HONG KONG.
PROBABLY. BUT SO WHAT? THAT CITY IS ONE OF THE MOST DENSELY POPULATED PLACES ON THE PLANET. THE GUY WILL JUST VANISH.
WELL, MAYBE. LET ME WORRY ABOUT THAT. FIRST, WE NEED TO GET THERE.
WHAT ARE YOU THINKING?
WELL, YOU KNOW HOW PEOPLE GET FROM MACAU TO HONG KONG? SOME FLY, BUT THAT'S EXPENSIVE. MOST PEOPLE...
"...TAKE THE HYDROFOIL."
I'M AMAZING.

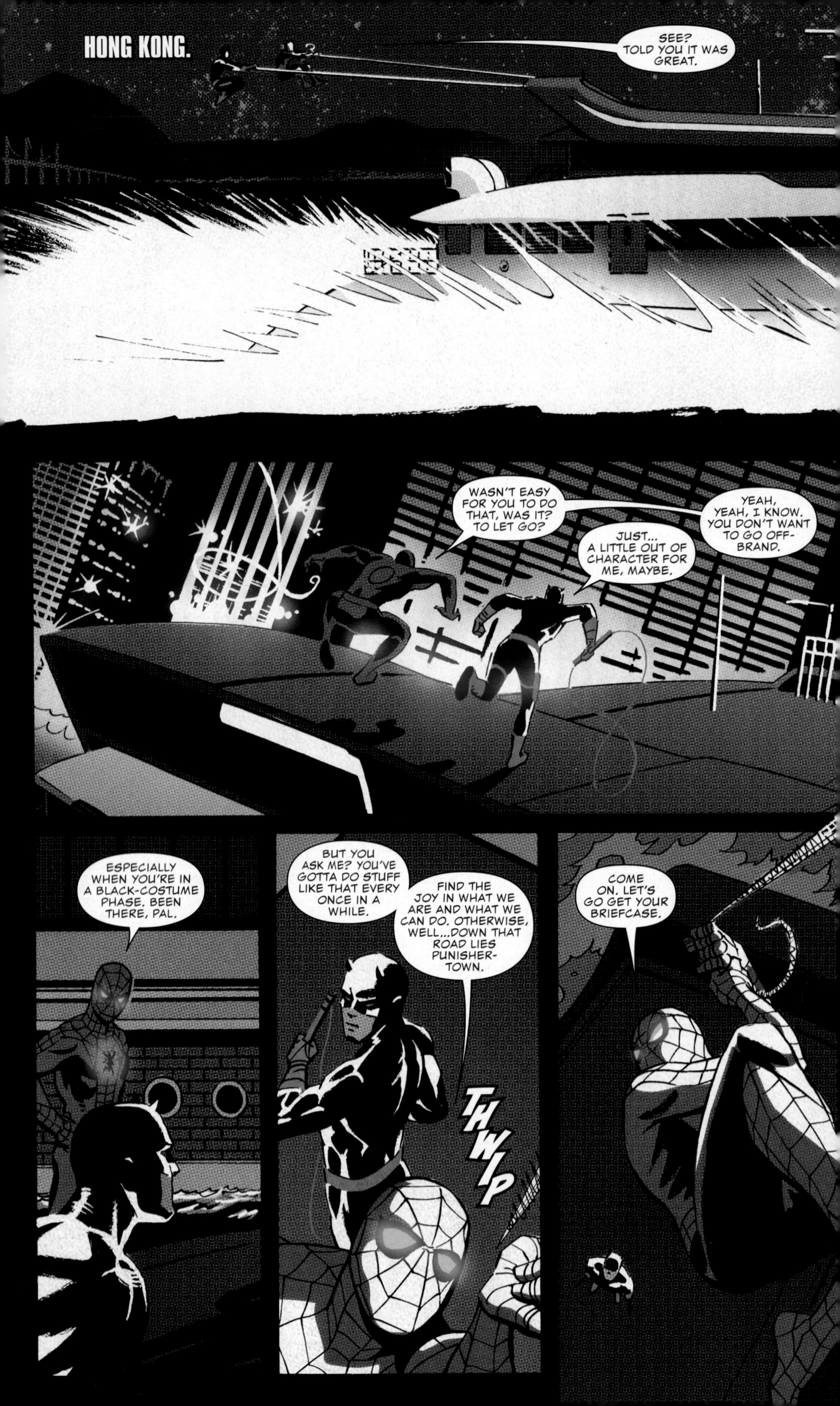
HONG KONG.
SEE? TOLD YOU IT WAS GREAT.
WASN'T EASY FOR YOU TO DO THAT, WAS IT? TO LET GO?
JUST... A LITTLE OUT OF CHARACTER FOR ME, MAYBE.
YEAH, YEAH, I KNOW. YOU DON'T WANT TO GO OFF-BRAND.
ESPECIALLY WHEN YOU'RE IN A BLACK-COSTUME PHASE. BEEN THERE, PAL.
BUT YOU ASK ME? YOU'VE GOTTA DO STUFF LIKE THAT EVERY ONCE IN A WHILE.
FIND THE JOY IN WHAT WE ARE AND WHAT WE CAN DO. OTHERWISE, WELL...DOWN THAT ROAD LIES PUNISHER-TOWN.
THWIP
COME ON. LET'S GO GET YOUR BRIEFCASE.

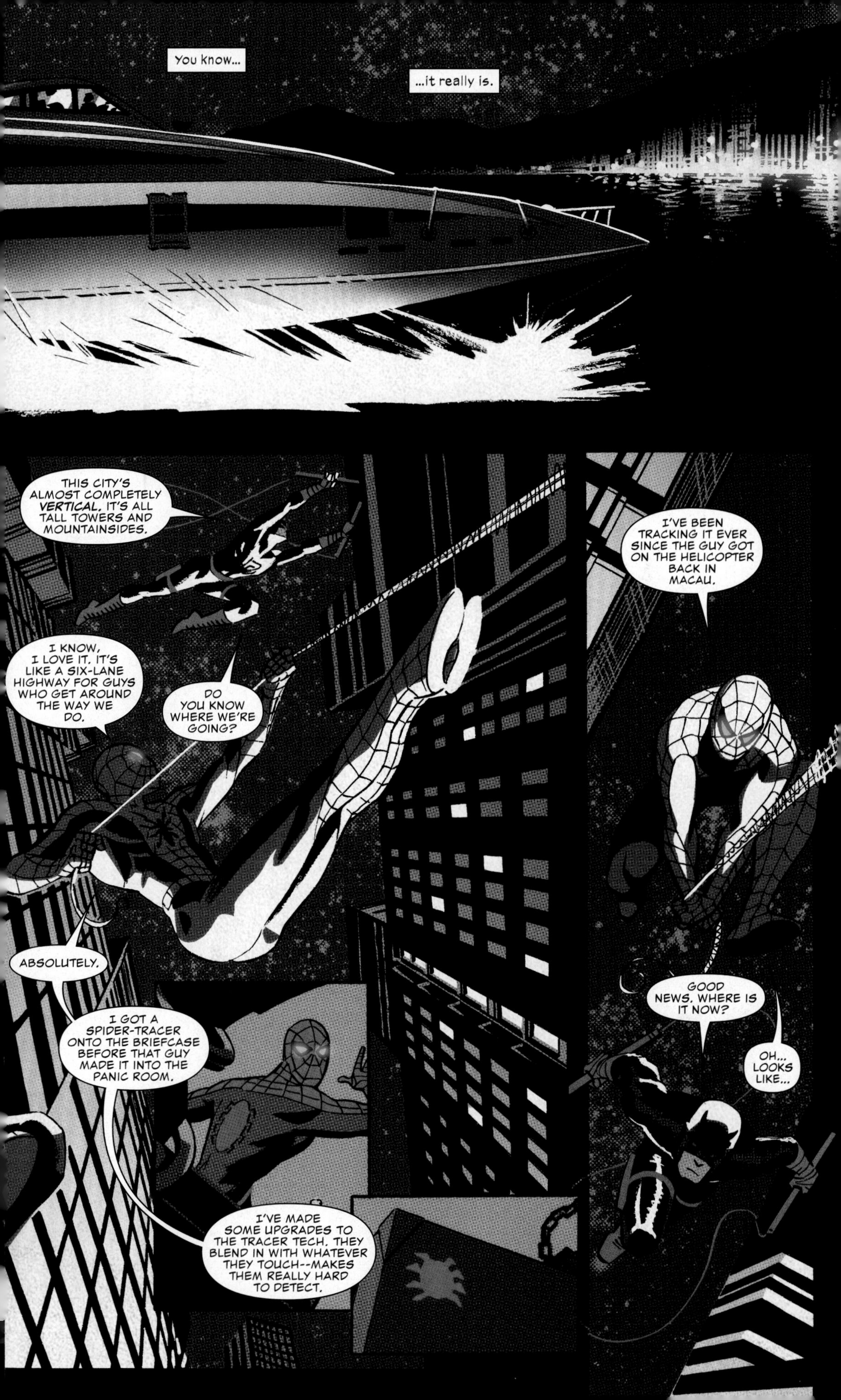
You know...
...it really is.
THIS CITY'S ALMOST COMPLETELY VERTICAL. IT'S ALL TALL TOWERS AND MOUNTAINSIDES.
I KNOW, I LOVE IT. IT'S LIKE A SIX-LANE HIGHWAY FOR GUYS WHO GET AROUND THE WAY WE DO.
DO YOU KNOW WHERE WE'RE GOING?
ABSOLUTELY.
I GOT A SPIDER-TRACER ONTO THE BRIEFCASE BEFORE THAT GUY MADE IT INTO THE PANIC ROOM.
I'VE MADE SOME UPGRADES TO THE TRACER TECH. THEY BLEND IN WITH WHATEVER THEY TOUCH--MAKES THEM REALLY HARD TO DETECT.
I'VE BEEN TRACKING IT EVER SINCE THE GUY GOT ON THE HELICOPTER BACK IN MACAU.
GOOD NEWS. WHERE IS IT NOW?
OH... LOOKS LIKE...

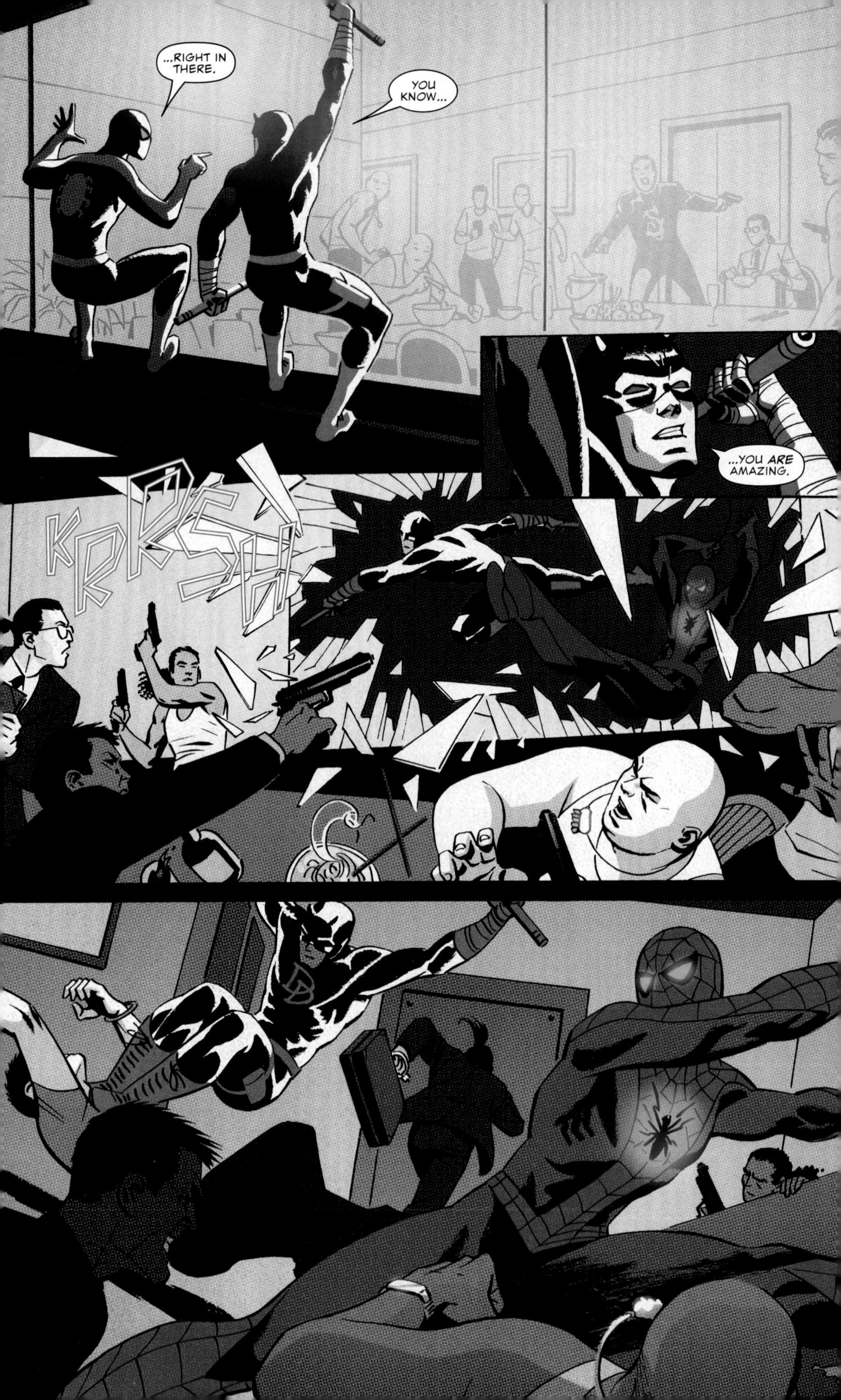
...RIGHT IN THERE.
YOU KNOW...
...YOU ARE AMAZING.
KRKRSSH

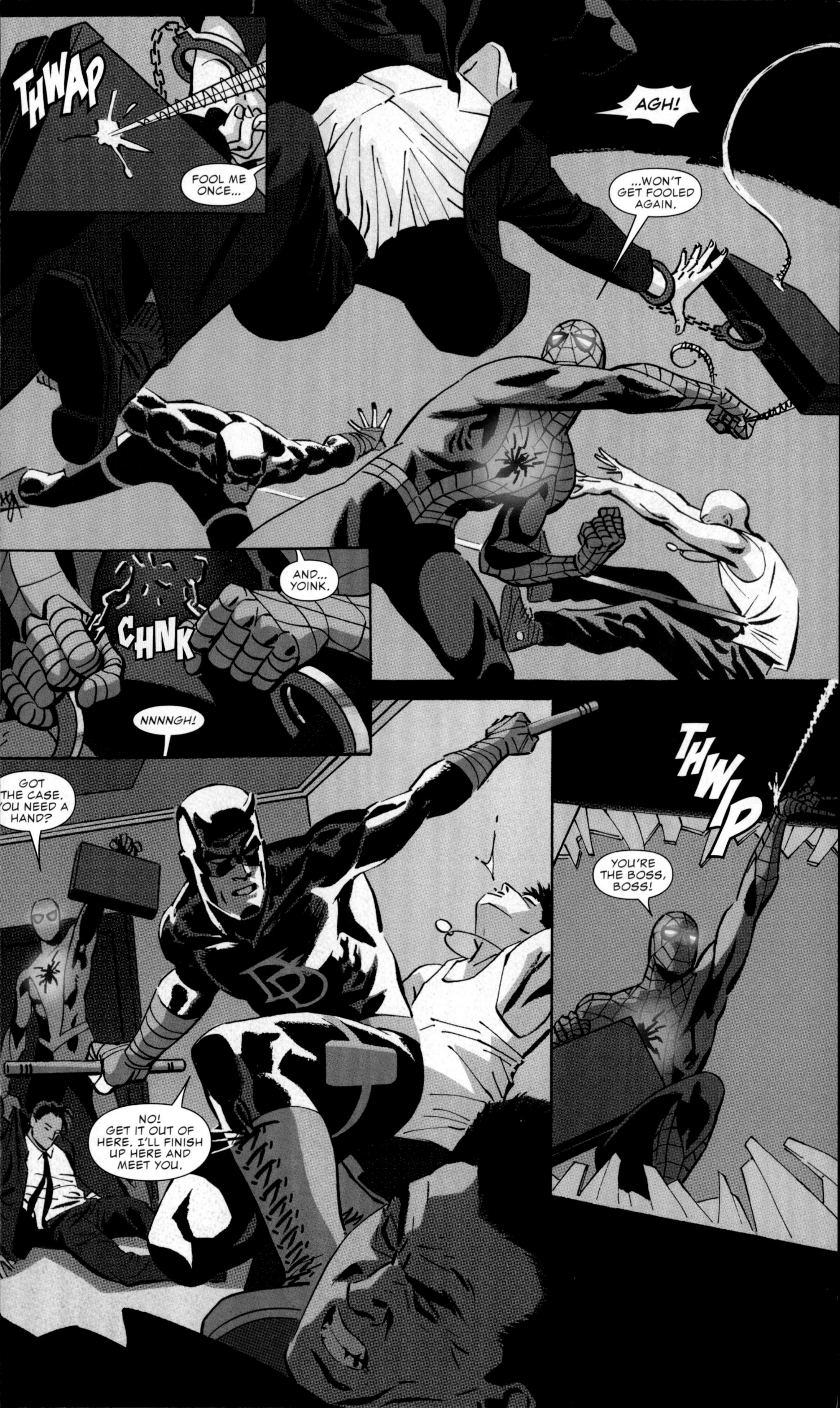

THWAP
FOOL ME ONCE...
AGH!
...WON'T GET FOOLED AGAIN.
AND... YOINK.
CHNK
NNNNGH!
THWIP
GOT THE CASE. YOU NEED A HAND?
NO! GET IT OUT OF HERE. I'LL FINISH UP HERE AND MEET YOU.
YOU'RE THE BOSS, BOSS!

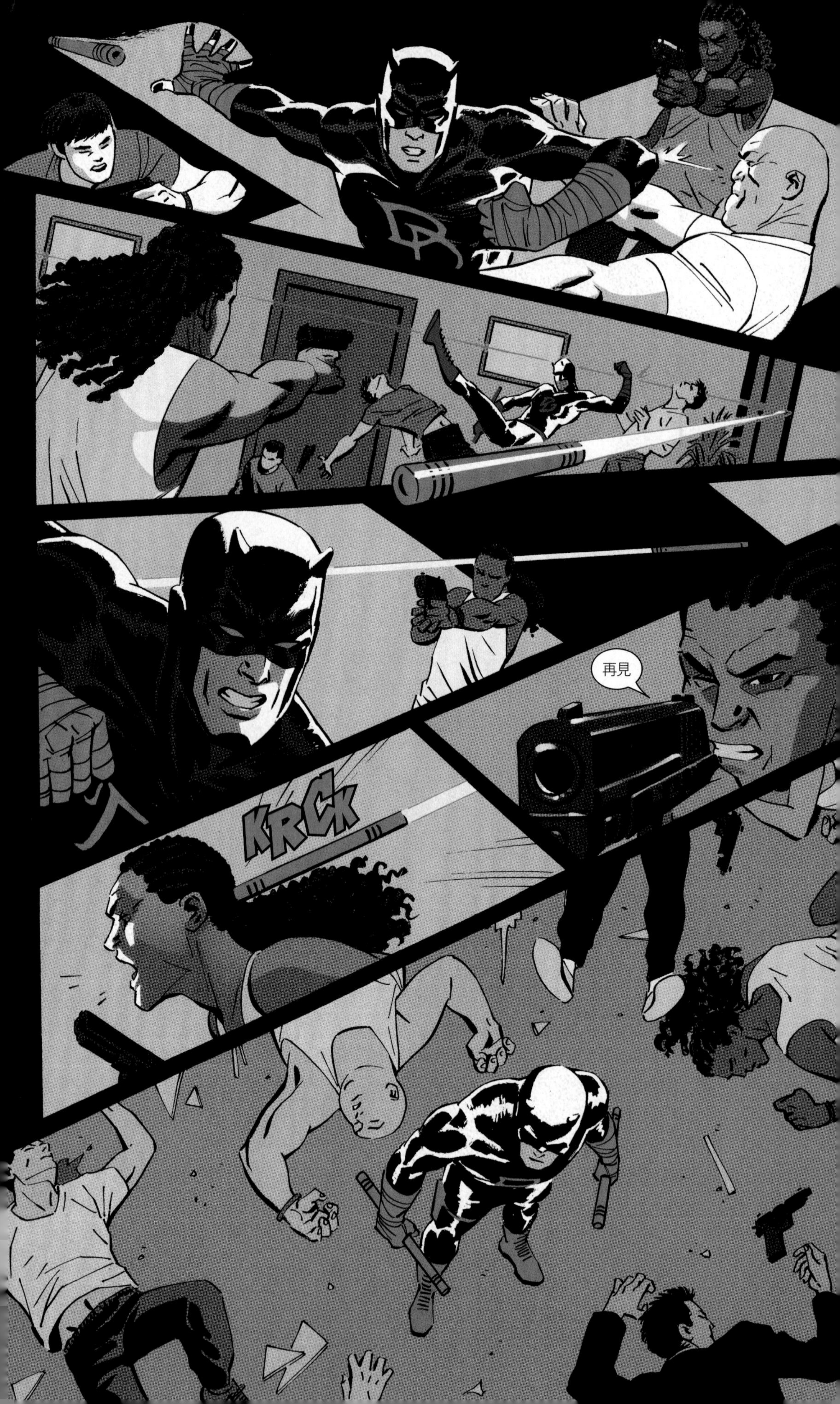
再見
KRCK

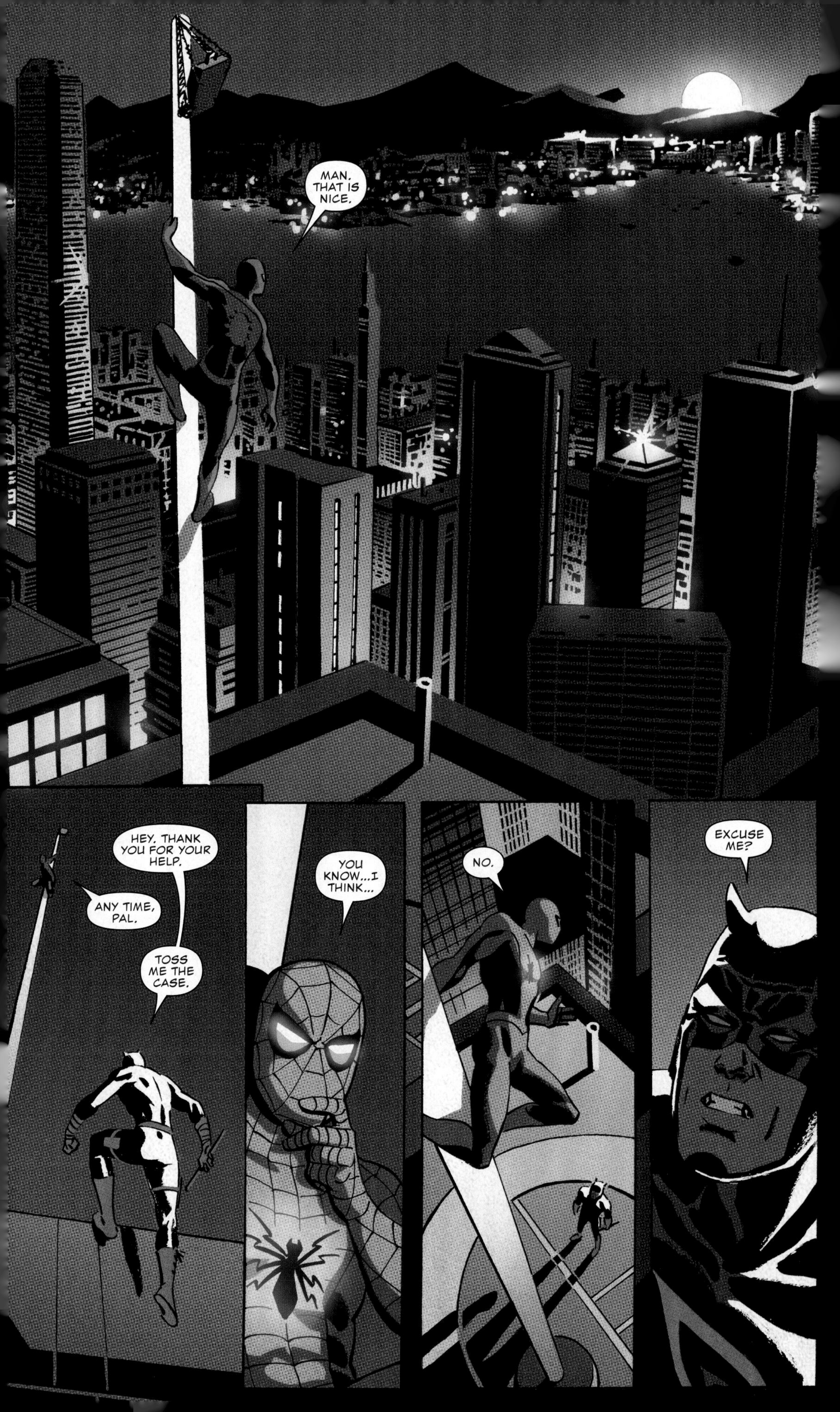
MAN. THAT IS NICE.
HEY, THANK YOU FOR YOUR HELP.
ANY TIME, PAL.
TOSS ME THE CASE.
YOU KNOW...I THINK...
NO.
EXCUSE ME?

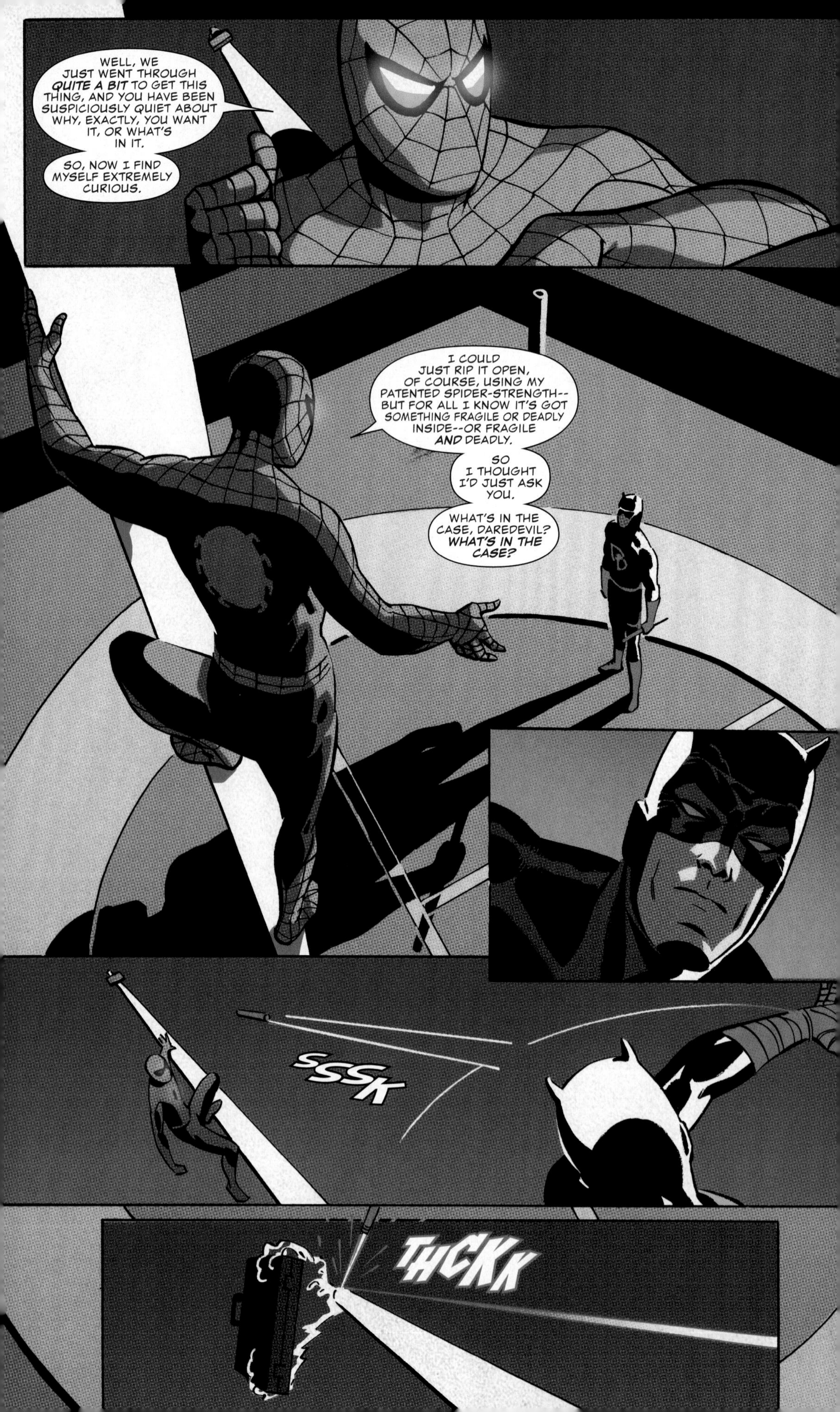
WELL, WE JUST WENT THROUGH QUITE A BIT TO GET THIS THING, AND YOU HAVE BEEN SUSPICIOUSLY QUIET ABOUT WHY, EXACTLY, YOU WANT IT, OR WHAT'S IN IT.
SO, NOW I FIND MYSELF EXTREMELY CURIOUS.
I COULD JUST RIP IT OPEN, OF COURSE, USING MY PATENTED SPIDER-STRENGTH--BUT FOR ALL I KNOW IT'S GOT SOMETHING FRAGILE OR DEADLY INSIDE--OR FRAGILE AND DEADLY.
SO I THOUGHT I'D JUST ASK YOU.
WHAT'S IN THE CASE, DAREDEVIL? WHAT'S IN THE CASE?
SSSK
THCKK

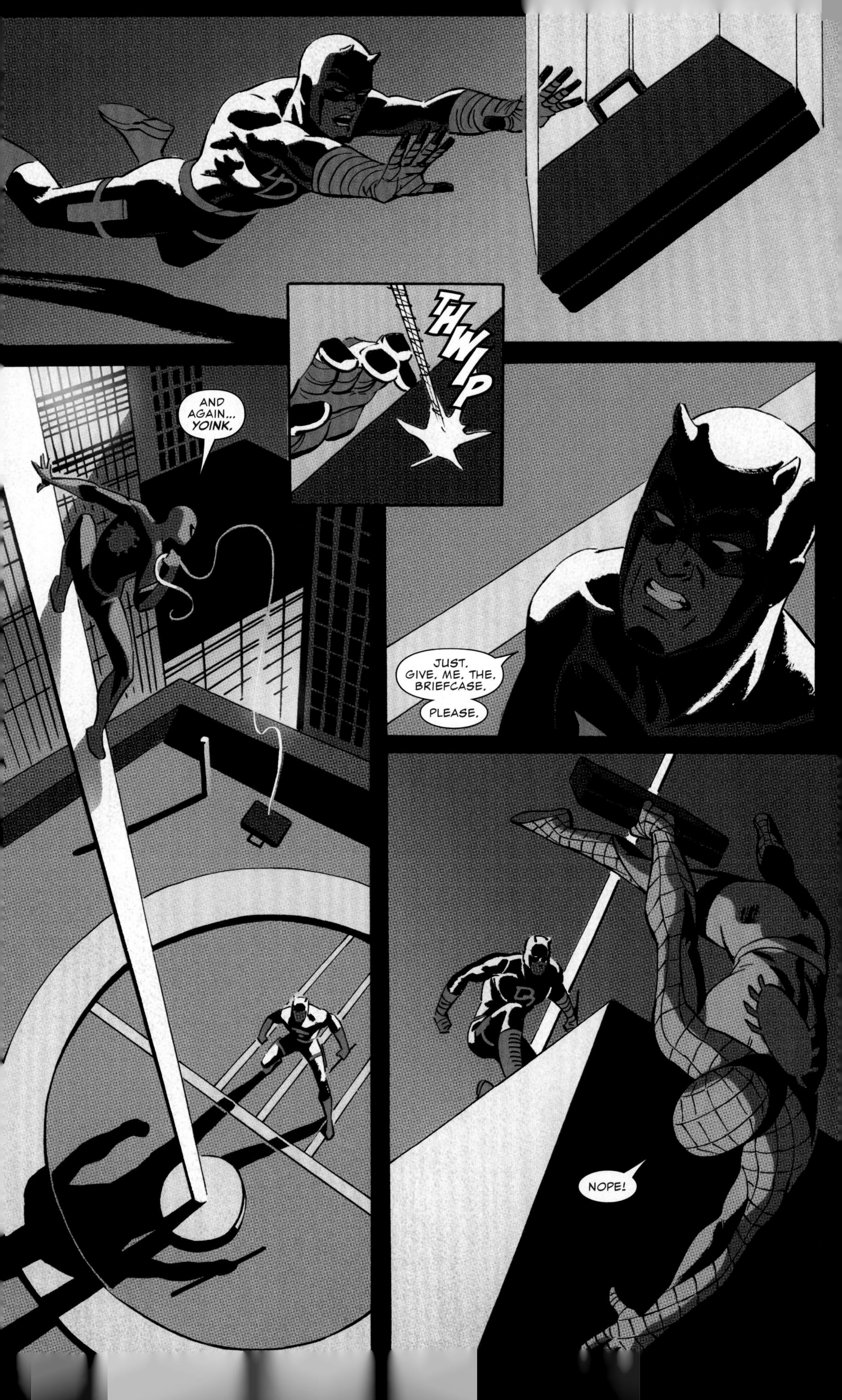
THWIP
AND AGAIN... YOINK.
JUST. GIVE. ME. THE. BRIEFCASE.
PLEASE.
NOPE!

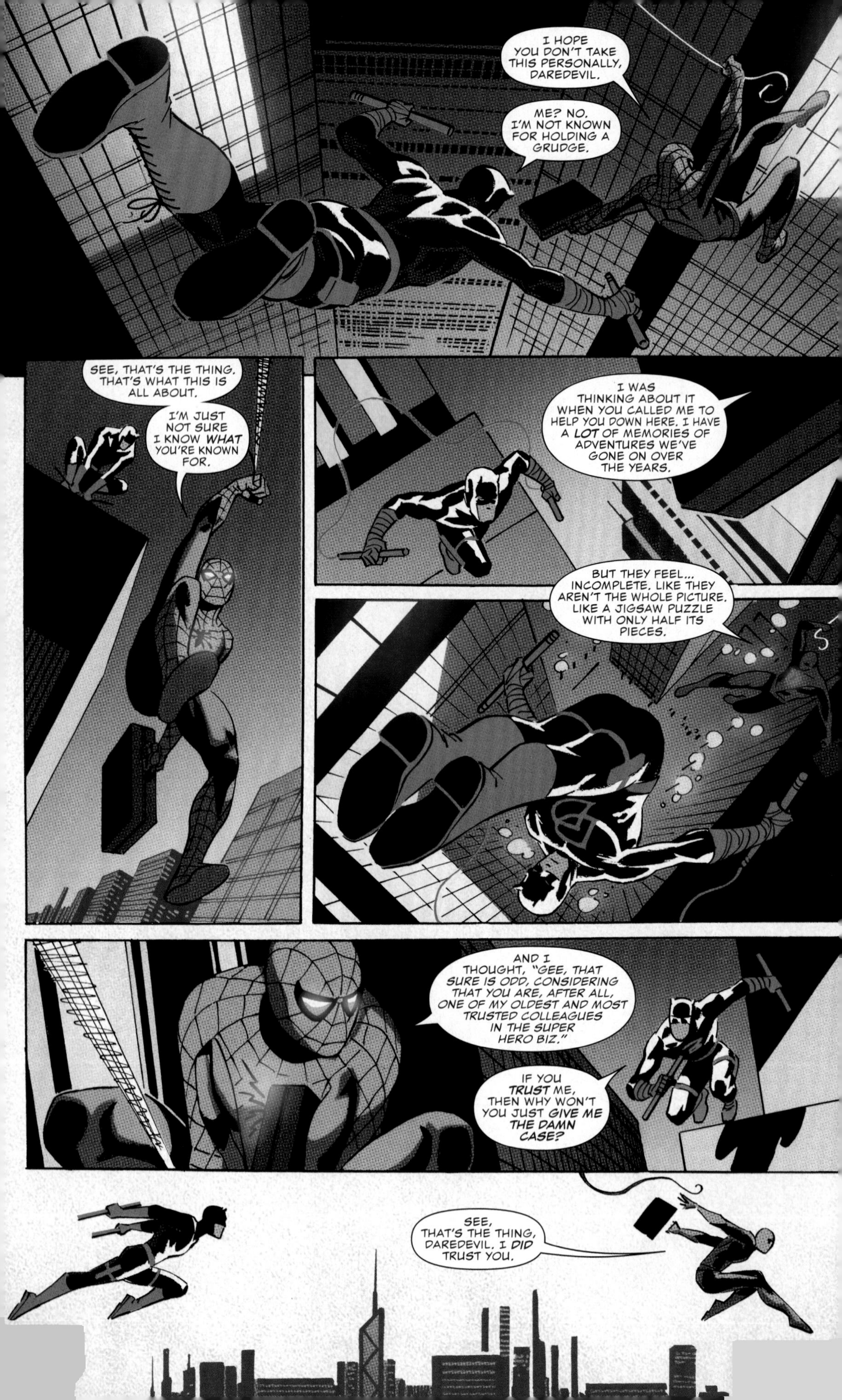
I HOPE YOU DON'T TAKE THIS PERSONALLY, DAREDEVIL.
ME? NO. I'M NOT KNOWN FOR HOLDING A GRUDGE.
SEE, THAT'S THE THING. THAT'S WHAT THIS IS ALL ABOUT.
I'M JUST NOT SURE I KNOW *WHAT* YOU'RE KNOWN FOR.
I WAS THINKING ABOUT IT WHEN YOU CALLED ME TO HELP YOU DOWN HERE. I HAVE A *LOT* OF MEMORIES OF ADVENTURES WE'VE GONE ON OVER THE YEARS.
BUT THEY FEEL... INCOMPLETE. LIKE THEY AREN'T THE WHOLE PICTURE. LIKE A JIGSAW PUZZLE WITH ONLY HALF ITS PIECES.
AND I THOUGHT, "GEE, THAT *SURE* IS ODD, CONSIDERING THAT YOU ARE, AFTER ALL, ONE OF MY OLDEST AND MOST TRUSTED COLLEAGUES IN THE SUPER HERO BIZ."
IF YOU *TRUST* ME, THEN WHY WON'T YOU JUST *GIVE ME THE DAMN CASE?*
SEE, THAT'S THE THING, DAREDEVIL. I *DID* TRUST YOU.

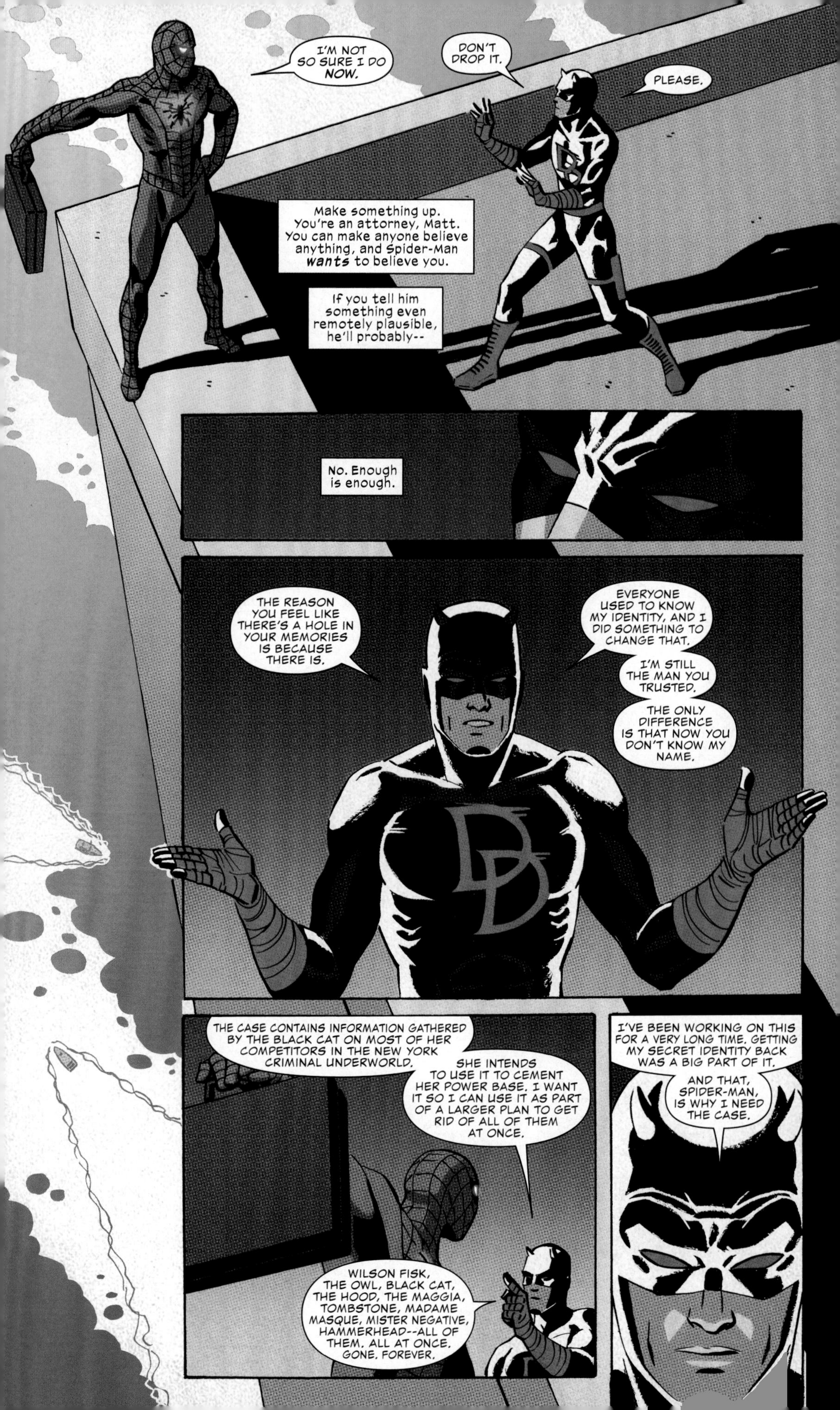
I'M NOT SO SURE I DO NOW.
DON'T DROP IT.
PLEASE.
Make something up. You're an attorney, Matt. You can make anyone believe anything, and Spider-Man wants to believe you.
If you tell him something even remotely plausible, he'll probably--
No. Enough is enough.
THE REASON YOU FEEL LIKE THERE'S A HOLE IN YOUR MEMORIES IS BECAUSE THERE IS.
EVERYONE USED TO KNOW MY IDENTITY, AND I DID SOMETHING TO CHANGE THAT.
I'M STILL THE MAN YOU TRUSTED.
THE ONLY DIFFERENCE IS THAT NOW YOU DON'T KNOW MY NAME.
THE CASE CONTAINS INFORMATION GATHERED BY THE BLACK CAT ON MOST OF HER COMPETITORS IN THE NEW YORK CRIMINAL UNDERWORLD.
SHE INTENDS TO USE IT TO CEMENT HER POWER BASE. I WANT IT SO I CAN USE IT AS PART OF A LARGER PLAN TO GET RID OF ALL OF THEM AT ONCE.
WILSON FISK, THE OWL, BLACK CAT, THE HOOD, THE MAGGIA, TOMBSTONE, MADAME MASQUE, MISTER NEGATIVE, HAMMERHEAD--ALL OF THEM. ALL AT ONCE. GONE. FOREVER.
I'VE BEEN WORKING ON THIS FOR A VERY LONG TIME. GETTING MY SECRET IDENTITY BACK WAS A BIG PART OF IT.
AND THAT, SPIDER-MAN, IS WHY I NEED THE CASE.

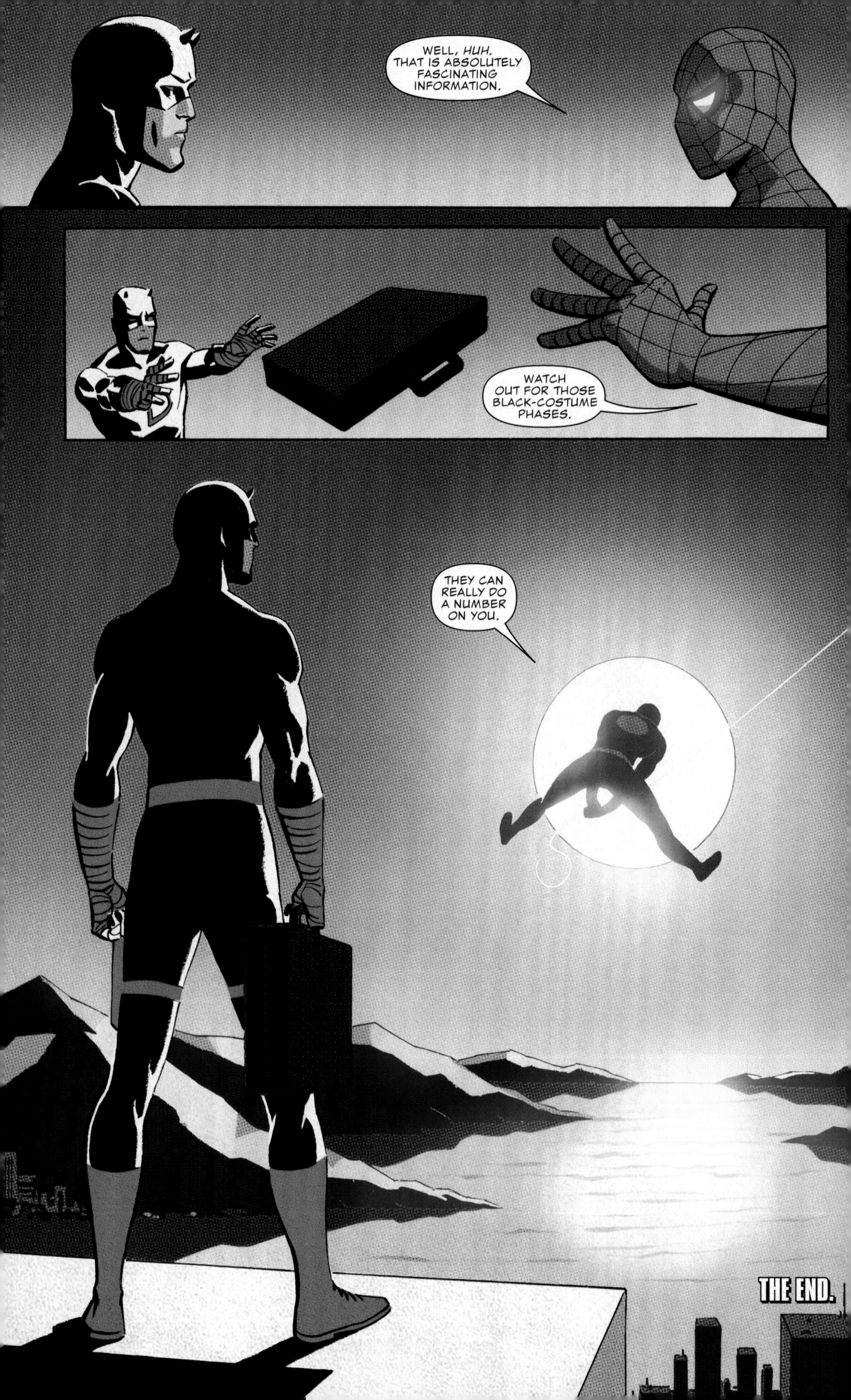
WELL, *HUH*, THAT IS ABSOLUTELY FASCINATING INFORMATION.
WATCH OUT FOR THOSE BLACK-COSTUME PHASES.
THEY CAN REALLY DO A NUMBER ON YOU.
THE END.

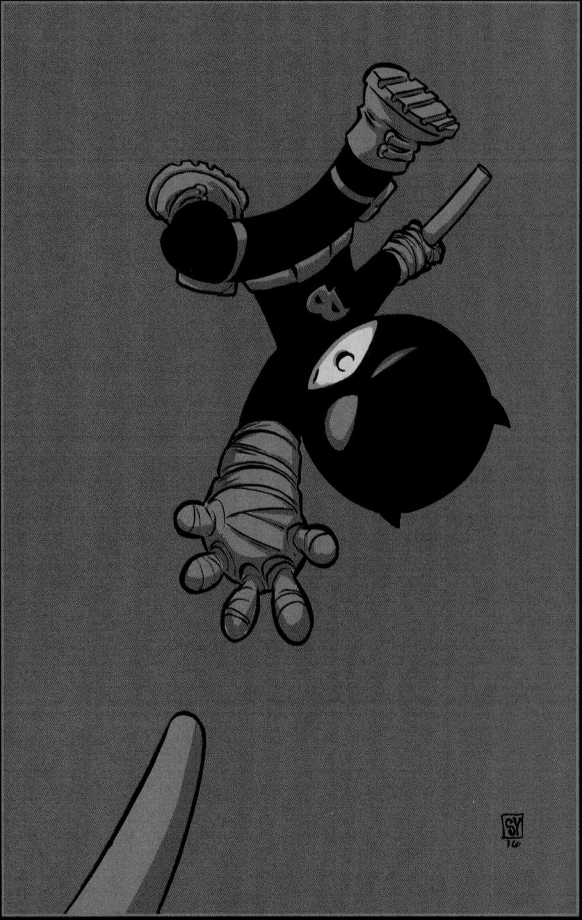

SKOTTIE YOUNG
ANNUAL No. 1 VARIANT

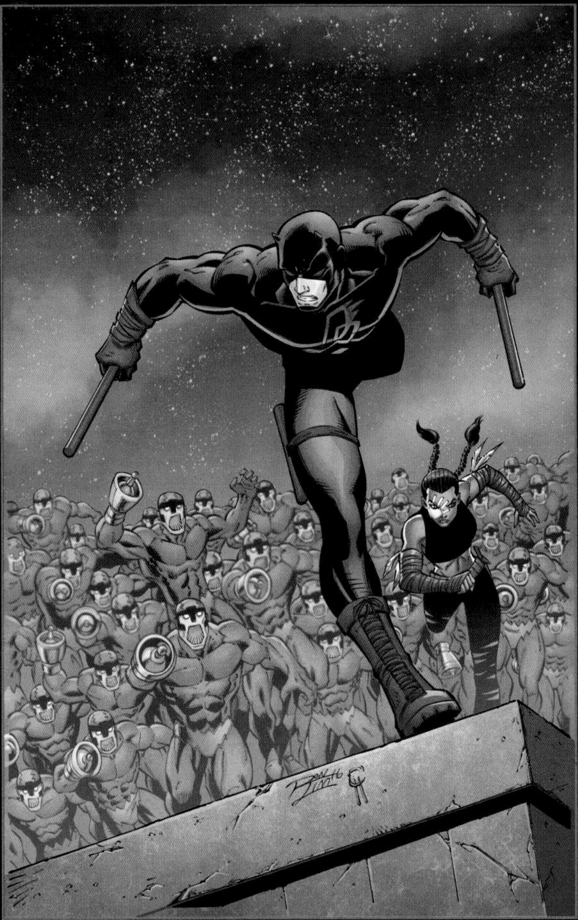

RON LIM,
CORY HAMSCHER & MATT YACKEY
ANNUAL No. 1 VARIANT

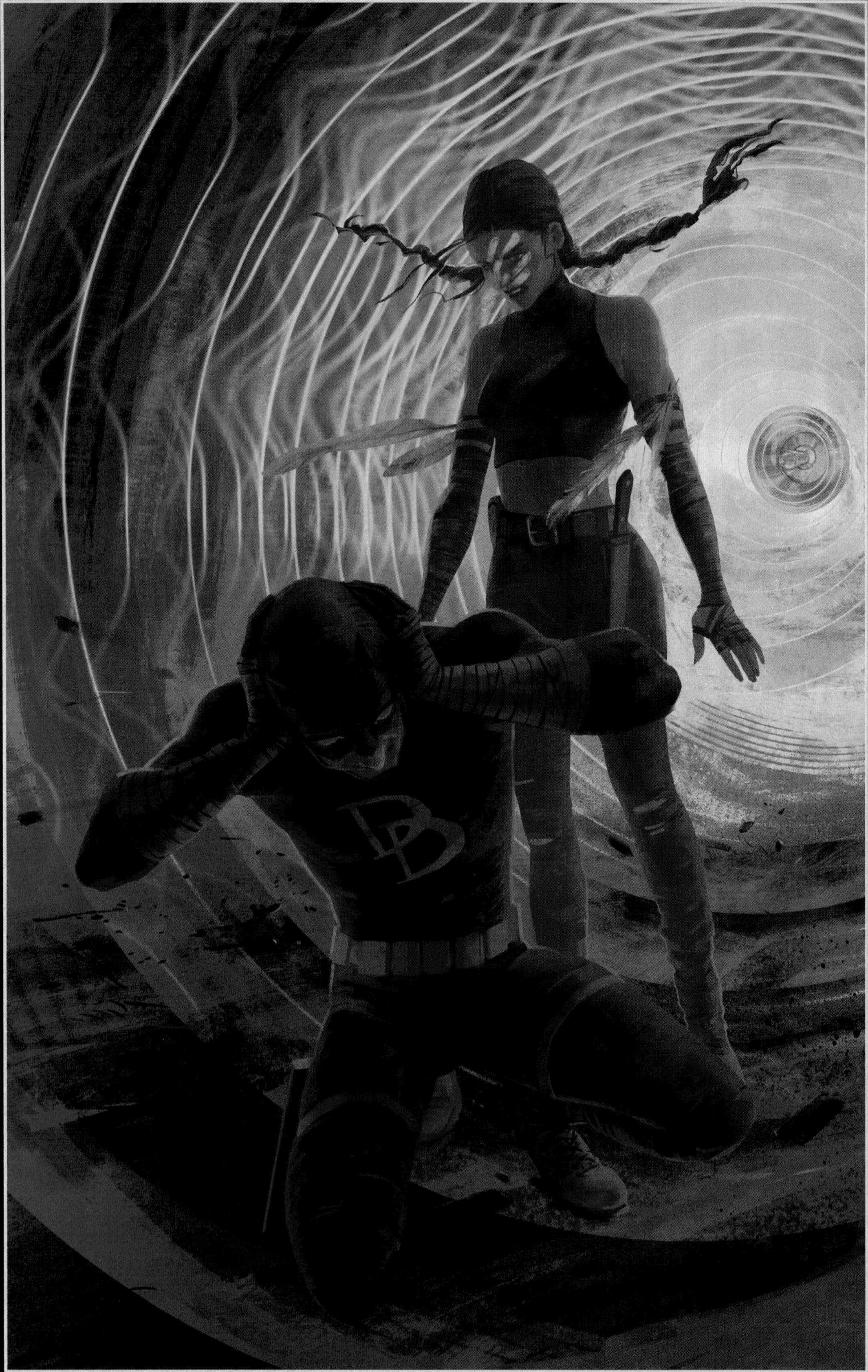

ANNUAL 1

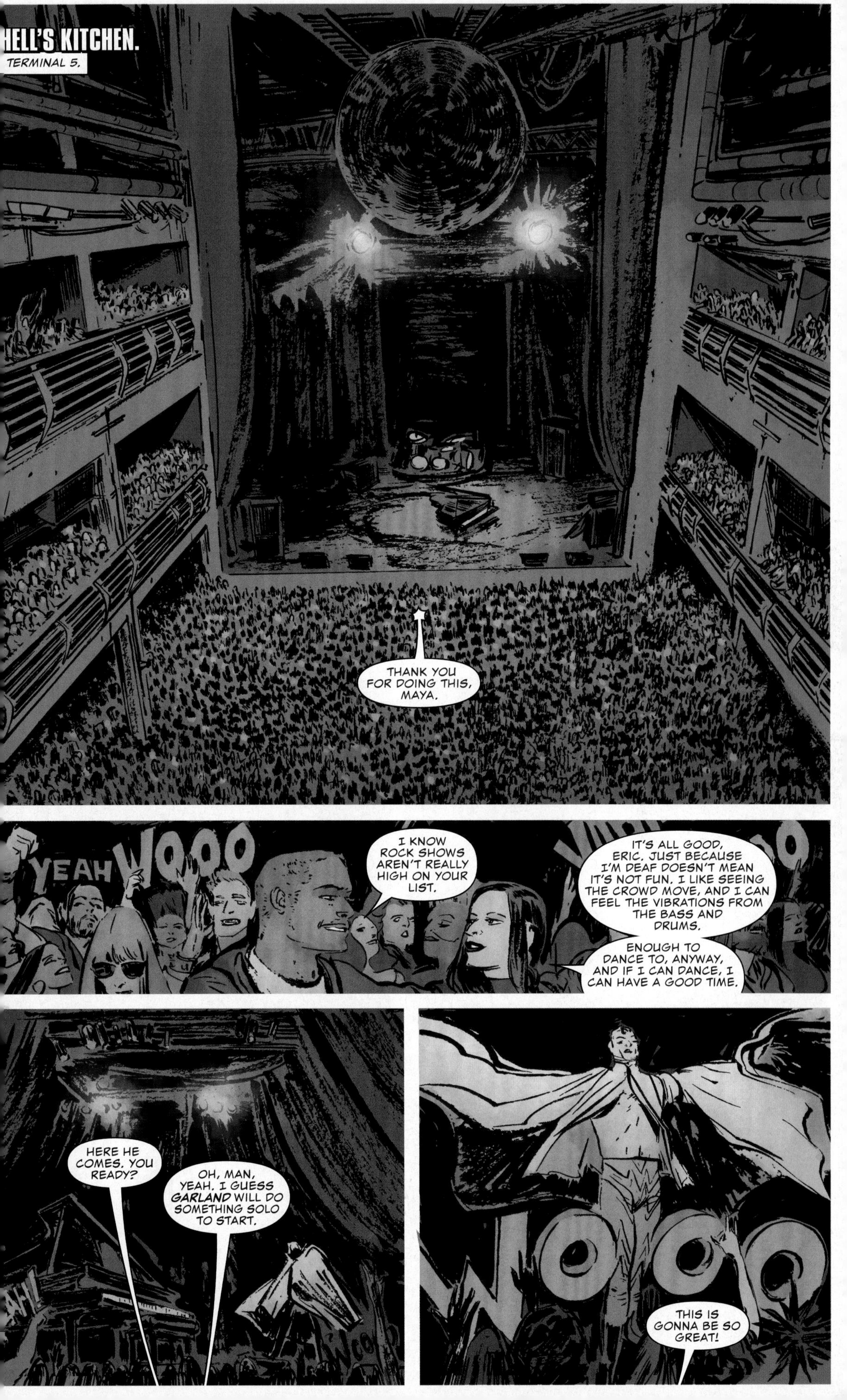
HELL'S KITCHEN.
TERMINAL 5.
THANK YOU FOR DOING THIS, MAYA.
YEAH
WOOO
I KNOW ROCK SHOWS AREN'T REALLY HIGH ON YOUR LIST.
IT'S ALL GOOD, ERIC. JUST BECAUSE I'M DEAF DOESN'T MEAN IT'S NOT FUN. I LIKE SEEING THE CROWD MOVE, AND I CAN FEEL THE VIBRATIONS FROM THE BASS AND DRUMS.
ENOUGH TO DANCE TO, ANYWAY, AND IF I CAN DANCE, I CAN HAVE A GOOD TIME.
HERE HE COMES. YOU READY?
OH, MAN, YEAH. I GUESS GARLAND WILL DO SOMETHING SOLO TO START.
WOOO
THIS IS GONNA BE SO GREAT!

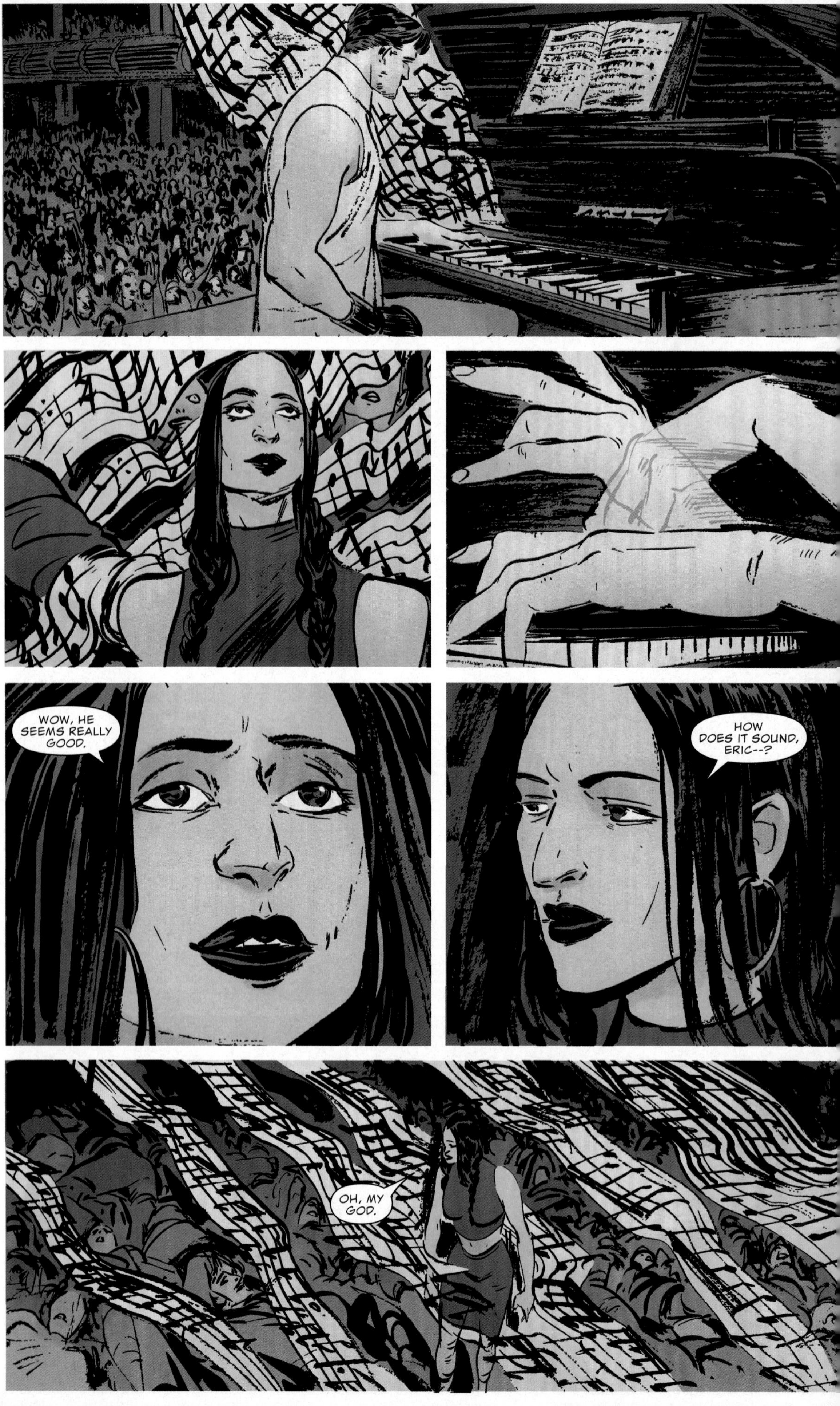
WOW, HE SEEMS REALLY GOOD.
HOW DOES IT SOUND, ERIC--?
OH, MY GOD.

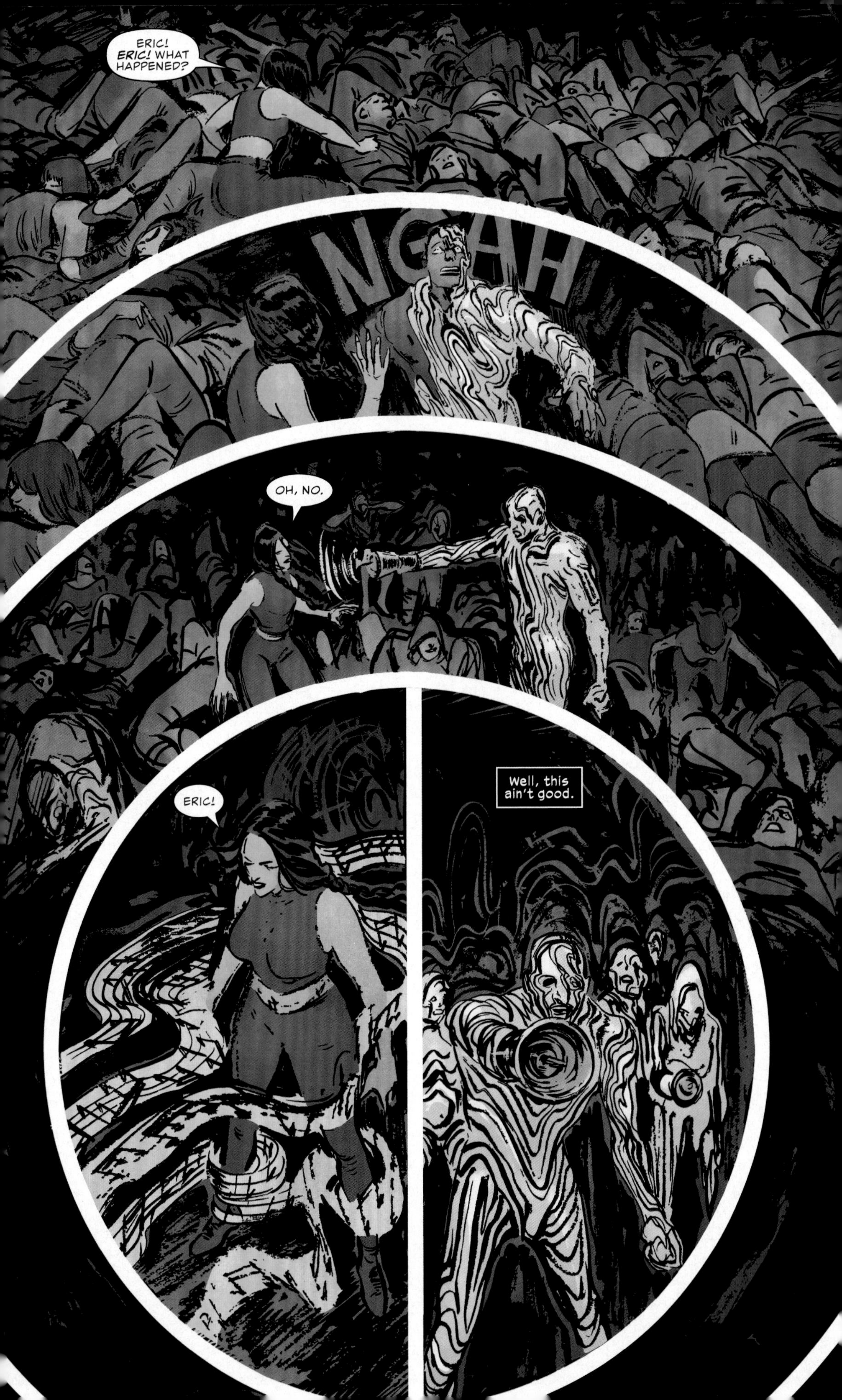
ERIC! ERIC! WHAT HAPPENED?
NGYAH
OH, NO.
ERIC!
Well, this ain't good.

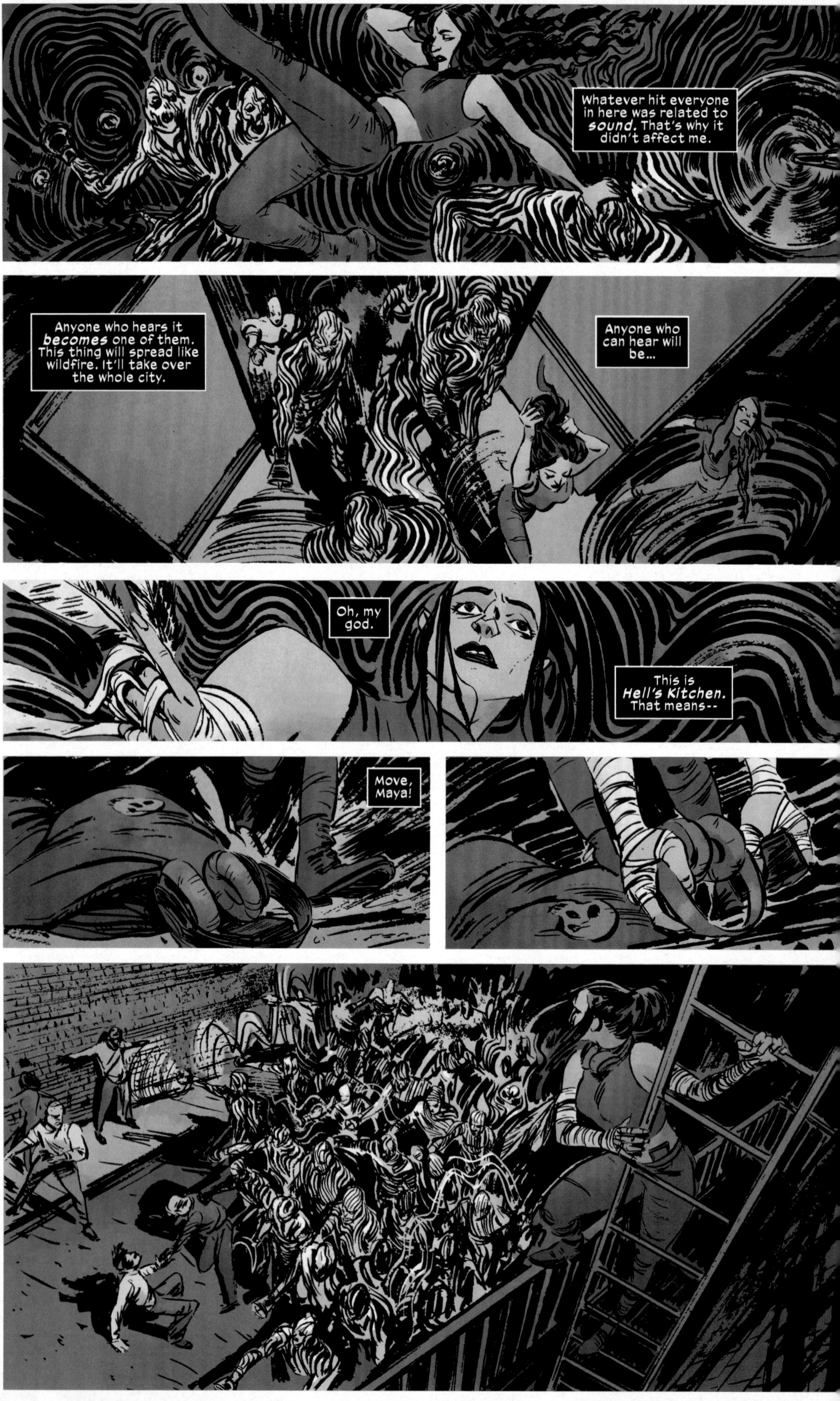
Whatever hit everyone in here was related to *sound.* That's why it didn't affect me.
Anyone who hears it *becomes* one of them. This thing will spread like wildfire. It'll take over the whole city.
Anyone who can hear will be...
Oh, my god.
This is *Hell's Kitchen.* That means--
Move, Maya!

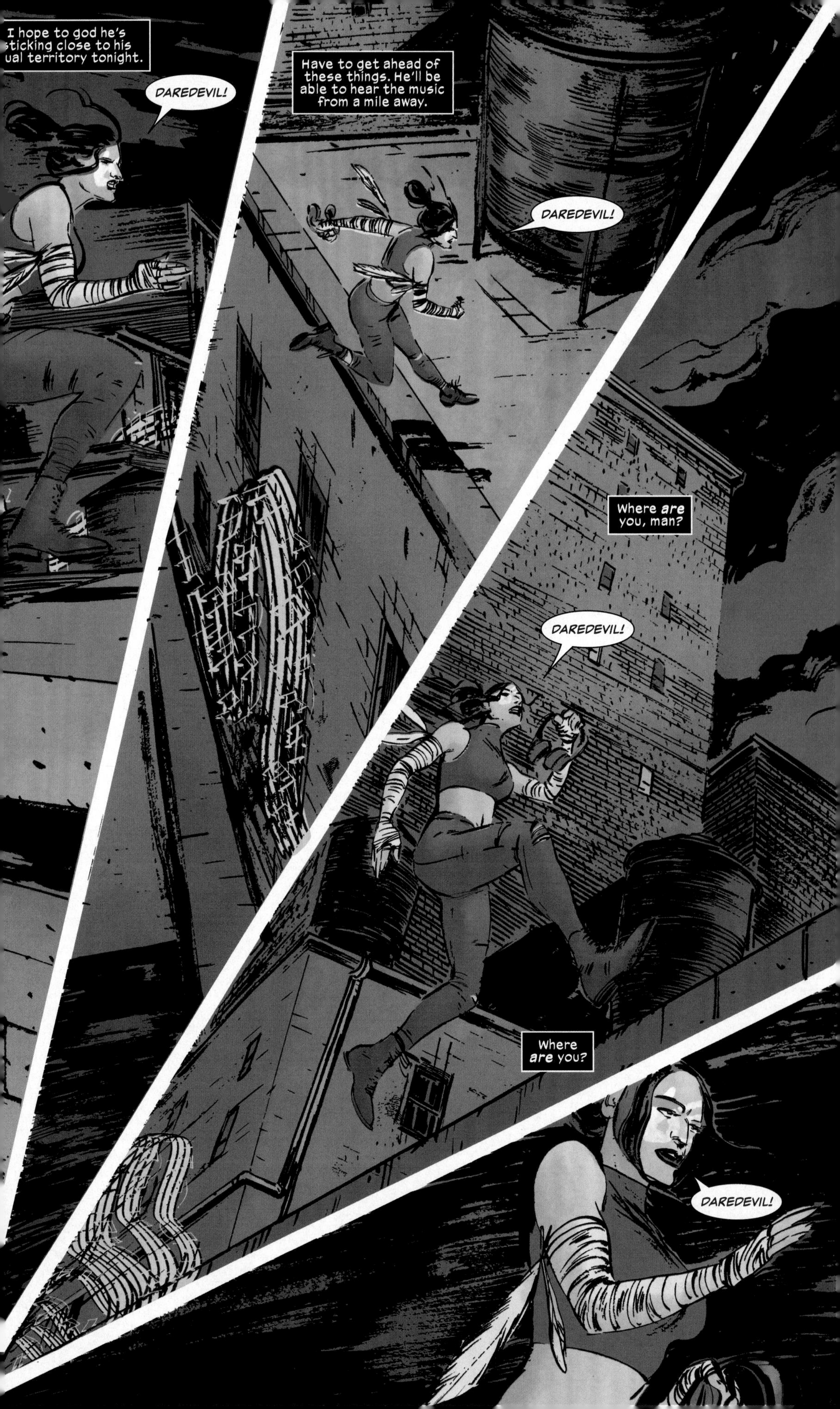
I hope to god he's
sticking close to his
ual territory tonight.
DAREDEVIL!
Have to get ahead of these things. He'll be able to hear the music from a mile away.
DAREDEVIL!
Where are you, man?
DAREDEVIL!
Where are you?
DAREDEVIL!

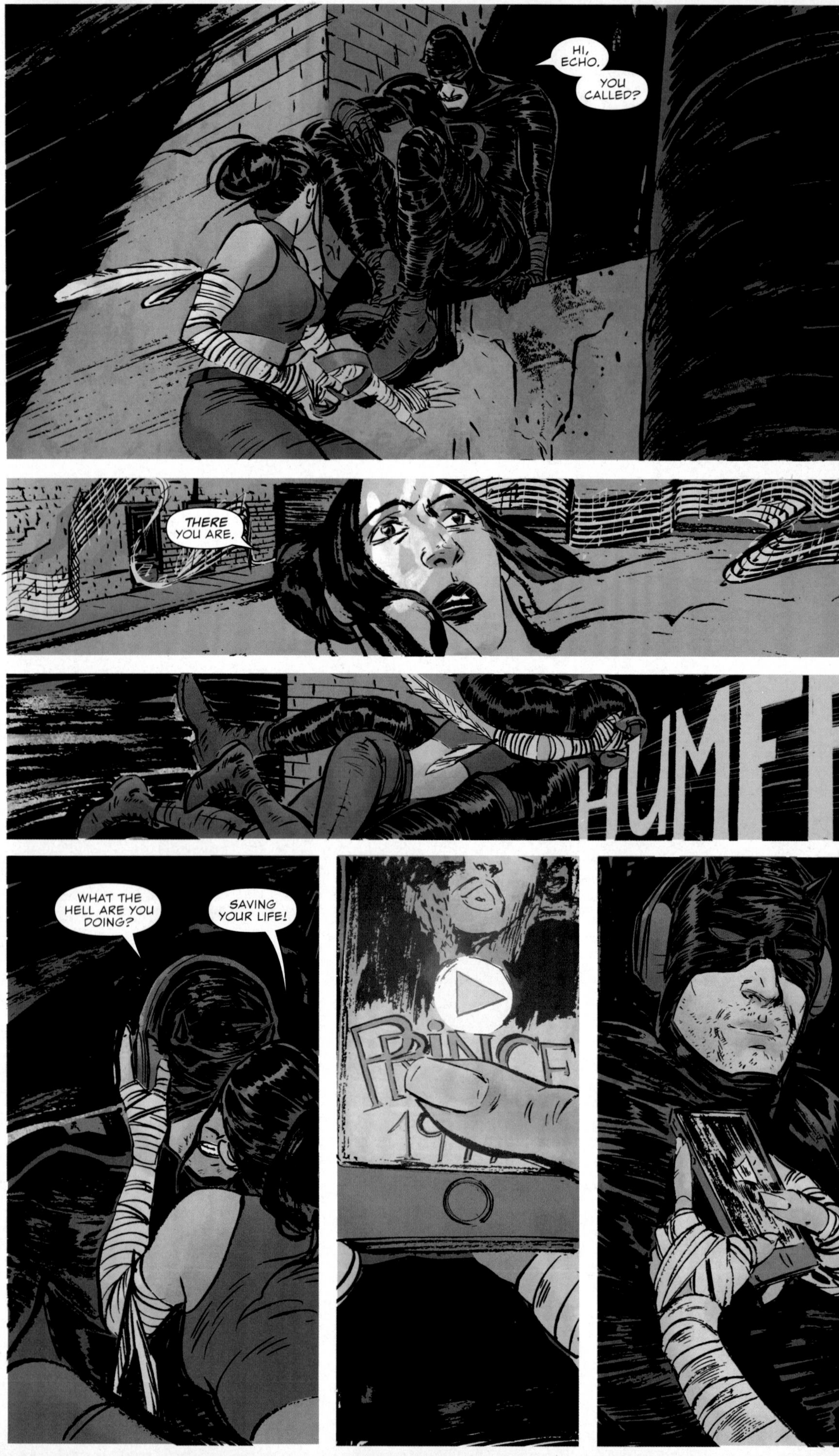
HI, ECHO.
YOU CALLED?
THERE YOU ARE.
HUMFF
WHAT THE HELL ARE YOU DOING?
SAVING YOUR LIFE!
PRINCE

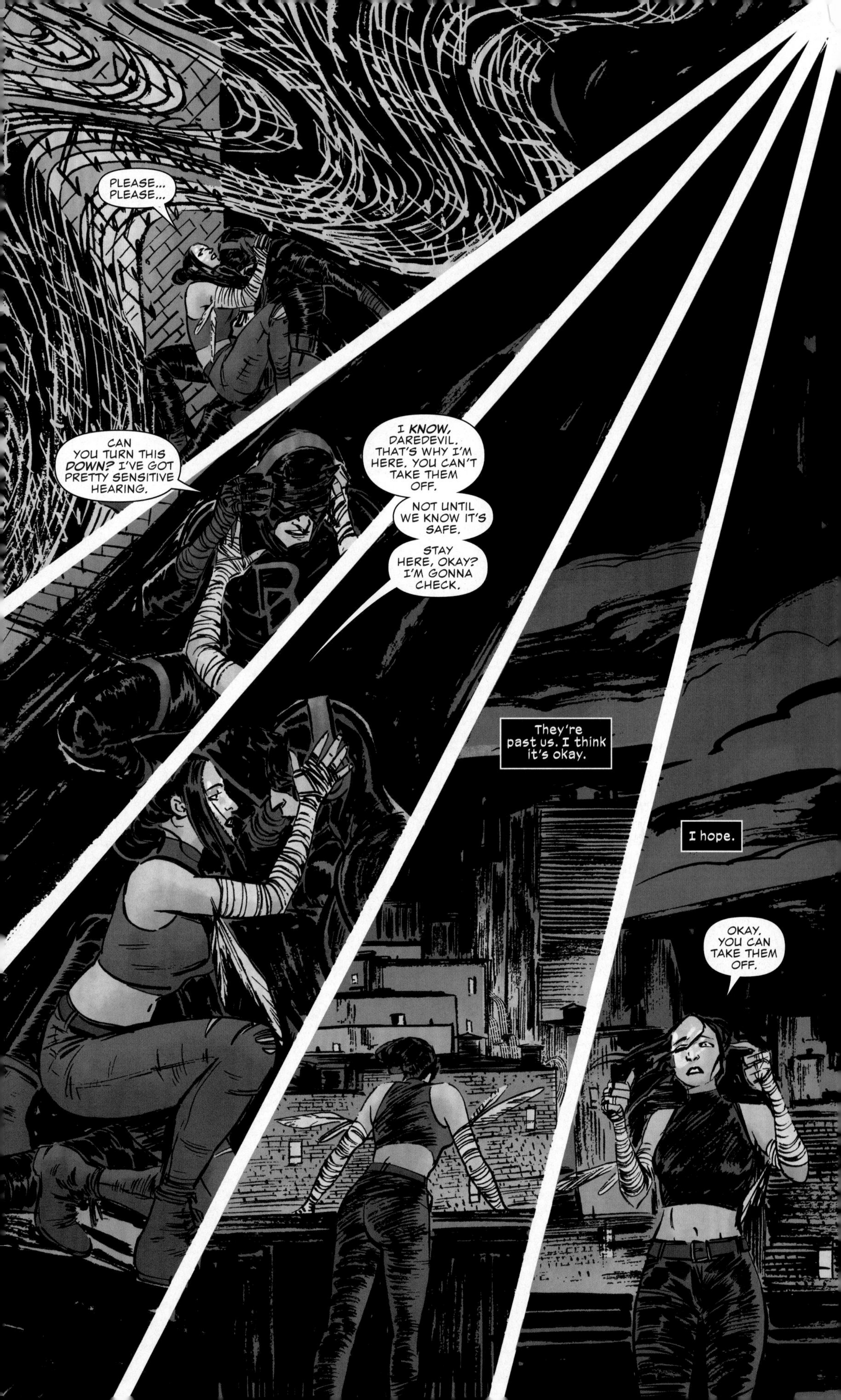
PLEASE... PLEASE...
CAN YOU TURN THIS DOWN? I'VE GOT PRETTY SENSITIVE HEARING.
I KNOW, DAREDEVIL. THAT'S WHY I'M HERE. YOU CAN'T TAKE THEM OFF.
NOT UNTIL WE KNOW IT'S SAFE.
STAY HERE, OKAY? I'M GONNA CHECK.
They're past us. I think it's okay.
I hope.
OKAY. YOU CAN TAKE THEM OFF.

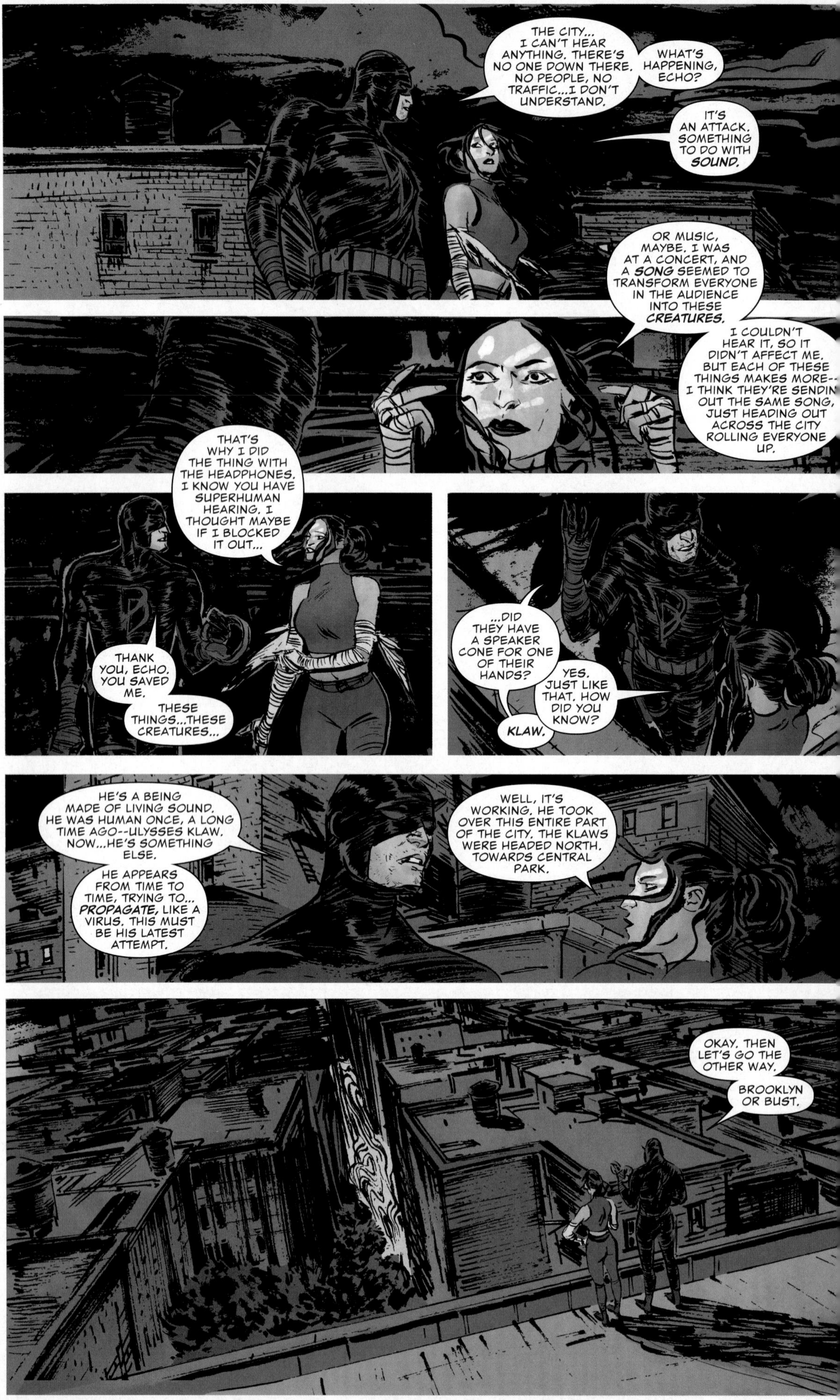

THE CITY... I CAN'T HEAR ANYTHING. THERE'S NO ONE DOWN THERE. NO PEOPLE, NO TRAFFIC...I DON'T UNDERSTAND.
WHAT'S HAPPENING, ECHO?
IT'S AN ATTACK. SOMETHING TO DO WITH SOUND.
OR MUSIC, MAYBE. I WAS AT A CONCERT, AND A SONG SEEMED TO TRANSFORM EVERYONE IN THE AUDIENCE INTO THESE CREATURES.
I COULDN'T HEAR IT, SO IT DIDN'T AFFECT ME. BUT EACH OF THESE THINGS MAKES MORE--I THINK THEY'RE SENDIN OUT THE SAME SONG, JUST HEADING OUT ACROSS THE CITY ROLLING EVERYONE UP.
THAT'S WHY I DID THE THING WITH THE HEADPHONES. I KNOW YOU HAVE SUPERHUMAN HEARING. I THOUGHT MAYBE IF I BLOCKED IT OUT...
THANK YOU, ECHO. YOU SAVED ME.
THESE THINGS...THESE CREATURES...
...DID THEY HAVE A SPEAKER CONE FOR ONE OF THEIR HANDS?
YES. JUST LIKE THAT. HOW DID YOU KNOW?
KLAW.
HE'S A BEING MADE OF LIVING SOUND. HE WAS HUMAN ONCE, A LONG TIME AGO--ULYSSES KLAW. NOW...HE'S SOMETHING ELSE.
HE APPEARS FROM TIME TO TIME, TRYING TO... PROPAGATE, LIKE A VIRUS. THIS MUST BE HIS LATEST ATTEMPT.
WELL, IT'S WORKING. HE TOOK OVER THIS ENTIRE PART OF THE CITY. THE KLAWS WERE HEADED NORTH, TOWARDS CENTRAL PARK.
OKAY. THEN LET'S GO THE OTHER WAY.
BROOKLYN OR BUST.

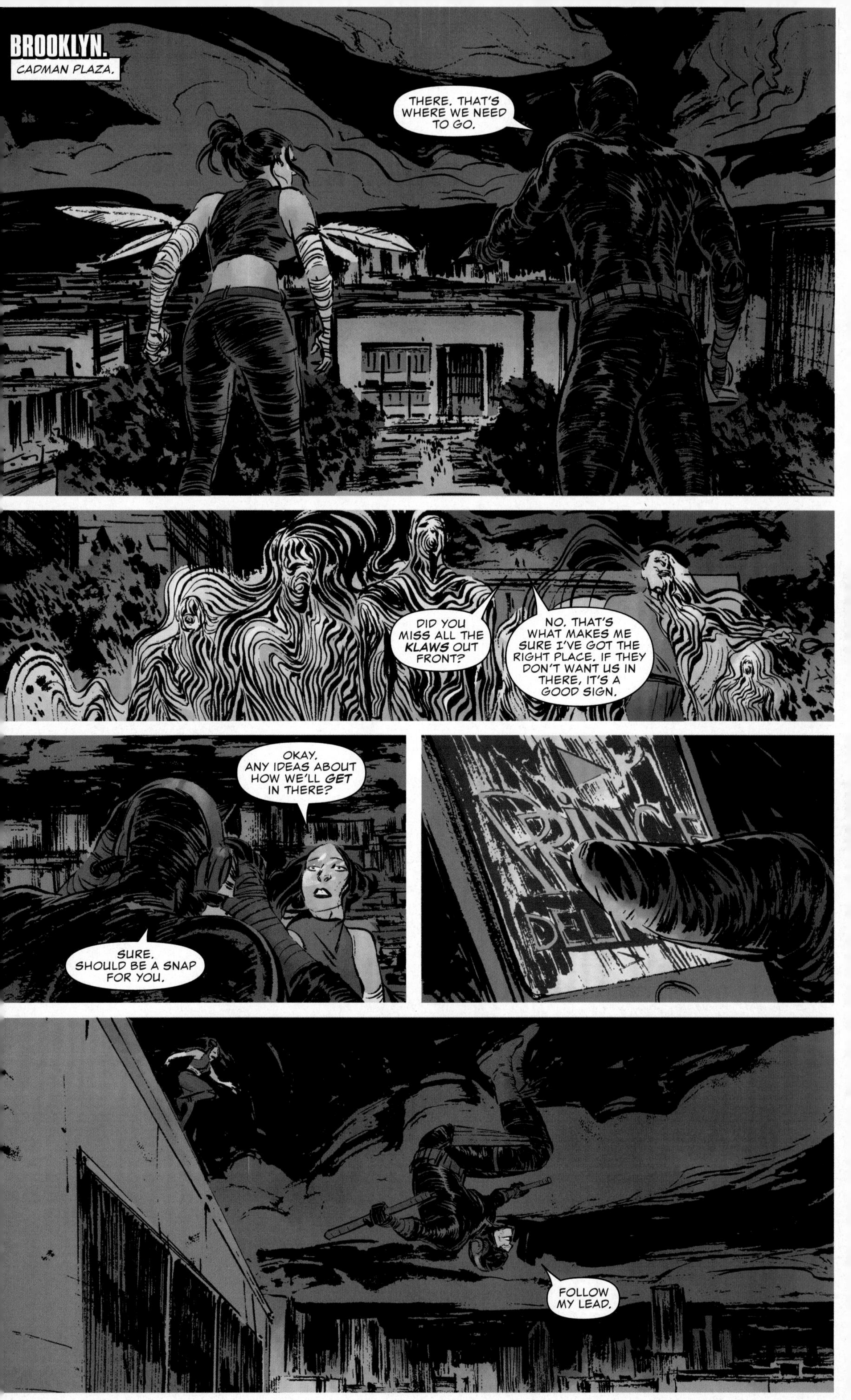

BROOKLYN.
CADMAN PLAZA.
THERE. THAT'S WHERE WE NEED TO GO.
DID YOU MISS ALL THE KLAWS OUT FRONT?
NO. THAT'S WHAT MAKES ME SURE I'VE GOT THE RIGHT PLACE. IF THEY DON'T WANT US IN THERE, IT'S A GOOD SIGN.
OKAY. ANY IDEAS ABOUT HOW WE'LL GET IN THERE?
SURE. SHOULD BE A SNAP FOR YOU.
FOLLOW MY LEAD.

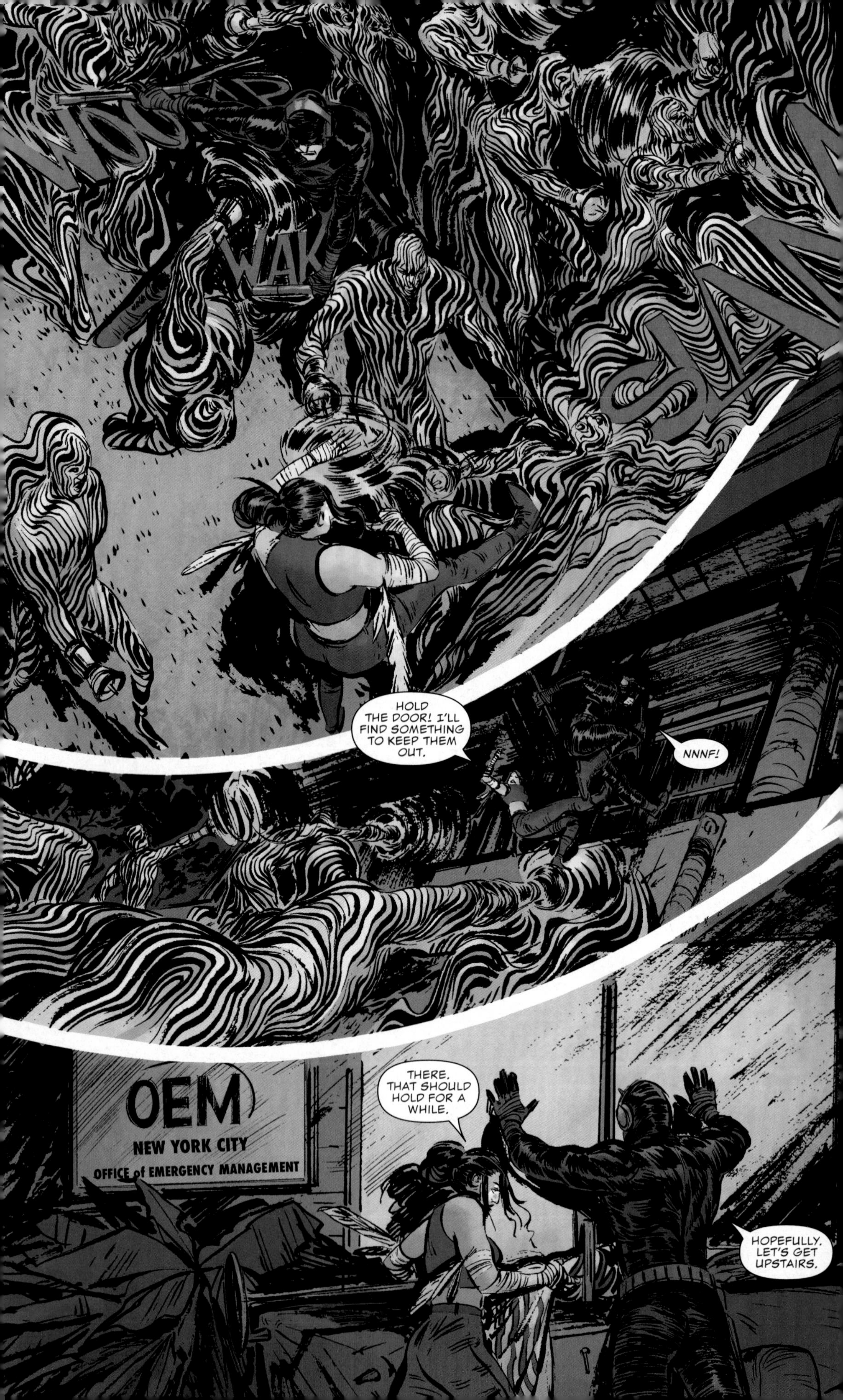
WAK
HOLD THE DOOR! I'LL FIND SOMETHING TO KEEP THEM OUT.
NNNF!
OEM
NEW YORK CITY
OFFICE of EMERGENCY MANAGEMENT
THERE. THAT SHOULD HOLD FOR A WHILE.
HOPEFULLY. LET'S GET UPSTAIRS.

THE EMERGENCY BROADCASTING SYSTEM?

YEAH. THEY CAN SEND AN AUDIO SIGNAL THROUGH ALMOST EVERY SPEAKER, PHONE, TV AND RADIO IN THE CITY.

NEW YORK CITY EMERGENCY BROADCASTING SYSTEM

OKAY... BUT WHAT SIGNAL?

STILL WORKING ON THAT.

ARE YOU... MY GOD, ARE YOU DAREDEVIL?

I AM. AND THIS IS ECHO.

HEY.

WE NEED YOUR HELP.

A CRIMINAL NAMED KLAW IS BROADCASTING AN AUDIO SIGNAL. ANYONE WHO HEARS IT FALLS UNDER HIS CONTROL. IT'S SPREADING LIKE A VIRUS.

WHAT? WHY HAVEN'T I...THAT SOUNDS LIKE ONE HELL OF AN EMERGENCY. YOU'D THINK SOMEONE WOULD HAVE CALLED TO ACTIVATE THE SYSTEM.

WHOEVER NORMALLY CALLS YOU MIGHT ALREADY HAVE BEEN TAKEN. IT'S MOVING REALLY FAST.

OEM
NEW Y...
OFFICE OF EMERGE...

OEM
NEW YORK CITY
...ERGEN... MANAGEMENT

HOW CAN I HELP?

THESE ARE NOISE-CANCELLING HEADPHONES. THEY WORK BY TAKING IN A FREQUENCY AND GENERATING ITS EXACT OPPOSITE WAVEFORM TO CANCEL OUT BOTH SOUNDS, RIGHT?

YEAH, I SEE WHERE YOU'RE GOING. IF WE COULD SEND OUT THE OPPOSITE OF KLAW'S SIGNAL, IT WOULD SHUT IT DOWN--BUT WE'D NEED THE ORIGINAL SIGNAL TO INVERT.

AND EVEN IF WE HAD THE SIGNAL, WORKING WITH IT MIGHT CONVERT US.

I JUST DON'T SEE HOW...

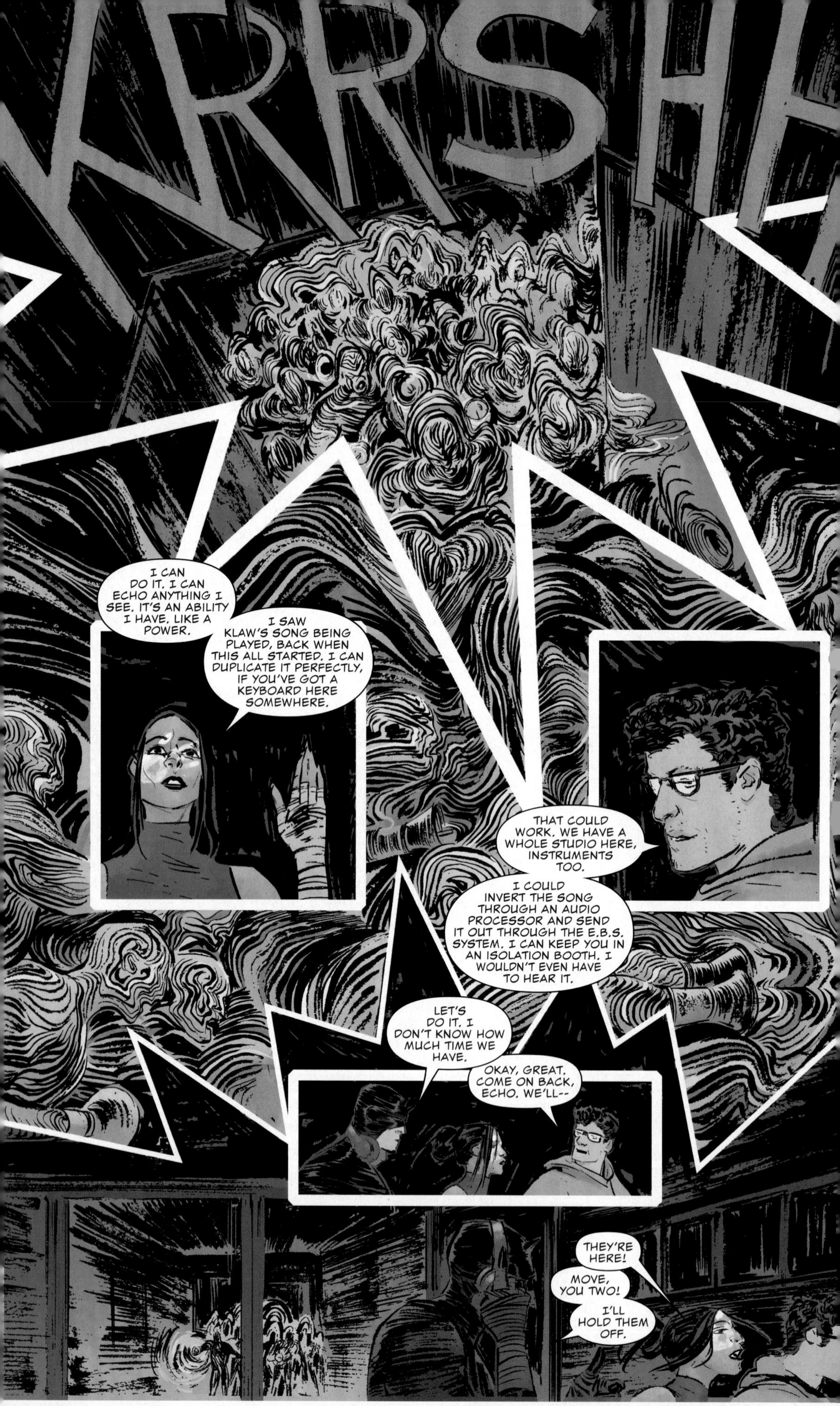
KRRSHH-
I CAN DO IT. I CAN ECHO ANYTHING I SEE. IT'S AN ABILITY I HAVE. LIKE A POWER.
I SAW KLAW'S SONG BEING PLAYED, BACK WHEN THIS ALL STARTED. I CAN DUPLICATE IT PERFECTLY, IF YOU'VE GOT A KEYBOARD HERE SOMEWHERE.
THAT COULD WORK. WE HAVE A WHOLE STUDIO HERE, INSTRUMENTS TOO.
I COULD INVERT THE SONG THROUGH AN AUDIO PROCESSOR AND SEND IT OUT THROUGH THE E.B.S. SYSTEM. I CAN KEEP YOU IN AN ISOLATION BOOTH. I WOULDN'T EVEN HAVE TO HEAR IT.
LET'S DO IT. I DON'T KNOW HOW MUCH TIME WE HAVE.
OKAY, GREAT. COME ON BACK, ECHO. WE'LL--
THEY'RE HERE!
MOVE, YOU TWO!
I'LL HOLD THEM OFF.

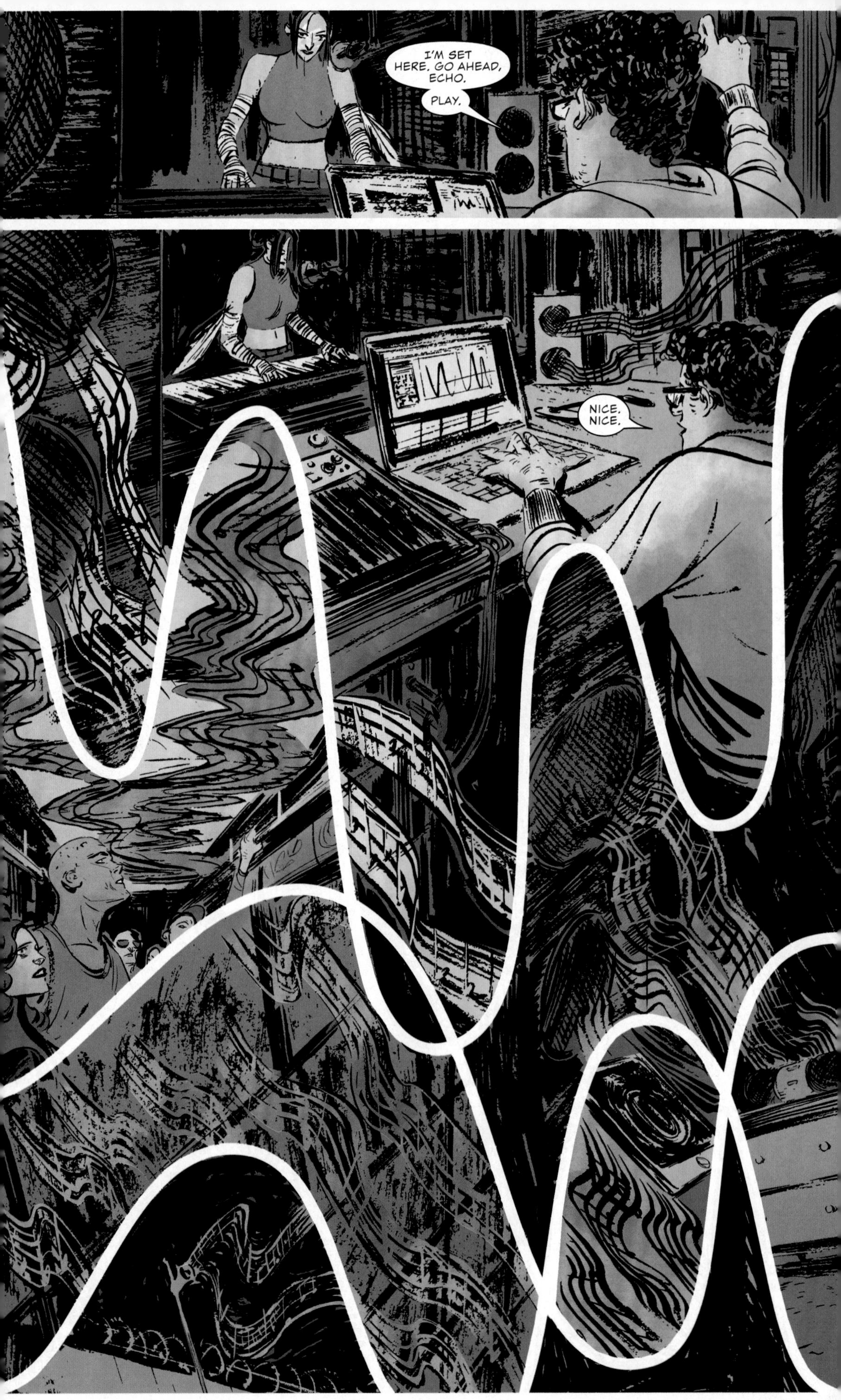
I'M SET HERE. GO AHEAD, ECHO.
PLAY.
NICE. NICE.

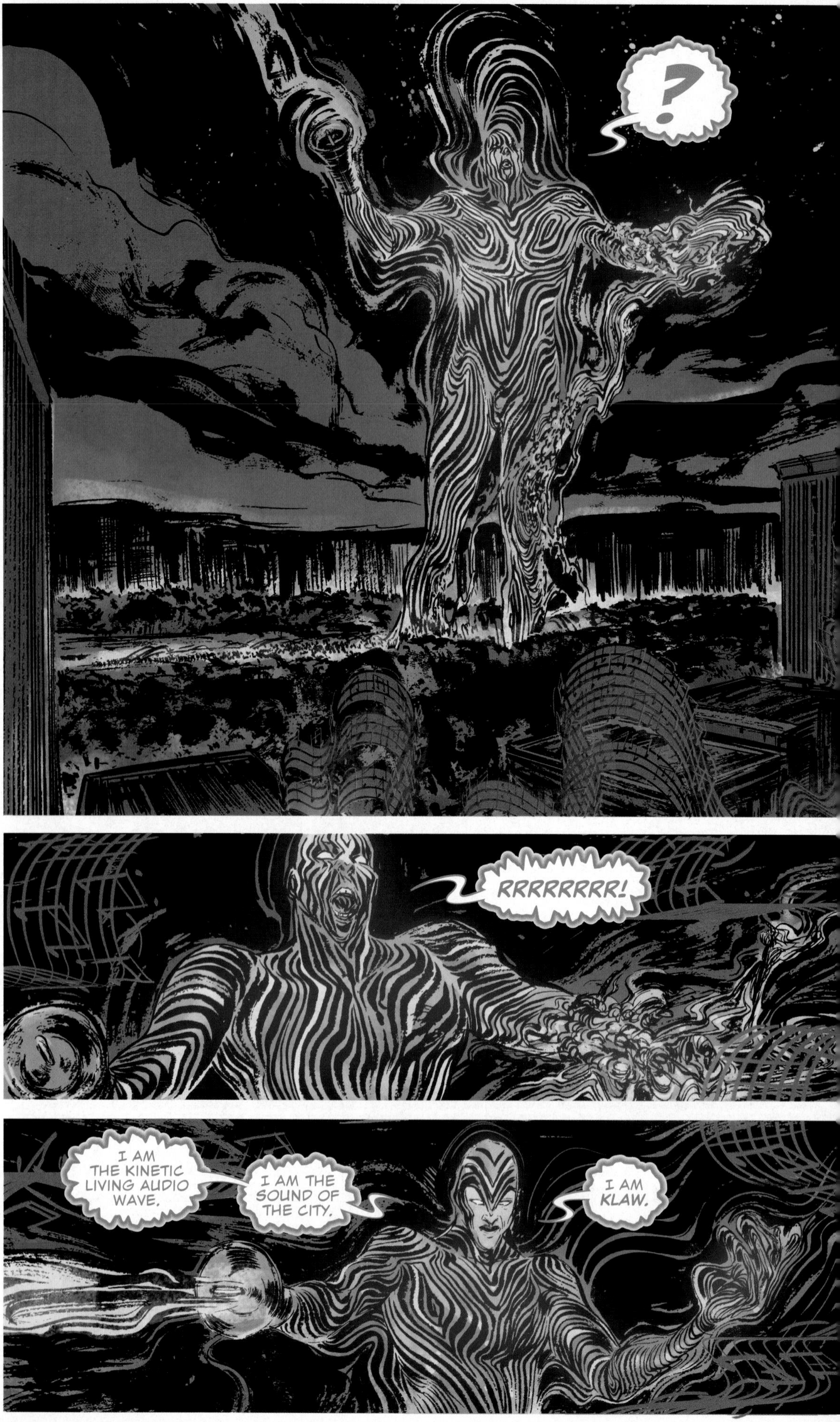
?
RRRRRRRR!
I AM THE KINETIC LIVING AUDIO WAVE.
I AM THE SOUND OF THE CITY.
I AM KLAW.

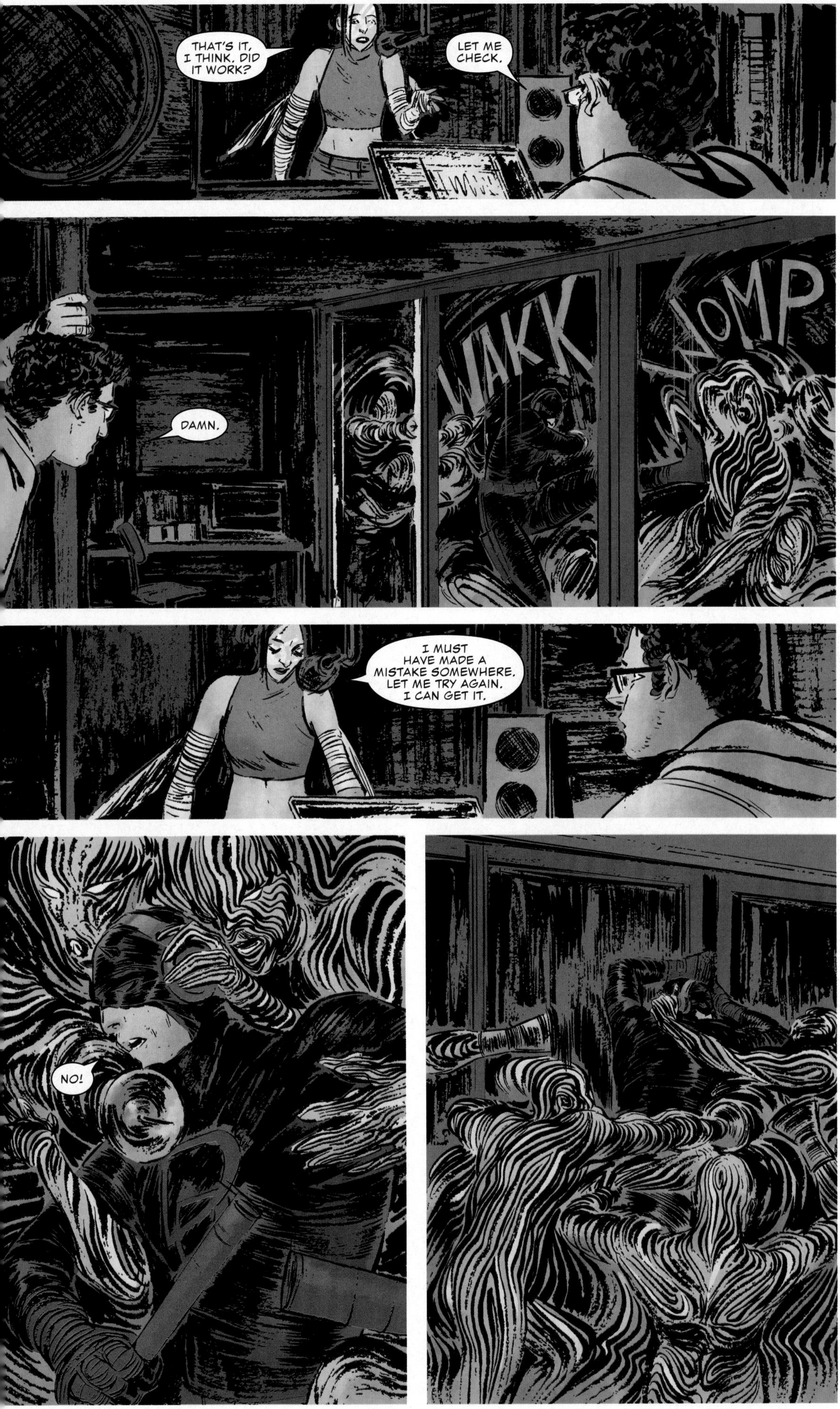
THAT'S IT, I THINK. DID IT WORK?
LET ME CHECK.
DAMN.
WAKK
WOMP
I MUST HAVE MADE A MISTAKE SOMEWHERE. LET ME TRY AGAIN. I CAN GET IT.
NO!

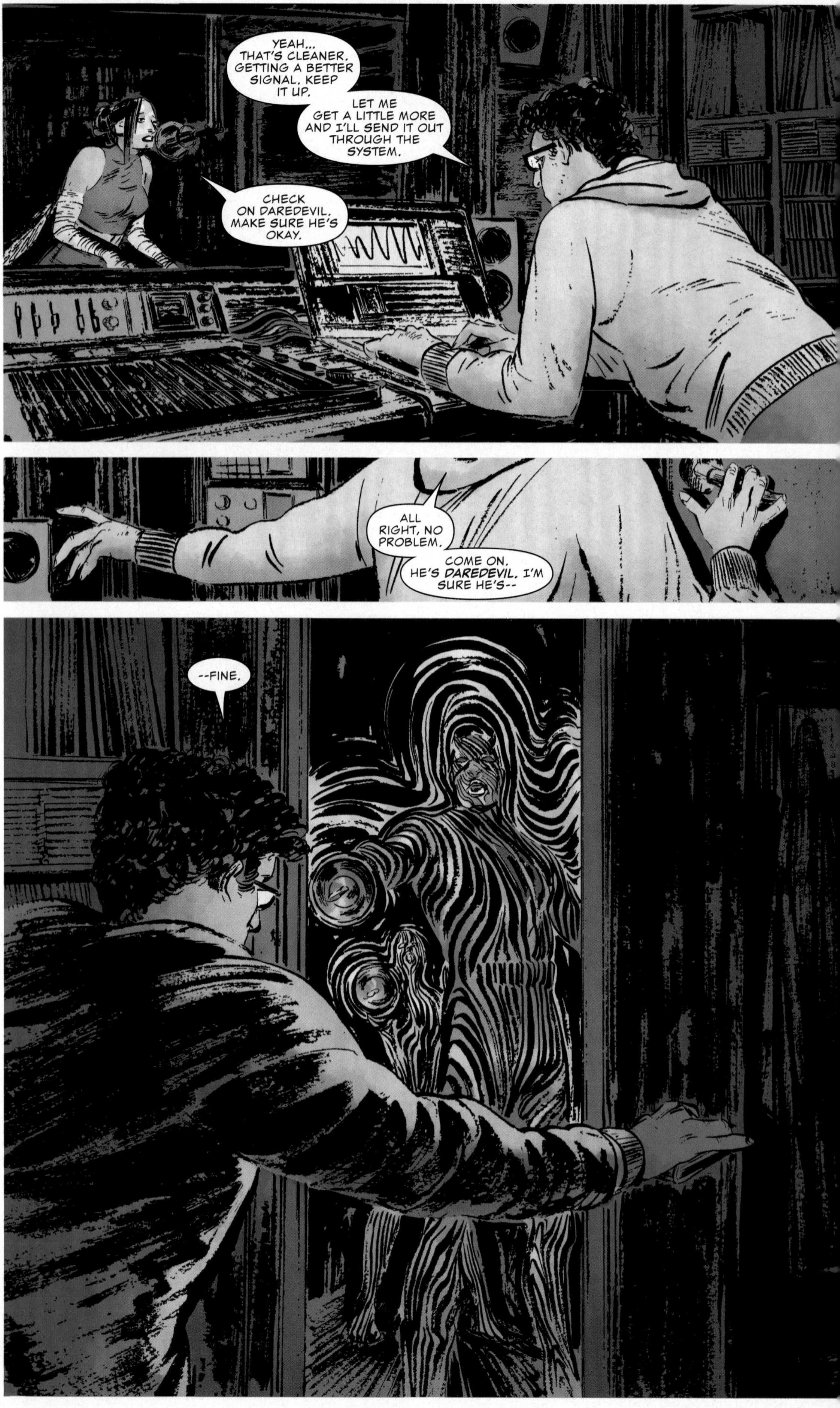
YEAH... THAT'S CLEANER. GETTING A BETTER SIGNAL. KEEP IT UP.
LET ME GET A LITTLE MORE AND I'LL SEND IT OUT THROUGH THE SYSTEM.
CHECK ON DAREDEVIL. MAKE SURE HE'S OKAY.
ALL RIGHT, NO PROBLEM.
COME ON. HE'S *DAREDEVIL*. I'M SURE HE'S--
--FINE.

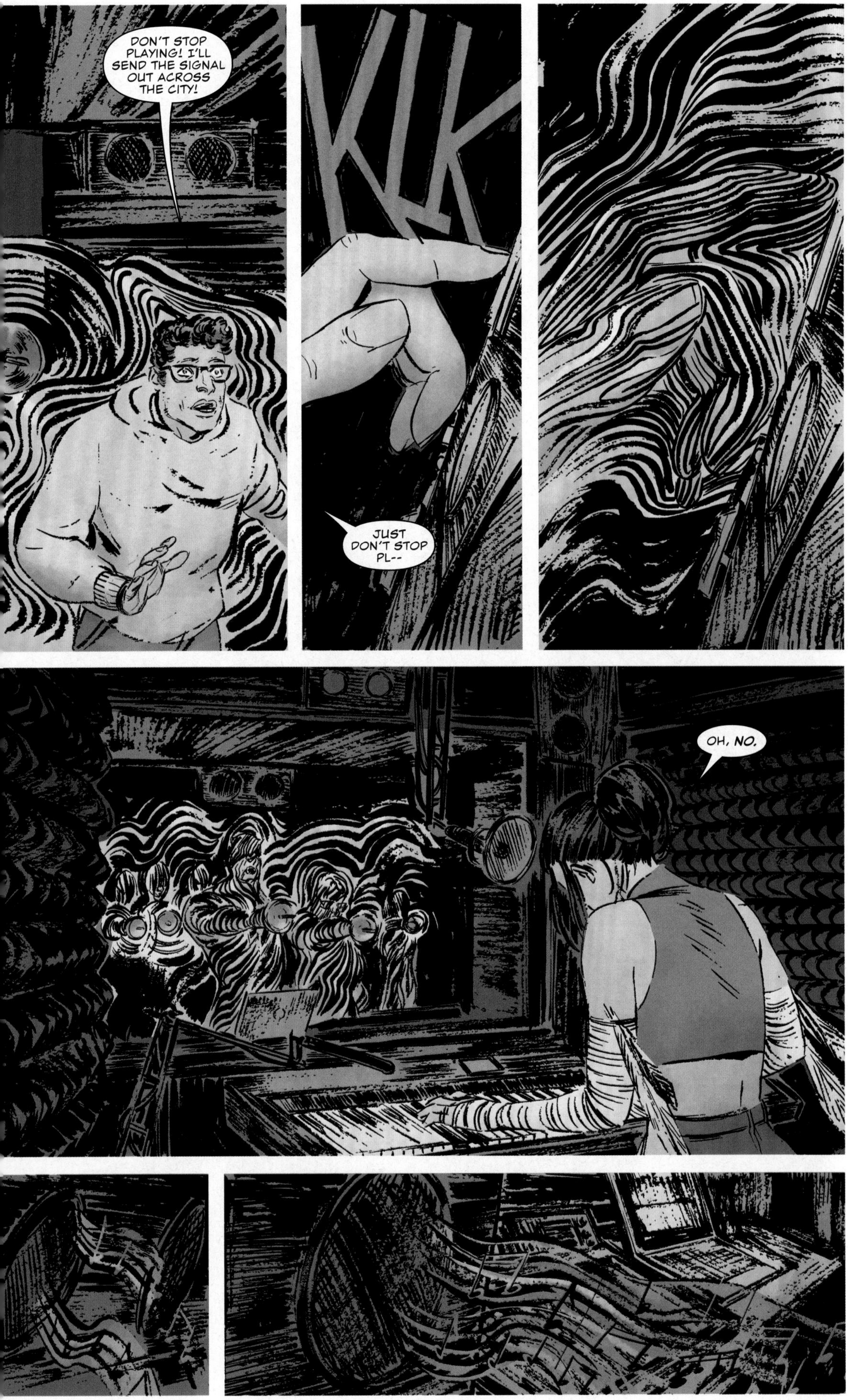
DON'T STOP PLAYING! I'LL SEND THE SIGNAL OUT ACROSS THE CITY!
KLIK
JUST DON'T STOP PL--
OH, NO.

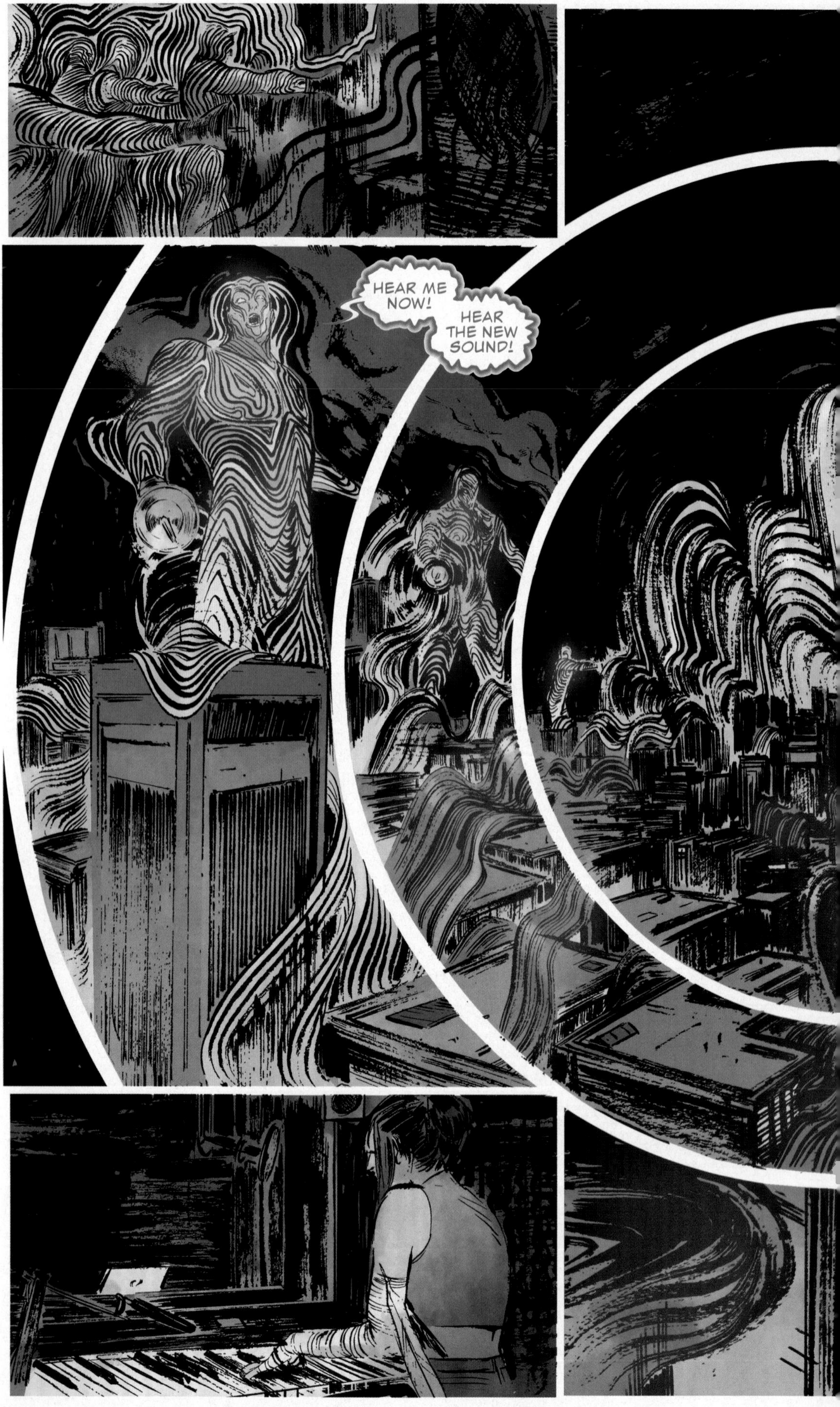
HEAR ME NOW!
HEAR THE NEW SOUND!

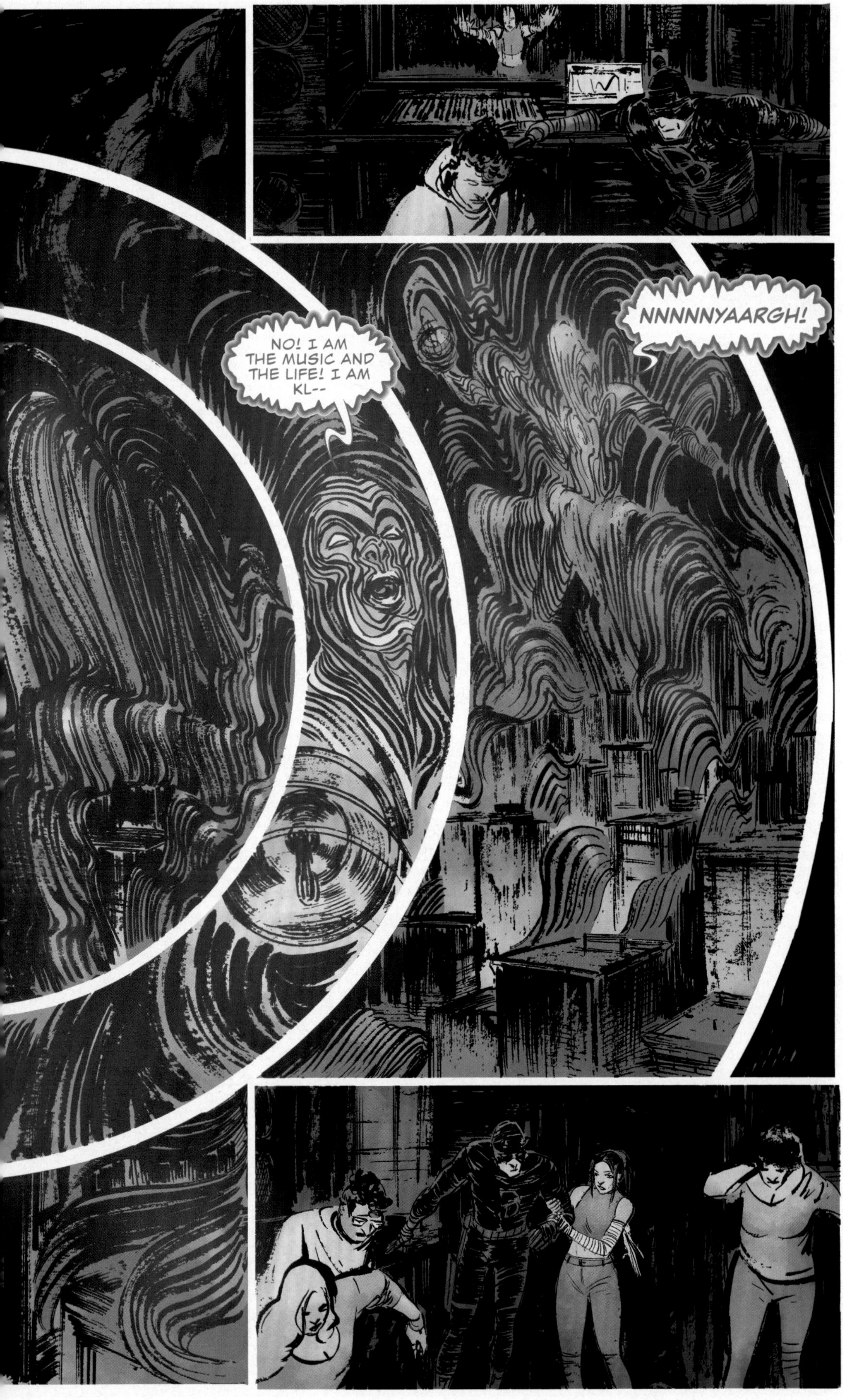
NO! I AM THE MUSIC AND THE LIFE! I AM KL--
NNNNNYAARGH!

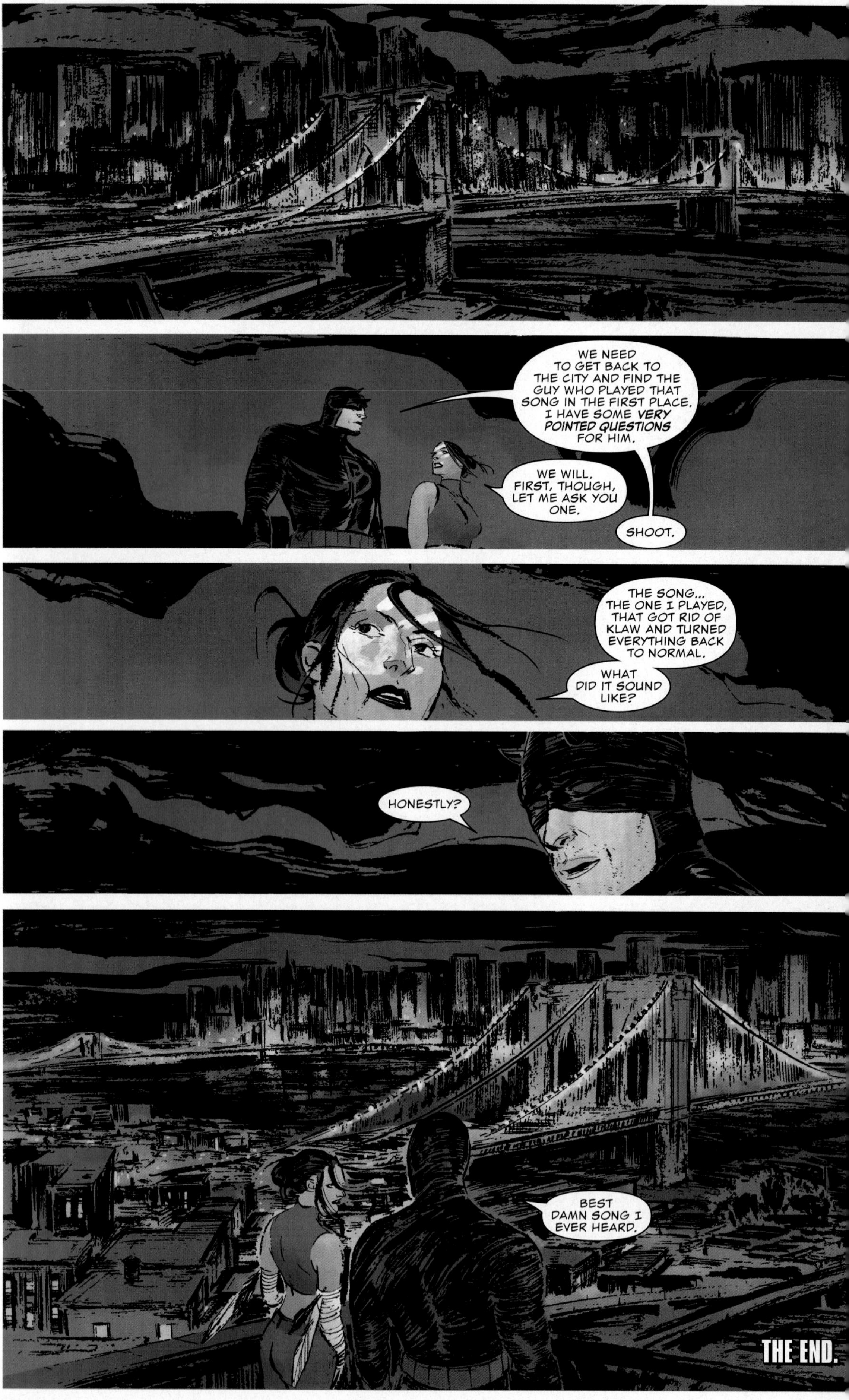

WE NEED TO GET BACK TO THE CITY AND FIND THE GUY WHO PLAYED THAT SONG IN THE FIRST PLACE. I HAVE SOME *VERY POINTED QUESTIONS* FOR HIM.
WE WILL. FIRST, THOUGH, LET ME ASK YOU ONE.
SHOOT.
THE SONG... THE ONE I PLAYED, THAT GOT RID OF KLAW AND TURNED EVERYTHING BACK TO NORMAL.
WHAT DID IT SOUND LIKE?
HONESTLY?
BEST DAMN SONG I EVER HEARD.
THE END.

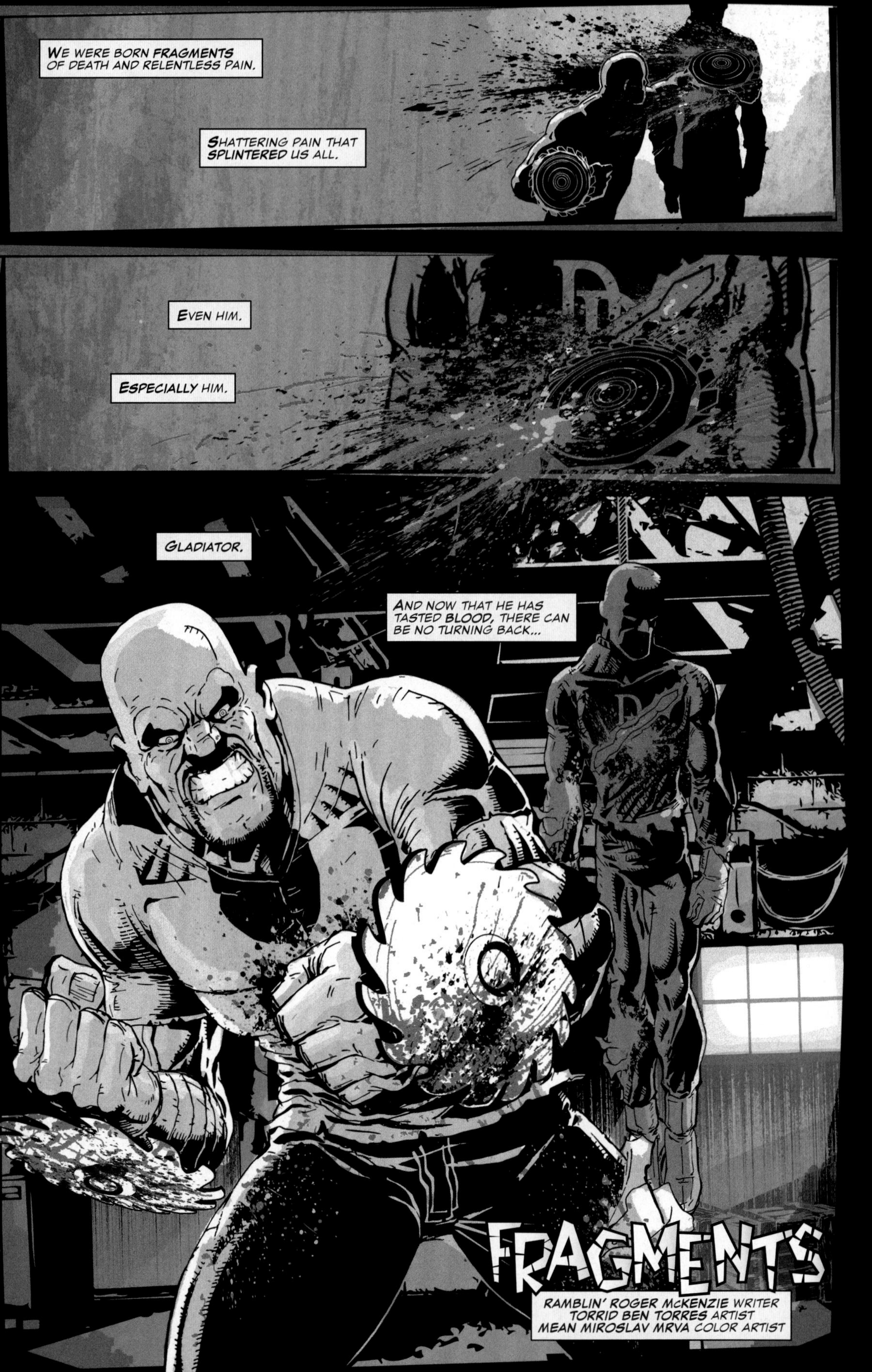
WE WERE BORN FRAGMENTS OF DEATH AND RELENTLESS PAIN.
SHATTERING PAIN THAT SPLINTERED US ALL.
EVEN HIM.
ESPECIALLY HIM.
GLADIATOR.
AND NOW THAT HE HAS TASTED BLOOD, THERE CAN BE NO TURNING BACK...
FRAGMENTS
RAMBLIN' ROGER McKENZIE WRITER
TORRID BEN TORRES ARTIST
MEAN MIROSLAV MRVA COLOR ARTIST

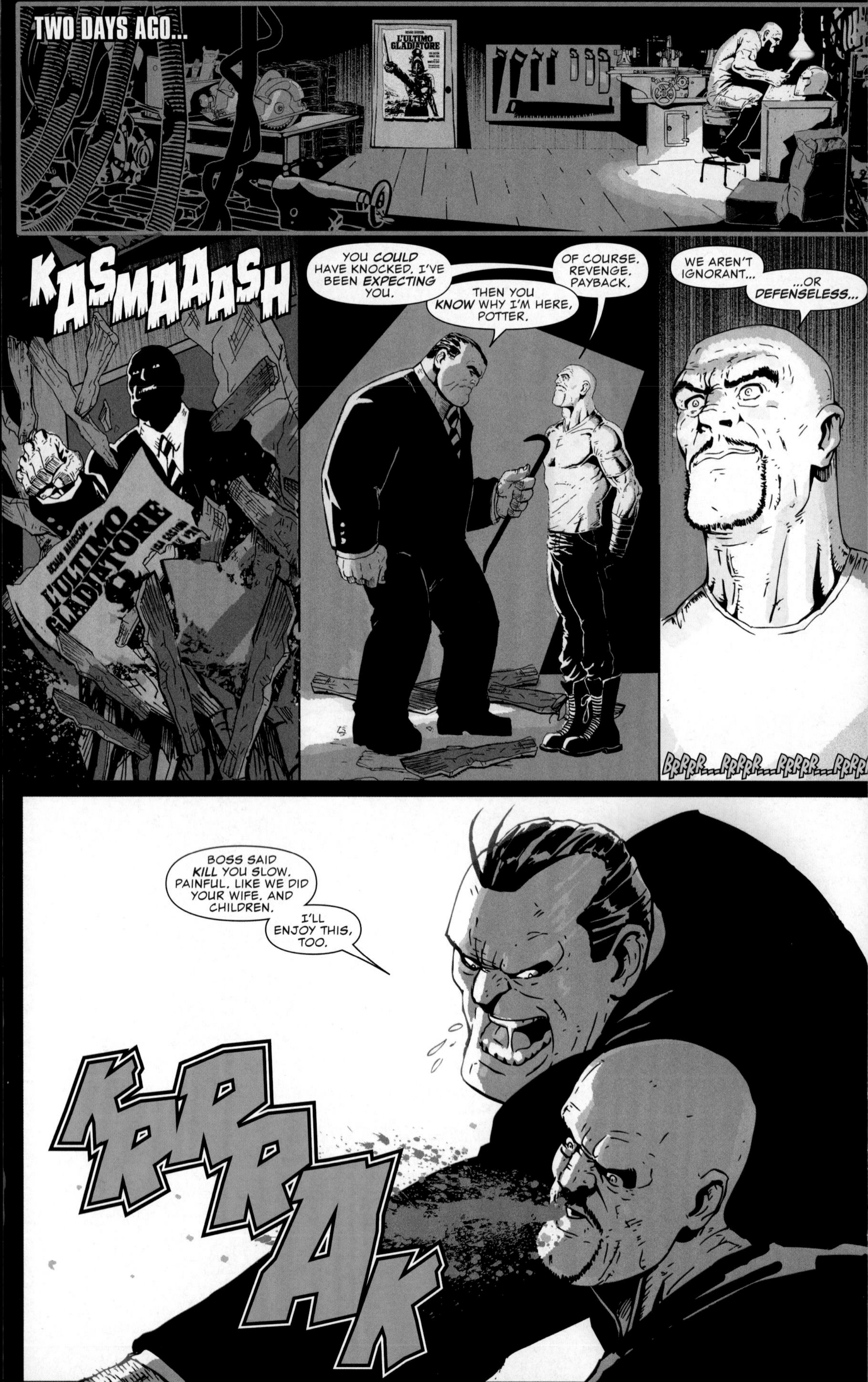
TWO DAYS AGO...
L'ULTIMO GLADIATORE
KASMAAASH
YOU COULD HAVE KNOCKED. I'VE BEEN EXPECTING YOU.
THEN YOU KNOW WHY I'M HERE, POTTER.
OF COURSE. REVENGE. PAYBACK.
WE AREN'T IGNORANT...
...OR DEFENSELESS...
BRRRR...RRRR...RRRRR...RRRR
BOSS SAID KILL YOU SLOW. PAINFUL. LIKE WE DID YOUR WIFE. AND CHILDREN.
I'LL ENJOY THIS, TOO.
KRRAK

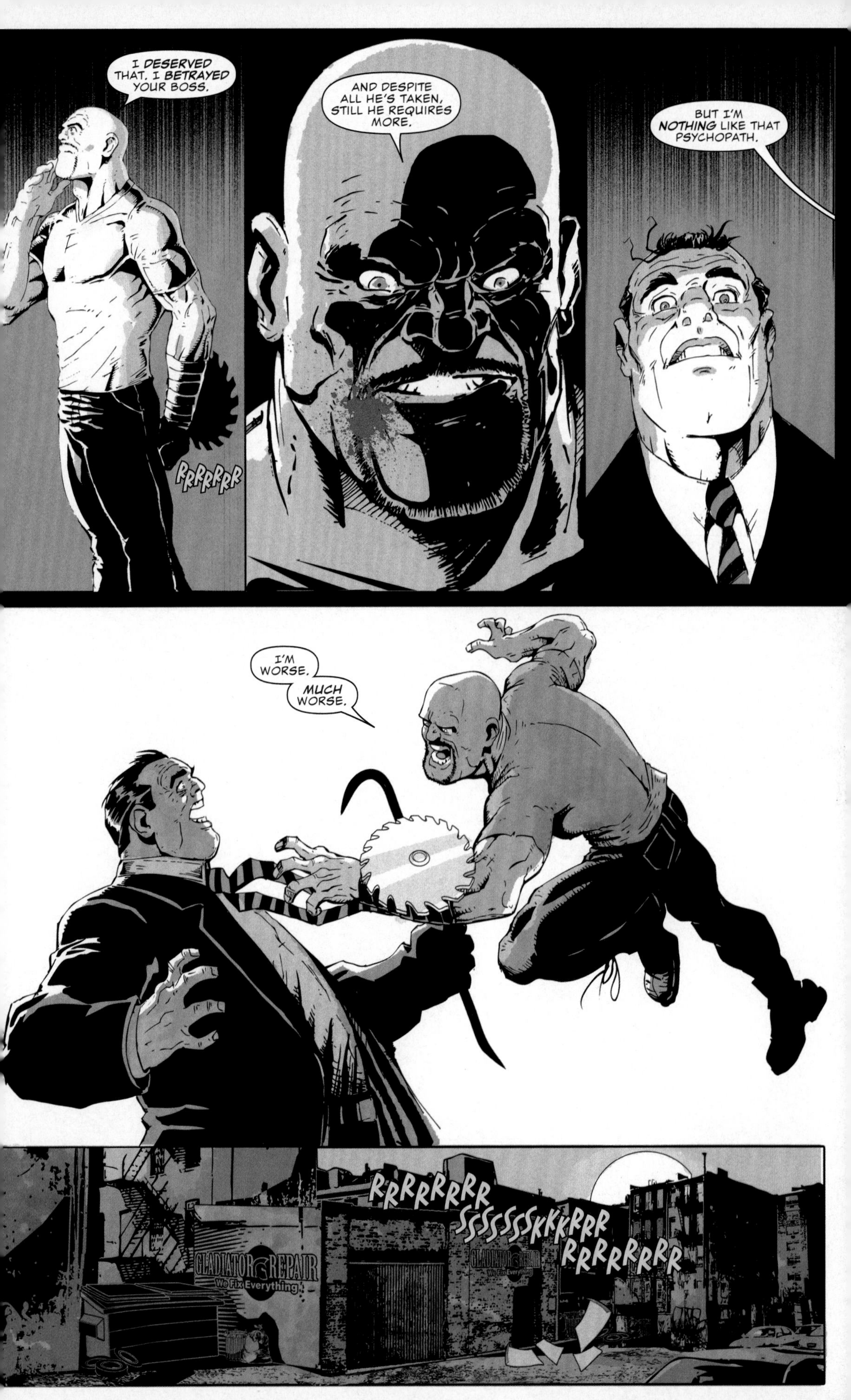
I DESERVED THAT. I BETRAYED YOUR BOSS.
RRRRRRR
AND DESPITE ALL HE'S TAKEN, STILL HE REQUIRES MORE.
BUT I'M NOTHING LIKE THAT PSYCHOPATH.
I'M WORSE.
MUCH WORSE.
GLADIATOR REPAIR
We Fix Everything
RRRRRRRR
SSSSSSKKKRRR
RRRRRRRR
GLADIATOR REPAIR
We Fix Everything

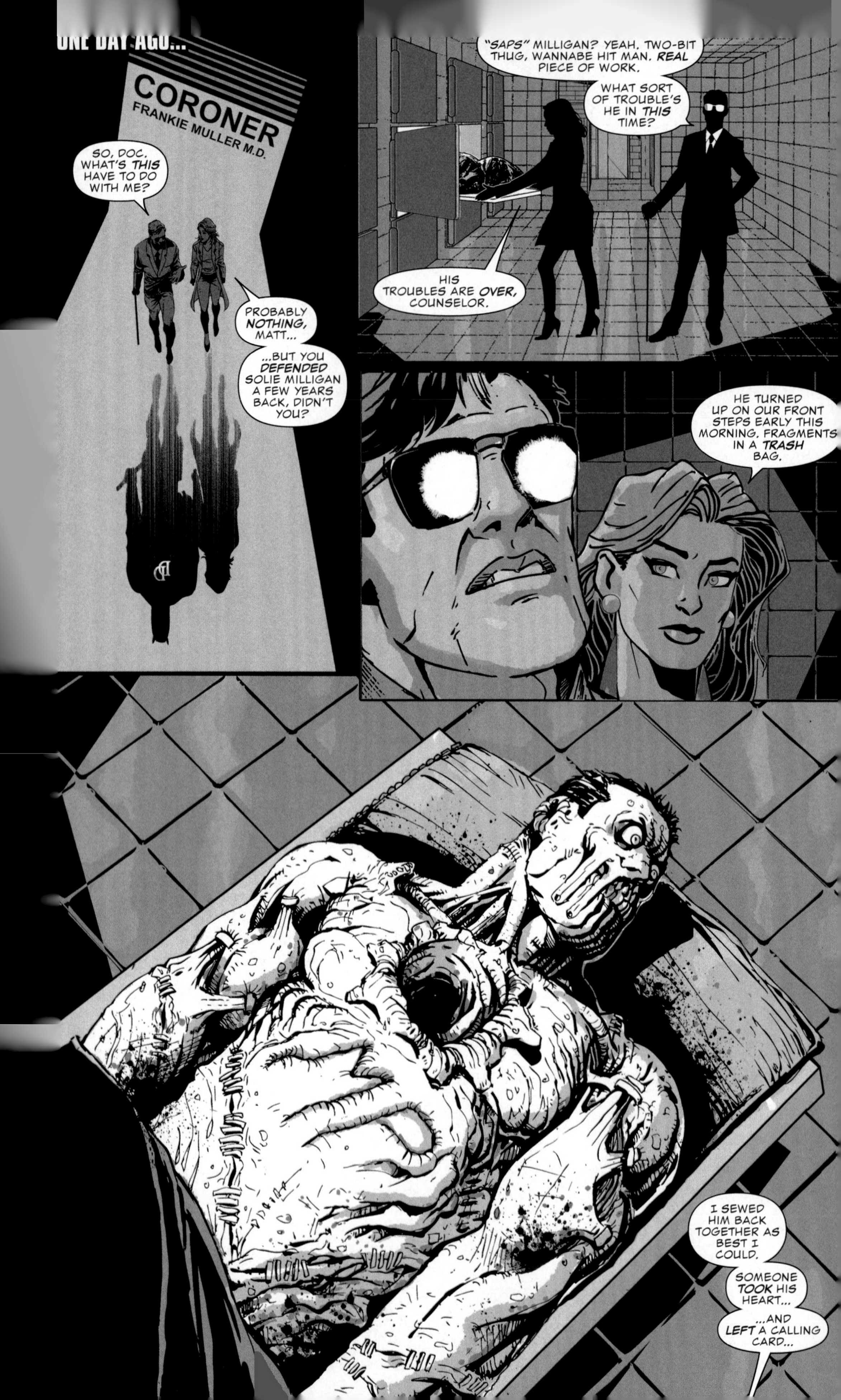

ONE DAY AGO...
CORONER
FRANKIE MULLER M.D.
SO, DOC. WHAT'S THIS HAVE TO DO WITH ME?
PROBABLY NOTHING, MATT...
...BUT YOU DEFENDED SOLIE MILLIGAN A FEW YEARS BACK, DIDN'T YOU?
"SAPS" MILLIGAN? YEAH. TWO-BIT THUG, WANNABE HIT MAN. REAL PIECE OF WORK.
WHAT SORT OF TROUBLE'S HE IN THIS TIME?
HIS TROUBLES ARE OVER, COUNSELOR.
HE TURNED UP ON OUR FRONT STEPS EARLY THIS MORNING, FRAGMENTS IN A TRASH BAG.
I SEWED HIM BACK TOGETHER AS BEST I COULD.
SOMEONE TOOK HIS HEART...
...AND LEFT A CALLING CARD...

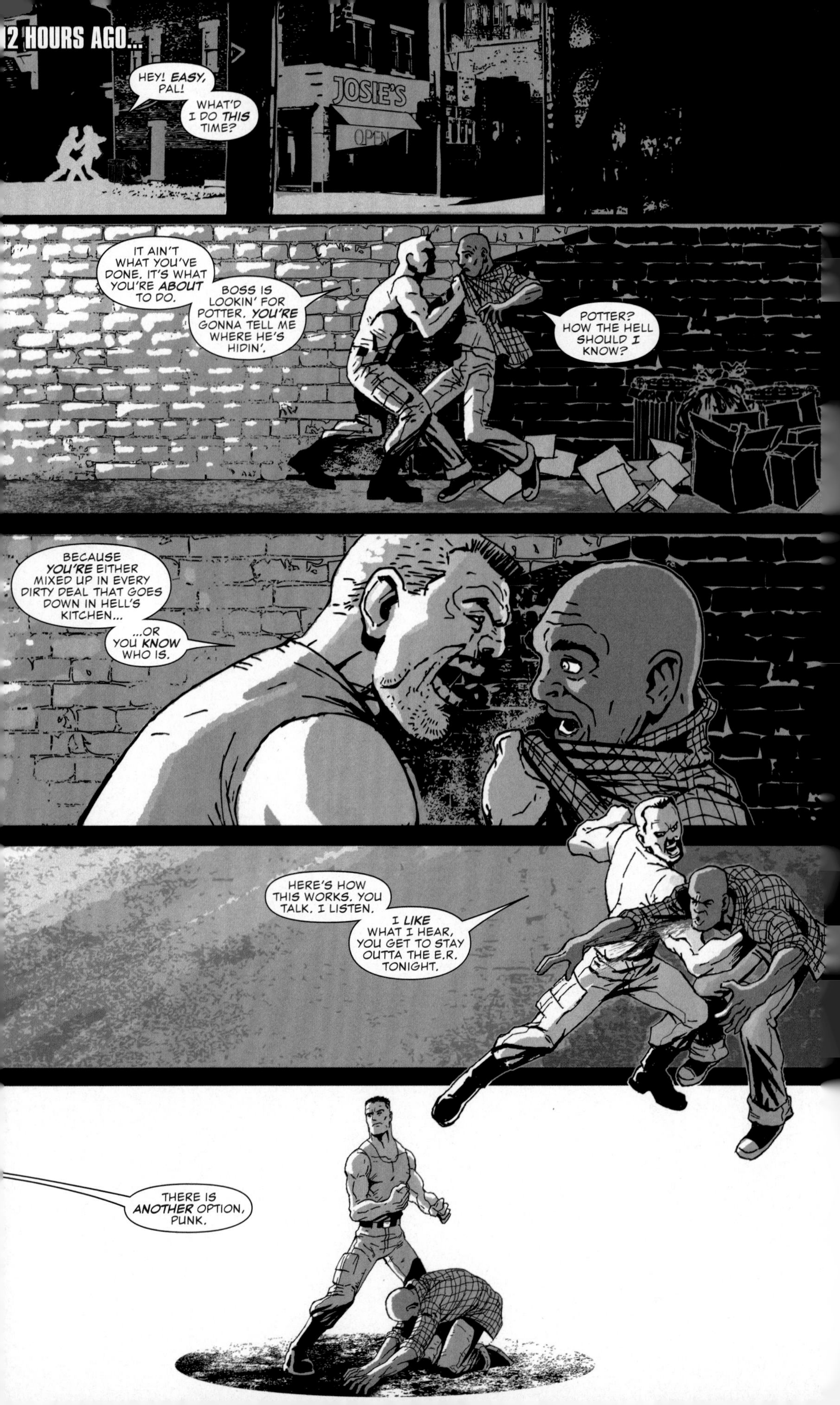

12 HOURS AGO...
HEY! EASY, PAL!
WHAT'D I DO THIS TIME?
JOSIE'S
OPEN
IT AIN'T WHAT YOU'VE DONE. IT'S WHAT YOU'RE ABOUT TO DO.
BOSS IS LOOKIN' FOR POTTER. YOU'RE GONNA TELL ME WHERE HE'S HIDIN'.
POTTER? HOW THE HELL SHOULD I KNOW?
BECAUSE YOU'RE EITHER MIXED UP IN EVERY DIRTY DEAL THAT GOES DOWN IN HELL'S KITCHEN...
...OR YOU KNOW WHO IS.
HERE'S HOW THIS WORKS. YOU TALK. I LISTEN.
I LIKE WHAT I HEAR, YOU GET TO STAY OUTTA THE E.R. TONIGHT.
THERE IS ANOTHER OPTION, PUNK.

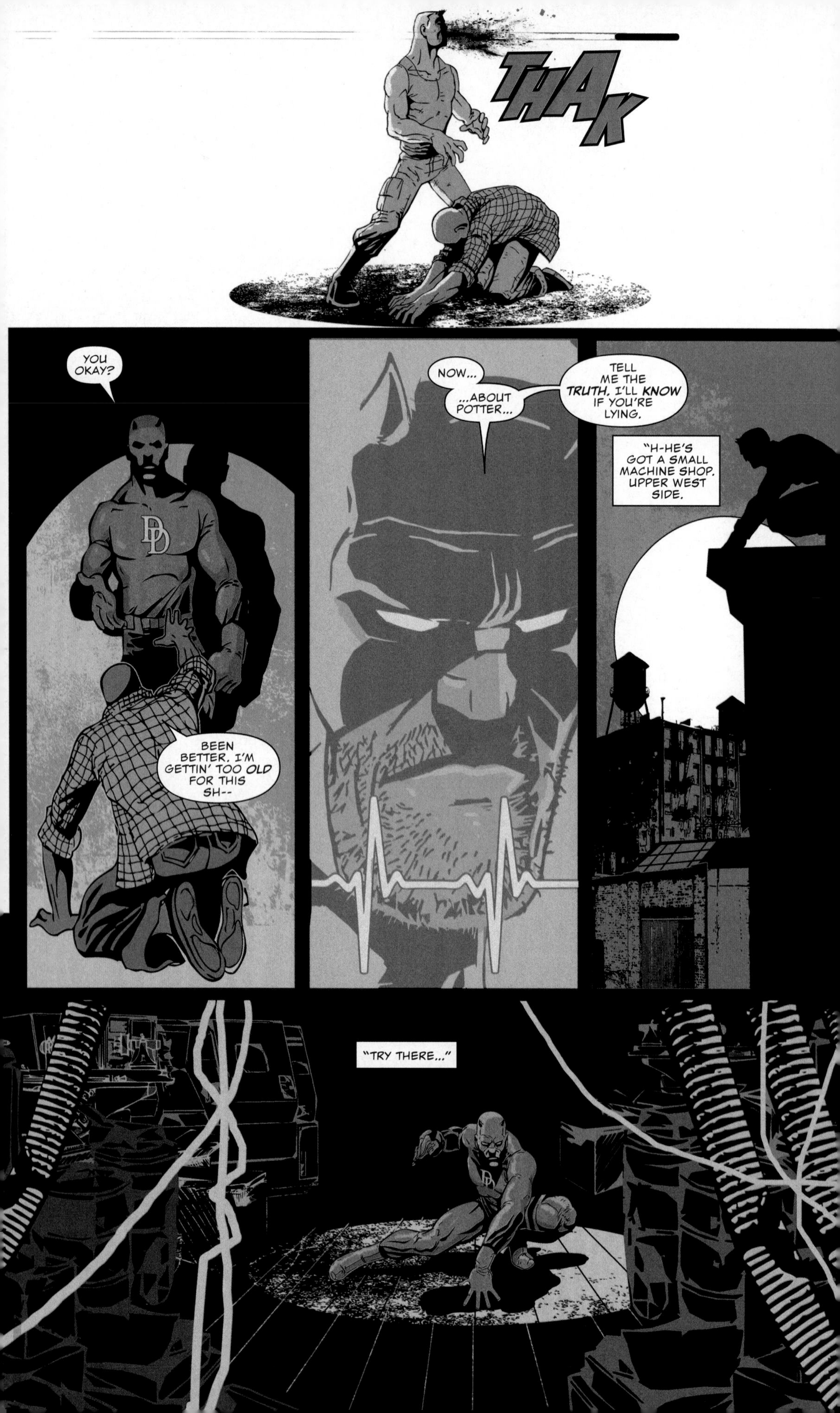
THAK
YOU OKAY?
BEEN BETTER. I'M GETTIN' TOO OLD FOR THIS SH--
NOW...
...ABOUT POTTER...
TELL ME THE TRUTH. I'LL KNOW IF YOU'RE LYING.
"H-HE'S GOT A SMALL MACHINE SHOP. UPPER WEST SIDE.
"TRY THERE..."

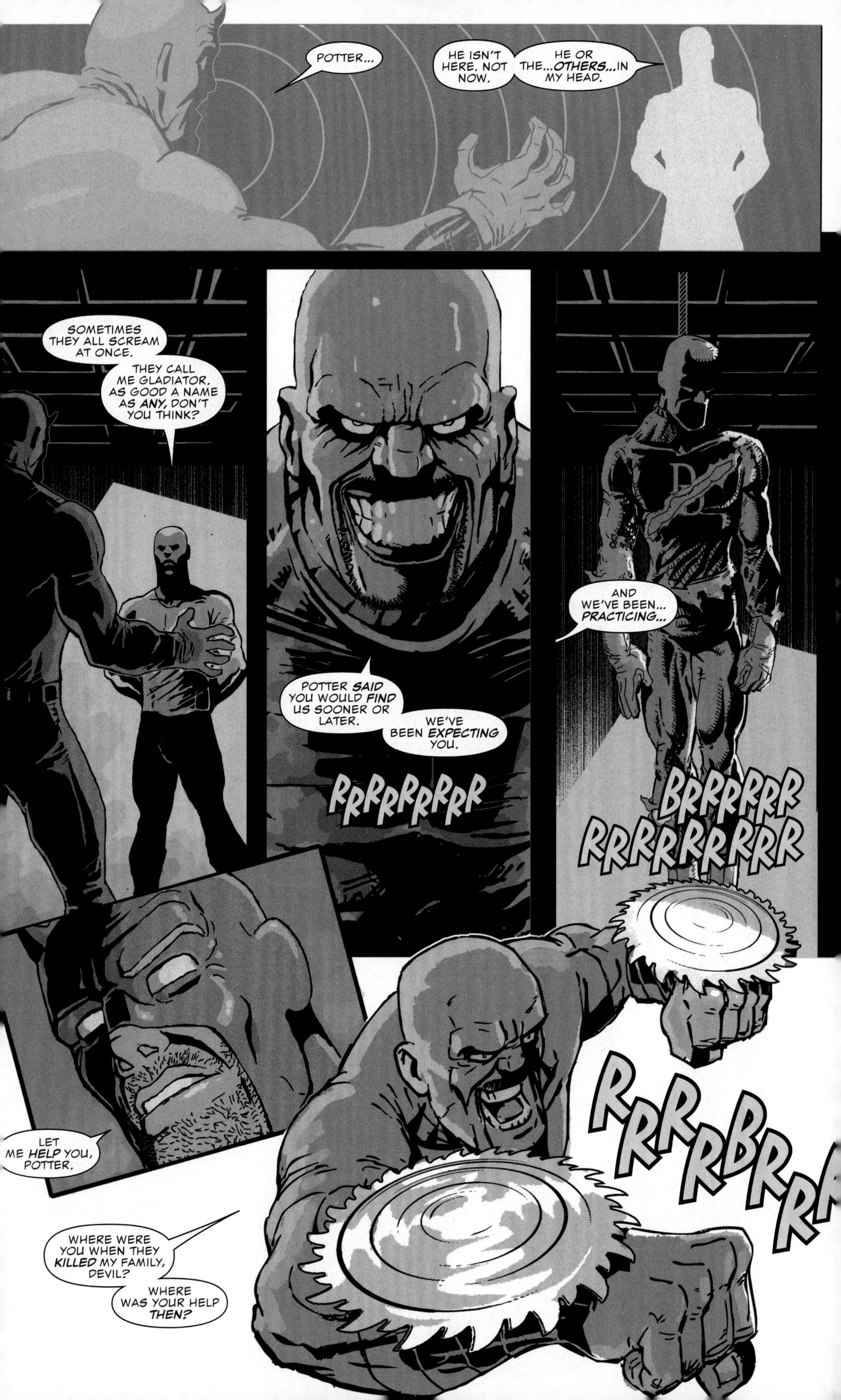
POTTER...
HE ISN'T HERE. NOT NOW.
HE OR THE...OTHERS...IN MY HEAD.
SOMETIMES THEY ALL SCREAM AT ONCE.
THEY CALL ME GLADIATOR. AS GOOD A NAME AS ANY, DON'T YOU THINK?
POTTER SAID YOU WOULD FIND US SOONER OR LATER.
WE'VE BEEN EXPECTING YOU.
RRRRRRRRR
AND WE'VE BEEN... PRACTICING...
BRRRRRR RRRRRRRRR
LET ME HELP YOU, POTTER.
RRRRBRRR
WHERE WERE YOU WHEN THEY KILLED MY FAMILY, DEVIL?
WHERE WAS YOUR HELP THEN?

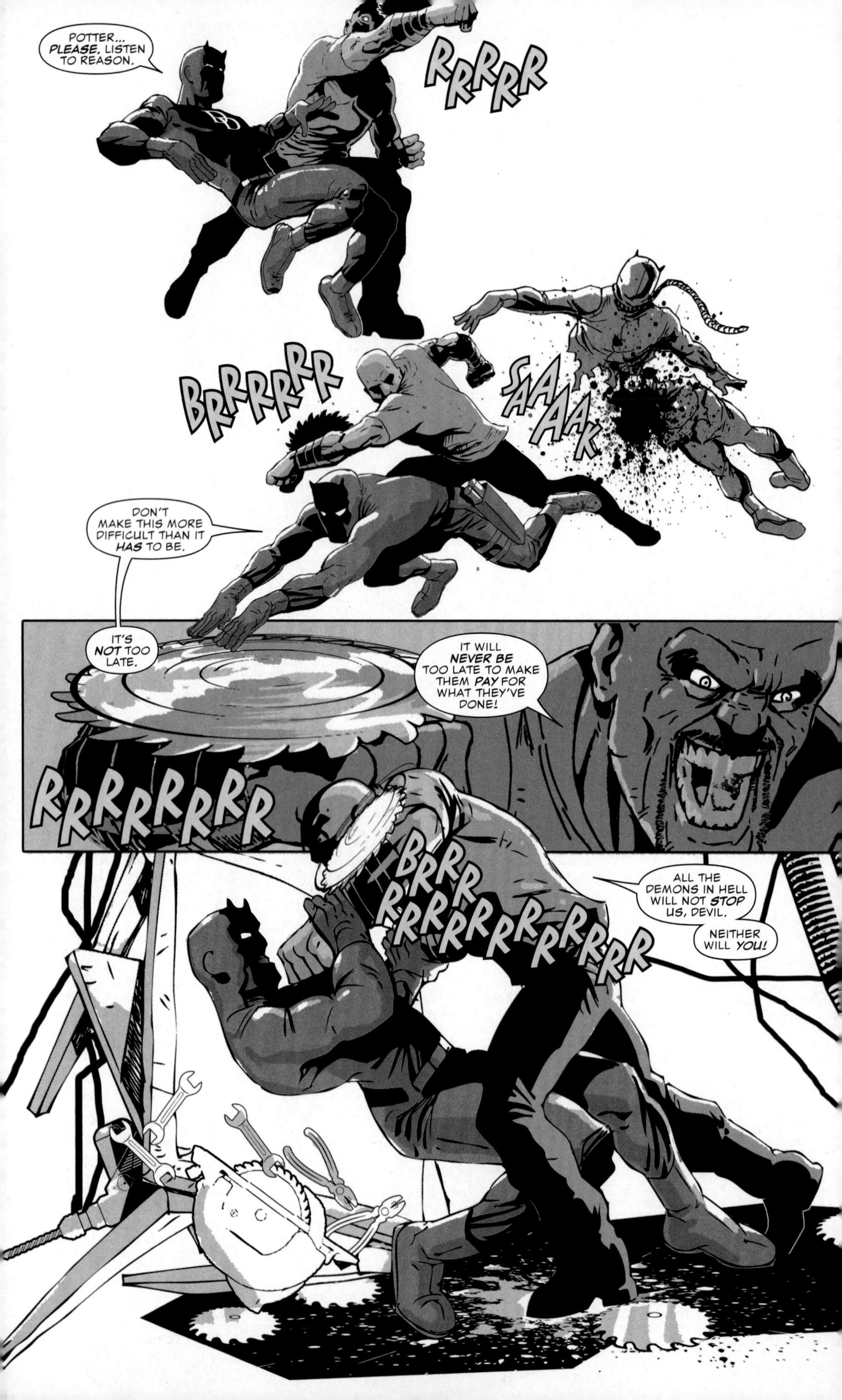
POTTER... PLEASE. LISTEN TO REASON.
RRRRR
BRRRRRR
SAAAAK
DON'T MAKE THIS MORE DIFFICULT THAN IT HAS TO BE.
IT'S NOT TOO LATE.
IT WILL NEVER BE TOO LATE TO MAKE THEM PAY FOR WHAT THEY'VE DONE!
RRRRRRRRR
BRRR
RRRRRRRRRRRRR
ALL THE DEMONS IN HELL WILL NOT STOP US, DEVIL.
NEITHER WILL YOU!

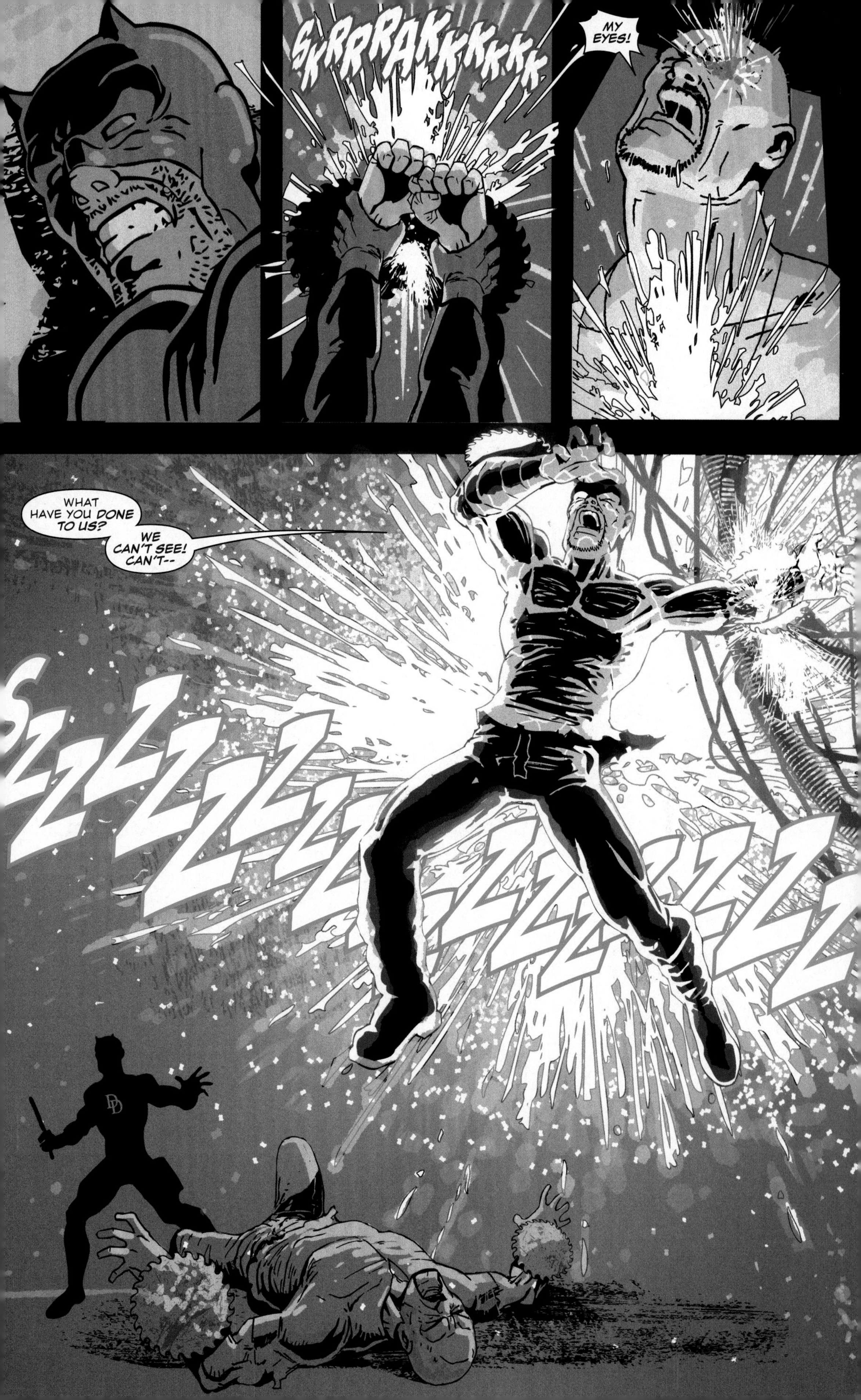
SKRRAKKKKKK
MY EYES!
WHAT HAVE YOU DONE TO US?
WE CAN'T SEE! CAN'T--
SZZZZZZZZZZZZZZZZZZ

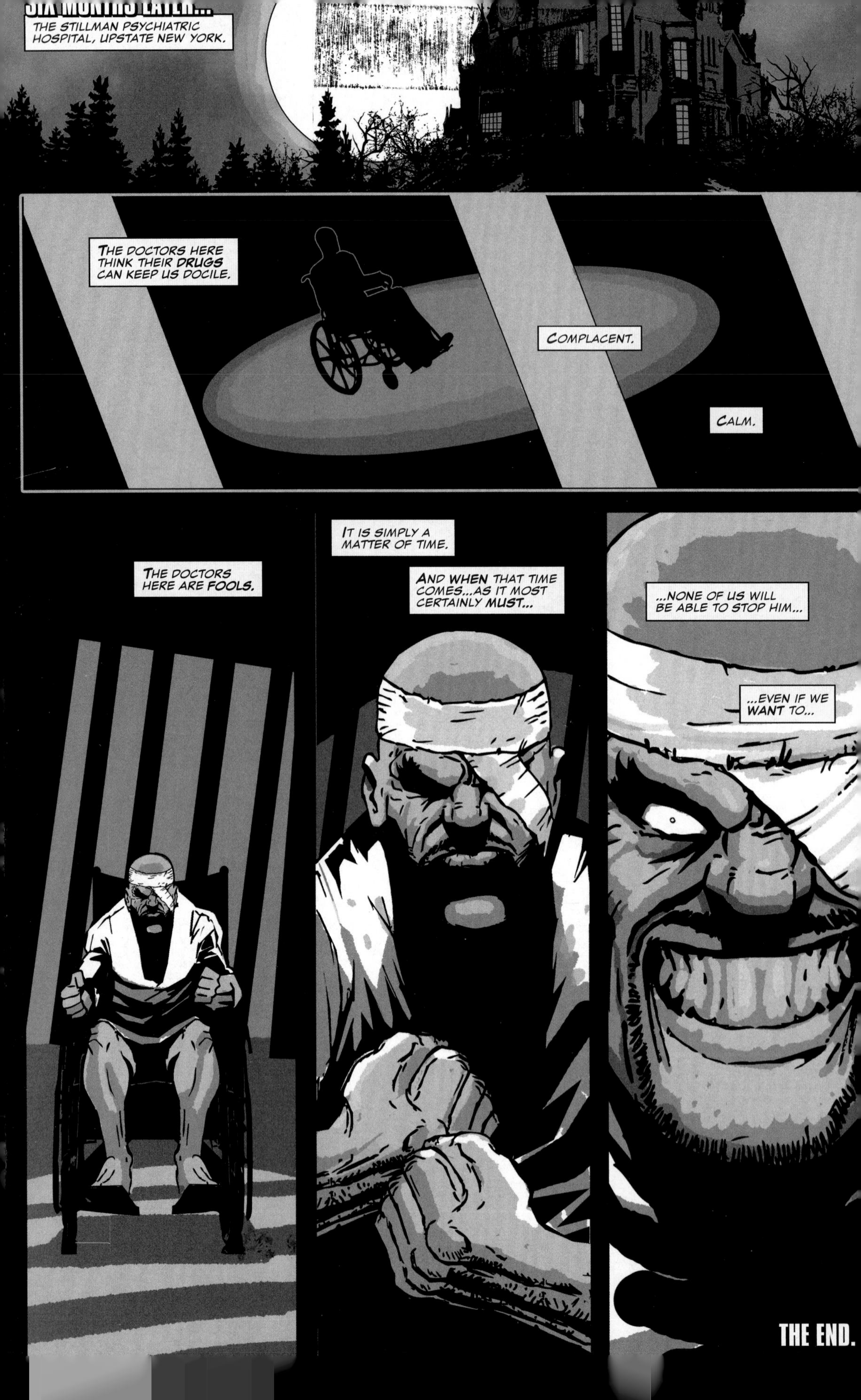
THE STILLMAN PSYCHIATRIC HOSPITAL, UPSTATE NEW YORK.
THE DOCTORS HERE THINK THEIR DRUGS CAN KEEP US DOCILE.
COMPLACENT.
CALM.
THE DOCTORS HERE ARE FOOLS.
IT IS SIMPLY A MATTER OF TIME.
AND WHEN THAT TIME COMES...AS IT MOST CERTAINLY MUST...
...NONE OF US WILL BE ABLE TO STOP HIM...
...EVEN IF WE WANT TO...
THE END.